IN A BEGINNING

Concordant Version

of the

Old Testament

The Book of "Genesis"

IN A BEGINNING

CONCORDANT PUBLISHING CONCERN

15570 West Knochaven Road, Canyon Country, CA 91351, U.S.A.

First Printing, 1957
Second Printing, 1978

TABLE OF CONTENTS

Key to Abbreviations and Symbols given on inside Front and Back Covers.

PREFACE

Wherein does a concordant translation or version differ from others? It is generally acknowledged, first of all, that the inspired Original is the only infallible evidence for divine truth. Consequently the nearer we can get to that, the safer we are. It is also beyond question that, even in the Original, the meaning of any word or expression is determined by the *contexts* in which it is found. Hence the earnest truth seeker will not depend on learned lexicons, or scholarly commentaries to settle the sense in which any word is used, but upon a *concordance of the Original.* Comparatively few are able to use such a work intelligently except through the medium of their mother tongue, so *a concordance of the original words in any translation* which they understand is by far the best book for the sincere student of the Sacred Scriptures.

The concordances of George V. Wigram, which give every word of the Hebrew, Aramaic and Greek Scriptures in alphabetical order, and, under each, quote a line including the English equivalent of all of its occurrences as found in the Authorized Version, are, next to my copies of the Original, the most helpful books I have ever bought. My first copy, containing all the Greek words, was used so much it disintegrated over thirty years ago. When I started work on the Hebrew words I knew that the book, in its ordinary binding, would never last long enough to finish that version, so I had a cloth hinge put on every page, at a cost of forty dollars, so that it is in usable condition yet, though some pages are torn and all are worn.

But these, though they are *con*cordances so far as the arrangement is concerned, reflect the *dis*cordances of the Authorized Version, for they expose the grave inconsistencies of that translation, and the clashing cross wiring of its renderings. But this is true of all other versions known to us, including even the Revision, and all modern versions, some of which are much better than the revered English classic, as far as truth is concerned. I was especially fond of Rotherham's version, as he seemed to be the most consistent, and did not shrink from using "impossible" English in the service of the truth. The tables showing the renderings of "eon" and "eonian", at the end of our booklet, "All in All", will prove how much he excelled the others in consistency. At first I was strongly inclined to use the word *age* for the Greek aiōn, as Rotherham had done. But in the language of the ordinary man, an *age* is much shorter than an *eon*, for he has been taught that there were "middle ages" and "dark ages" (plural) in the present single eon. Then the compound "age-abiding" literally denotes abiding for *one* age, whereas *eonian* clearly includes *all* the eons clear up to the consummation. Now, when we have the actual words of inspiration, *eon* and *eonian*, in our own tongue, why muddle matters by using human substitutes which will only confuse the ordinary person? Our Lord spoke of *eonian*, not age-abiding or eternal or everlasting life. Why alter it?

At first I tried to use Rotherham as an aid in making a concordant version, but I soon found him a hindrance rather than a help, as he did not seem to have any apparent system in forming his vocabulary, nor had he made a concordance of his version. I greatly admire his motive and his scholarship and would trust him rather than any other translator. But my object was the very opposite of this. I did not want to lean on *any* man, least of all on myself. Could we not have a *translation* which exhibits the *facts* of God's revelation in such a way that no one is dependent on any intermediary? A *uniform, exclusive sublinear* comes as close to this as is humanly possible when it is complemented by a concordance of the Original. This is true of any language. I cannot conceive of any other plan which so nearly excludes the bias of the translator or puts the student into possession of the facts, subject to his own decision. Of course it cannot exclude the prejudices and predilections of its many readers, but it should help to correct them.

Should it be necessary to press the point that a Concordant Version, in any language, is to be differentiated from all others? By its uniform sublinear and its ultimate concordance of the original, it is not only unique, but allows the compiler to step back and say, "I implore you not to depend on my fallible and fleeting opinions, yet I do beseech you to consider the evidence which we have made so easy to consult, and base your conclusions on the facts alone. I am *not* an authority, but the facts presented have been checked by many aids, and may be depended upon." If you know of any other publication which gives you anything like this unbiased presentation, and does not depend on human opinion, I will be glad to know of it.

What version, after it was completed, made an exhaustive and detailed concordance of the minutest variations, not only of the words, but of every form of each word, just to check its accuracy? This alone meant many years of tedious toil. So far we have never had the means to publish this concordance, but the International Edition has benefited by this unexampled effort to obtain the highest degree of faithfulness to the Original.

In the *version*, however, there is a human element, but *far less in a concordant version based on a uniform sublinear and exhaustive concordance of the Original than in any other.* To make readable English demands a knowledge of figures of speech, especially idiom, in both the Original and in our own tongue. Moreover, even figures, including idiom, are by no means absolutely lawless, but can be classified and controlled by comparison with other occurrences of the same figure, or similar usages of the same word. In this respect the Concordant Version is unique also, for it indicates the common figures both in the text and in the concordance.

Moreover, uniformity and consistency can be greatly aided by marking all the figurative usages of each word at the same time in a concordance, rather than occasionally, at each occurrence in the text. We have already done most of the figures in the Hebrew Scriptures. They are entered in Wigram's concordance and in a card index first, so that they can be arranged in any order desired for study, and, God willing, will be published for the benefit of those whose hearts are set on digging deep into the treasures of God's Word. In doing this work we are learning much ourselves and are impressed by the clarity and certainty which it imparts to the realm of thought which is usually very vague in the minds of Western peoples. We know of no other version which provides such help.

Living in a land whose physical features, topography, climate and water supply are probably more like that of Palestine than any other place on earth, I could see that the Authorized Version had been translated by men who were strangers to the land of promise. A single word will confirm this. In this climate, with little rain for half the year, the streams are dry in summer, though they may be raging torrents in winter. The Spaniards, who settled this country, call them *arroyos*. This is the meaning of the Hebrew *nchl*, which the A.V. renders *brook*, *flood*, *river*, *stream*, and *valley*. Its most conspicuous feature to a Westerner they missed, for it is a sandy waste much of the year. We render it *watercourse*. Here we have many of these as well as high snow mountains, foothills, a lake below sea level, a desert to the east and the sea to the west.

We studied books and maps to get a clear conception of conditions which would affect translation, but were not satisfied, so made a trip nearly halfway round the world to get a firsthand view of the people as well as the land, on the spot. This has kept us from many a mistake in local coloring. After all, one who aspires to understand and reproduce God's revelation in the vernacular, should shun no effort to prepare himself for the task. How many modern Bible translators have *lived* in Palestine long enough to become familiar with the facts of the physical background in divine revelation?

In such a matter as idiom one who has had much experience has a great advantage. I have often thanked God that English was once a foreign language to me, and a very idiotic one in some ways it appeared to be at first. My mother tongue was almost as odd in other ways, but I did not notice that until I knew both. Now that I deal constantly with four languages, and have compared the Greek idiom of the Scriptures with the Hebrew Scriptures throughout, I do not try to make a literal English caricature of every idiom in the *version*. I let my readers know the facts in the *sublinear*, but I do not destroy the concordance of the version by altering all normal English idioms to conform to it, when the results might be misleading to the ordinary reader. The version is, of necessity, somewhat idiomatic when this is necessary to carry over the sense of the original. The sublinear, on the other hand, is perfectly uniform and literal.

The different departments of the work are done by specialists. One works on the grammar, another on the figures of speech, etc. This method makes them more expert than one man could possibly be. Almost all great achievements are accomplished by the cooperation of specialists. Although the compiler checks and passes upon all the work, he is by no means to be credited with all that is done, although he assumes responsibility for it.

The two principles underlying the vocabulary—each word of the original having an *exclusive, constant* English equivalent *when idiom allows*, and each English equivalent being assigned to represent only *one word* of the original language—leading to otherwise unattainable *accuracy* and *consistency*, are used in compiling the vocabulary of the Concordant Version, and no other.

The restoration of the Hebrew text has taken most of our time for the last fifteen years. We know of no version which has made a comparable effort to recover the ancient inspired readings. No one not actually engaged on it can have any apprehension of the labor involved. Thousands upon thousands of readings have been entered on slips, along with the evidence of the Septuagint. Vast concordances of the Greek version have been made in the past, but this appears to be the first comprehensive attempt to *use* them and incorporate and indicate their readings in an English version. If this had already been published we would not devote so much time and effort to it. In every case we seek to serve ordinary people, and present the facts in such form as they can easily understand.

There are many translations. Some seem to think that the C.V. is only another of the same kind, dependent on the authority or scholarship of the translator, instead of an entirely different combination of a concordance coupled with a uniform, literal translation and a version, which provides ordinary folk with the facts needed to ascertain what is in the inspired Original. We will not allow anyone to depend upon our ability or lack of it. We will not come between them and God's revelation. Our long life has been devoted to the building of a bridge, like that which led to His sanctuary in Jerusalem, over which they *themselves* may cross into His holy temple, and hear His words with their own ears, and see His glory with their own eyes, without any mediator other than our Saviour, Christ Jesus, the Son of God's love.

A.E.K.

INTRODUCTION

THE CONCORDANT VERSION OF THE HEBREW AND CHALDEE SCRIPTURES

GOD HAS SPOKEN! He talks to us in foreign tongues. Nothing is so imperative as a firsthand knowledge of His inspired revelation, without the intervention of human faults and disabilities. This is made impossible by the usual methods of translation. We can come much nearer to the ideal through systematic obedience to the laws of language, because, first of all, it leads to much greater accuracy, and, secondly, it is self-corrective. A word uniformly translated absorbs its true intent from its contexts. The plan has been tested in translating the Greek Scriptures, in several languages. After a long trial it has proved most satisfactory. Many contradictions have vanished. Much fresh truth has been discovered. Difficult theological problems have been solved. It is invaluable for enlightening the heart with the glories of God and His Christ.

The plan of the Hebrew concordant version is essentially the same as that employed in translating the Greek. Wigram's Englishman's Concordance was used in the preliminary work. It contains every Hebrew word found in the Scriptures, usually followed by all of the passages in which it occurs, as rendered in the Authorized Version, as well as two indexes. The English index lists every English word used in the A.V., followed by every Hebrew word which it translates. The Hebrew index lists all the Hebrew words and every English word used to translate them.

The English vocabulary was formed as follows: The occurrences of each Hebrew word were studied as listed in Wigram, and the nearest English equivalent was written in his concordance. This was entered or underlined in the English and Hebrew indexes. Whenever it was discovered that a term had served as the translation of another Hebrew word it was crossed off, and all other translations of the Hebrew word chosen were likewise struck out. This process of elimination was continued with frequent changes and revisions, over a long period of time, until most of the words in the divine vocabulary seemed to have been given their nearest English equivalent.

As an example, we will take the well-known stem kphr, which sounds like our English word **cover**, and is generally given this meaning by scholars. This word is often translated "atonement" in our venerable Authorized Version. It may help us to grasp the basic meaning of this stem if we consider its renderings. These are: appease, atonement (make), bribe, camphire, cleanse, disannul, forgive, merciful (be), mercy seat, pacify, pardon, pitch, purge, put off, ransom, reconcile, satisfaction, sum of money, village; besides bason, hoarfrost, lion, and young. It will be seen from these that the stem does convey the general idea of a cover. But the examination of another stem, kse, will show that this must be rendered **cover**. It is almost always so translated in the Authorized Version. Only occasionally we find clad, close, conceal, hide, overwhelm, raiment, vesture, all of which are closely allied to cover. No other English word will do as well as cover for the Hebrew kse.

But we should not use the same term, cover, for both kphr and kse. A closer examination of kphr will show that it always refers to a protective cover, a **shelter**. This will be found a far more satisfactory equivalent. The word atonement does not convey the full sense. The Greek translation uses propitiation, which is far better To keep the connection between this and later revelation and, at the same time, show the simple force of the stem, we render it "propitiatory **shelter**."

In this way the vocabulary of this version was built up before it was used in translation. This method forces us to be more consistent and accurate than would be possible without it. The chief advantage, however, is this, that it largely eliminates private opinion in the rendering of any particular passage. The words have already been fixed before the compiler comes to turn the sentence into English.

The usual lexicons and other works of reference were not neglected, although, in most cases, they proved too inaccurate to be helpful. The fauna and flora were given special attention, including a sojourn in the Holy Land, and a study of the dress, customs and manners, many of which remain today as they were in ancient times. A number of other translations were consulted, but little help was obtained from them because their vocabularies are discordant.

When the meaning of a word or a reading of the text is not certain, we strive to incorporate the evidence in our rendering. Thus the word lbb **heart** (2 Sa. 13:8) evidently refers to baked bread of some kind. So we render it **heart** shaped ⁷cakes⁰. This shows that the Hebrew was **heart** and the Septuagint has cakes. The word shape is not in either, but is needed in the verb (2 Sa. 13:6) to indicate the action, shape heart ⁷cakes⁰. With this evidence the student can form his own conclusion.

In order to secure uniformity, a card index was made of every form of every Hebrew word, and to each was added its English standard. The whole Hebrew text was copied, on special sheets, in English, or Latin, letters, so that the standards in the index could be placed beneath each word, making the sublinear uniform. As a companion to this, a complete Hebrew lexicon was written in loose leaf form, to record the standards and register further improvements.

After the vocabulary and grammar had been settled in this manner, about half of the Hebrew Scriptures were translated tentatively, using Ginsburg's Masoretico-Critical edition of the text as a basis, in order to test the vocabulary and the state of the text. The poetical portions were chosen because they contain many literary forms, especially parallelisms, with their synonyms, which are a great help in further refining the vocabulary, and in recovering the ancient text. Not many changes were needed in the vocabulary, but the consistent renderings revealed the fact that even the Masoretic text, in many cases, has failed to preserve the original rendering. The rabbis seem to have realized that the text was gradually becoming more corrupt, so they sought to stereotype the form it had in their day. They did not change it, even when they knew that it was wrong, but put some of these mistakes on record in the margin.

HOW THE WORK WAS DONE

It is practically impossible to understand or appreciate this version without knowing something of the method and the tools used in producing it. For clarity's sake, these will be discussed under the following heads:

1. The Restoration of the Text and its Pronunciation.
2. The Revision of the Hebrew Grammar.
3. The Compilation of the Vocabulary.
4. Idiomatic English, Spelling, etc.
5. The Function of the Signs, Type Faces, etc.
6. Figures of Speech, including Skeletons.
7. The Select References.

1. THE RESTORATION OF THE HEBREW TEXT AND ITS PRONUNCIATION

The Hebrew Text we have today differs considerably from that which was originally given. Since the days of the Masorites, the preservers of the traditional text, there seem to have been no great number of vital changes, for their system of counting the letters and cataloguing other facts has tended to stabilize their text. This is especially true since the invention of printing. But the very fact that it was deemed necessary to protect the text by "putting a fence about it" suggests that corruption had been at work for a thousand years before. No Hebrew manuscript (except Isaiah) goes back more than a thousand years. Before that, old copies were usually destroyed when new ones took their place. The Greek and other translations, some of which go back a thousand years earlier, reflect a text which often differs from the one now used in making our Bibles.

THE ANCIENT FORM OF THE LETTERS

We can go back to the days of Hezekiah for the forms of the Hebrew letters. We have the recently unearthed Lachish letters and the Siloam inscription, which once was in the wall of the tunnel running under Ophel, about twenty feet from the pool of Siloam, to show us just how they wrote Hebrew before this time and until the deportation. This alphabet is shown on the fly leaf. With the return from the deportation the Jews brought with them the Aramaic dialect and the square characters which are now generally known as "Hebrew." These letters were probably used in writing the Syriac or Aramaic portions of the Scriptures, but not for the rest. The original forms were abandoned because the people no longer were acquainted with them.

HEBREW PRONUNCIATION

The ancient Hebrew letters are no longer in use. So-called "Hebrew" Bibles really employ an entirely different alphabet, which is variously termed Chaldee or Syriac or Aramaic. In the course of time the pronunciation of the vowels changed, so a new and different pronunciation was added by means of so-called "points," little dots and dashes beneath, in, or over the letters. The original vowels, however, were retained, except that u and i were often omitted in spelling, because their sounds were already indicated by the points. Today, however, the vowel points themselves are variously pronounced by different classes of Jewish scholars, and the whole matter is in confusion. We avoid this difficulty in the simplest way. We use a Latin (or English) character for each ancient Hebrew letter, including the vowels, and ignore the uninspired "points," which add nothing to the sense, but only duplicate the vowels, as a rule. When the vowel has dropped out, we replace it.

The following examples will make this clear. The first is all vowels, the second mixed, and the third all consonants. The word "oue," depraved, was doubtless pronounced just as it is spelled, in ancient Israel. Now that two little characters, like capital T's, have been added under the o and u, the usual way of transliterating it into English would entirely ignore the real vowels in the word. The word "adm", **human**, also has two small T's beneath it. In English we spell Adam with two a's, but the second a is not pronounced. We say ad*u*m. This slight *u* sound is often needed in Hebrew to pronounce a word and must be supplied. We call it the "involuntary vowel," because it comes of itself when we try to pronounce two consonants one after another. Our next example calls for two of these. The word "nphsh" **soul** has points that would make it nephesh, which is almost the same as n*u*ph*u*sh. It is possible that words like nphsh are defective. We may insert u, as in nuphsh or nphush, if we discover evidence that it has dropped out.

The original pronunciation of Hebrew, the manner in which David and Abraham and Adam spoke the tongue of inspiration, is a problem which we thought far beyond our range. As we did not deem it essential we gave it small attention at first. Later, when it seemed wise to put the inspired text before our readers in well-known Latin in place of Chaldee characters, we found it necessary to determine, to some degree of accuracy, what are the nearest equivalents, so that there would be at least an approximation to the facts. The efforts made in this direction have been far more convincing than we anticipated, hence we will give a short account of the means used and the results attained.

Wouldn't it be marvelous if we could read the Hebrew psalms as David did? Of one thing we may be sure. If he listened to the liturgy of a Hebrew synagogue, he would probably find it difficult to understand his own compositions, even if they were read in faultless Hebrew, according to the standards of the Jewish rabbis. The reason is that the language has changed so much, especially in the vowels, that it sounds very different. In fact, I am told that the various classes of Jews cannot understand one another because of their clashing pronunciations. The very same text read by an Ashkenazim, or German Jew, sounds quite unlike the reading by a Sephardim, or Spanish Jew.

HEBREW A NATURE LANGUAGE

Sounds in nature do not change. The peoples of the earth are continually varying their mode of talking, but the voices of the animals and the sounds made by inanimate objects continue as they were in the beginning. A stranger in a foreign land, who is homesick because the voices all about are barbarous, can cure it by going among the animals, for these speak the same language as those at home. The dogs bark, the hens cackle, the roosters crow, the donkeys bray in the same dialect wherever we find them. In its close connection with nature we may find a key to the pronunciation of the Hebrew tongue, as it was spoken in the days of old, before the Jews learned many other languages and adapted their own to these outlandish tongues.

The first hint of this that I came across was the word bqbq. This is the name they gave to a **bottle**. If we empty a fluid out of a narrow-necked container which has no means of allowing air to enter it to displace the fluid withdrawn, the flow will stop occasionally so that a bubble of air may slip by. In doing this it makes a characteristic sound, buq-buq, which gives the vessel its name in Hebrew. Now an American bottle, or an English one, or even a Chinese flask all make the same sound if they are shaped the same, and this has always been the case. We may, then, conclude that all bottles or narrow-necked containers can speak one word of Hebrew **correctly**, and it will be our duty and pleasure to learn it from them.

But we can learn much more than that. We know what letters were used to represent this sound in Hebrew, b, u and q, so we have a clue to their true and ancient pronunciation, especially if this is confirmed by other similar cases. Just lately a worker on the Hebrew called my attention to the word heart, which we have made lbub. (It is usually shortened to lb). Now listen to a heart beat. Is not this as close as we can get to the sound made by it? This is hardly clear enough to base much upon, but it seems to confirm what we have learned before. We now know the sounds of four letters in Hebrew.

Now let us inquire of the birds. The partridge seems to know one word of Hebrew. Its **call** is qra, and this is also its **name** (1 Sam. 26:20). And this is the sound it still makes after thousands of years. So once again we have a q sound, besides r and a.

Though we cannot feel nearly so safe in basing anything upon them, it does seem that some words have come down to us altered but very little by the course of time. Such a one is ebuni, which is practically the same as our **ebony**. This adds to our list e and n and i, though we will find that i is ee rather than ih. The word qnmun means **cinnamon**, so is nearly Hebrew, and adds the letter m to our list. Some English words from the Hebrew are helpful, as iubl **jubilee**. Amn (**Amen**) corroborates what has been said.

COMPARISON WITH THE GREEK

Perhaps the best human means of checking the ancient pronunciation is to be found in the transcription of Hebrew names in the Septuagint. Being human, we cannot place much reliance on details, but a general view should give us an idea how Hebrew was spoken in the third century before Christ, when the Septuagint was translated. Where this agrees with our findings in other fields it should be final. This we find to be true for most of the letters. A vowel or two and the labials are the only exceptions. We find that the comparison breaks down, however, where the Greek has no equivalent, or where the vowels have already begun to vary in Hebrew.

I am indebted to friends for a list of over five hundred proper names which gives the spelling of the Greek and the Hebrew, and a column for every Hebrew letter showing which Greek letter was used in transcribing it.

The easiest way to examine this table will be to check off those letters first which are settled beyond a doubt by the figures. Thus Hebrew b is rendered by the Greek b 112 times with only six departures, and g is g 27 times with only two. The following letters are likewise determined once for all by this table: d 80(2 off), z 28(1), th 60(9), i 194(14), l 128(3), m 149(4), n 123(4), r 155(2), ph 47(only 3 p). About half of the letters need no further examination because the evidence against them is not of sufficient weight to warrant it.

Some of these, however, are of special interest because the Greek distinguishes closely related sounds. Thus th is used only once for t, while t is so transcribed 13 times, though 9 times it is also made th. Scholars today, while they would probably acknowledge that these letters were quite distinct in primitive Hebrew (in which alone we are interested) would give th both sounds, that is, almost identical with t when it has a dot within it. This, however, seems to be the result of contact with other languages, as this table shows, and not the pure Hebrew we are after.

Modern Hebrew has both p and ph (or f). The difference is indicated by a dot in the letter, which hardens it to p. Independent investigation led me to conclude that ancient Hebrew had no p. It was always soft, ph (or f). But this was challenged, so a friend went through the proper names in the Septuagint at my request, and found that p was never used in pure transcriptions. While in Palestine I was struck with the name of the Arab newspaper Falastin (in place of Palastin), and I found that the Arabs there could not pronounce the letter p. Evidently it is not used in modern Arabic. Further inquiries confirmed this. The table now made seems to settle the matter finally. Ph is used 47 times and p only 3 times. In these cases the Greeks did not transcribe, but spelled as was their custom, just as we do so often in English. We will not transcribe Phr in our translation, but make it Persia, for so we are accustomed to call the country in our own language.

The Hebrew letters s and sh have a story all their own. It seems that these letters are easily confused. In parts of Europe the colloquial dialect uses sh for s always, for the people cannot pronounce s. The opposite seems to have been the case in Ephraim in early times (Jd. 12:6). When Jephthah with his Gileadites defeated them and caught them at the fords of Jordan, he tested them to see if they were Ephraimites by asking them to say **Shibboleth**. But it seems that this tribe could not pronounce the sh sounds, so they said Sibboleth, and paid for it with their lives. Correct pronunciation may be more vital than it seems! For my part, I refuse to endanger my life, like most scholars do, by putting a dot on the top of the sh to make an s out of it. Remember the Ephraimites at the fords of the Jordan!

But Greek has no sh. How, then, could they translate this passage? Very simply! They left out a part and only said that the Ephraimites could not pronounce the word. The two versions of the LXX I have consulted carefully avoid the word shibboleth because the Greeks also could not pronounce it. Each one translates it by a different Greek word. Does not this show conclusively that there was no sh sound in Greek? Hence it is clear that we cannot get this sound through the LXX. So also with tz. Greek could not distinguish between these three letters. Therefore s does duty for them all. We are more fortunate. We have no letters, indeed, but we have combinations, and can pronounce the sounds of sh and tz, so can keep them distinct from s.

THE PALATAL LETTERS

In the palatal letters ch, k, q, we seem to have much confusion. Even today the western languages cannot really represent the sounds in Arabic by their alphabets, and few can readily pronounce them. I remember speaking to an Arab in Tiberias who was explaining to me the difference between the pronunciation of Semek, a wady right across the lake, and Semakh, the town at the southern end of the lake. To me the pronunciation seemed to be practically the same. I could not "frame to pronounce" the difference between the final k and kh, though I could discern it. The English have the same difficulty with the Scotch ch, which both the k and ḳh of the Arabic closely resemble. The best we can do is to have a distinct character for each, according to its location in the alphabet, and to assign to these characters the sounds of the Hebrew as they are ascertained.

It is said that k and q are very frequently interchanged in cognate languages. The same word spelled with k in one will be q in another. The usual idea is that q is "harder," being produced in the back part of the palate, with more effort than k. The difference seems to be beyond most westerners. As, however, we have the letter q as well as k, and it is quite possible that it differs in the right direction, minute as it may be, it seems most practical to use it to distinguish these two letters from each other. Anyone who will examine a number of Hebrew grammars, especially in different languages, will see how inconsistent their spelling is. The English works generally spell the name of the light class of Hebrew verbs kal, but on the continent some make it Qal. The latter appeals to me as more practical if k is to be used for k, but it is not worthwhile to differ with the textbooks on this ground.

As Greek has no q they sought to distinguish it from k by making the q k and the k ch as a rule. They then had no letter left for ch, so they usually omitted it, 51 times out of 71, and used ch when they carried it over, thus confusing ch and k, which they rendered ch 49 times out of 57. The lesson we should learn is that the Hebrew k should be sounded softly (perhaps kh will express it), but q hard. It would not be wise to follow the confusion of the Greek transliteration at this point. It arises from a lack of sufficient characters and the aspiration which they gave their initial vowel at times, without representing it in writing. After a vowel ch is usually ch. Before a consonant, at the beginning of a word, it is replaced by a vowel, probably with the aspirate implied. Chnne becomes Anna, English Hanna, which is often changed to Anna.

THE HEBREW VOWELS

Vowels are the most unstable sounds in any language. Even in the living languages, there is more difference in these few letters than in all the rest combined. The enunciation of an American differs from the literary English chiefly in this regard. Hebrew has changed greatly in the course of time. The alteration has been so great, indeed, that the old vowels are now silenced, and a new set has replaced them. Even when the Septuagint was made this process was well under way. In the names, a was rendered by a(78), e(20), ê(or ay)(22), o(9), and ō(or oo)(3). The letter e was made a(12), e(1), ê(2), o(7). U was transliterated a(5), e(2), i(1), o(5), u(20), ō(63). I was written a(2), e(6), ê(2), i(194), o(1), u(1), ō(2). O appears as a(35), e(16), ê(7), o(13), ō(2). So great is this confusion that it has hardly any weight in deciding the proper pronunciation of these letters. But, in contrast with present practise, u is a vowel (not v), and so is e (not h), and o (not ng).

If the transliteration of the proper names sheds little light, it at least shows that they are vowels, and that is most important at the present time, when a and o are denied even a letter, being given only apostrophies which have no sound at all. Hebrew **had** (and pure Hebrew **has**) vowels, just like other languages. These must be restored.

A glance at the order of these letters in the Hebrew alphabet will almost suffice to identify them and give each its proper sound.

In the alphabet on the fly leaf we have tried to show the corresponding letters in the Latin (or English), the ancient and modern Greek, the Aramaic (commonly called Hebrew) and the real original Hebrew as shown on the ancient remains, such as were found at Lachish. The recently found manuscript of Isaiah, which may go back to the century before the birth of Christ, has the vowels as we have restored them in the Concordant Hebrew text, on which this version is based. The location of the vowels in the alphabets (as they should be) seems to be the best indication of their pronunciation.

In each alphabet the most open of all the vowel sounds seems to come first. It is a(ah). That this was so in Hebrew seems to be settled by the cry of the partridge. This is the most-used sound in the proper names, so there seems to be little doubt that the Hebrew a was originally a[h], as in father.

The vowel **u** (now usually given as v or w) is found in the full spelling of buqbuq, hence it has the sound of long u. This is confirmed by the fact that the LXX transcription makes it either **u** or **o**.

That **i** (pronounced as long ee) is **i** seems settled by the Greek transcription. There is no case for the present method of making it ahee.

That the letter o (generally represented by a reversed apostrophe (') is a real vowel is clear, for it is always represented by one in the transcription. Coming between mn and p in the alphabet, it seems the only one for the missing o sound.

TRANSLITERATION OF THE HEBREW

Our system of transliteration is as simple as it can be. It may be used with any Hebrew text or lexicon, with the equivalents shown on the flyleaf.

THE RESTORATION OF THE ORIGINAL HEBREW TEXT

When the present traditional text is consistently translated, much of it makes no sense. Hitherto it has been left to scholars to extract a rational rendering by consulting the context of their own opinion of what was intended. In one of the most scholarly editions of modern times, the learned editors simply omitted many phrases and passages because they could not make anything out of the Hebrew text before them. In order to determine the true condition of the text and provide a basis for its restoration, the compiler translated most of the literary scrolls, from Job to the end, strictly according to the Masoretic edition by Christian D. Ginsburg, and published by the Trinitarian Bible Society. The result shows that the original text must be recovered before a concordant version is possible.

Now that it was clear that much work was needed to restore the text, various helps were consulted, such as Kennedy's "Aid to the Textual Amendment of the Old Testament," Davidson's "The Hebrew Text," as well as the notes in Ginsburg's Introduction and margin. As all of this fell far short of our expectations, a painstaking comparison was made with the three most ancient manuscripts of the Septuagint, and, in some parts, with other Greek versions, Aquila, Symmachus, Theodotion, and the Hexapla of Origen. As the Septuagint proved our best aid, it will be well to consider it more closely, and the relation of the later Greek versions to it. The books of Moses were also checked with the Samaritan Pentateuch, which supplied quite a few words which had dropped out.

After all this work was done, the whole was checked by the evidence provided by the ancient manuscript of Isaiah, recently discovered. It also uses the so-called silent consonants as vowels.

THE SAMARITAN PENTATEUCH

After carefully comparing the Samaritan text with the Masoretic, as printed in modern editions, as well as with the tentative Concordant Hebrew Text, we have come to some conclusions which may be valuable in the recovery of the primitive original. The text used was that found in Kennicott's great edition, dated 1776, which seems to be based on a collation of about a dozen manuscripts for the whole and several more, on occasion. It is not printed in full. Only the variations from the Hebrew are shown. This makes it easy to see the differences and judge of their character.

The Concordant Hebrew Text is much fuller than the Masoretic because we have restored thousands of vowels which have dropped out. Many words are admittedly "defective" in many of their occurrences, the lacking letters having been replaced by the modern vowel points. These being gone, we replace the lost letters in the text. These letters had gradually disappeared. Thousands of them are still present in the Samaritan text and this again lacks some that are in the Masoretic copies. They all were undoubtedly present in the text from which both of these were derived. The fact that we, without the Samaritan text, were able to restore so many letters which it retains, shows that we are on the right track in our efforts to reconstruct the original. This assurance alone is worth all the labor expended on the comparison. As these letters affect only the spelling of the Hebrew, there is no way of showing this in a version.

The principal value of the Samaritan text for a version lies in the recovery of the words and passages which have dropped out of the common text. These are marked $^{s}\ldots^{n}$ in the version. In many cases they agree with the Septuagint, the ancient Greek version. In that case the restoration is practically proved to be correct. Throughout the five books of Moses, to which the Samaritan text is confined, the symbol $^{7}\ldots^{n}$ will be found. This denotes that the Septuagint and the Samaritan agree in restoring to the text the word or words between the ^{7} and ^{n}. We feel that they must have belonged to the original, hence value them as most precious treasures and vital parts of God's revelation, which have been lost a long, long time, but now have been restored to the ordinary reader of the Scriptures.

THE GREEK VERSIONS

The Greek version of the Hebrew, which was made by Jewish rabbis about the third century before Christ, differs considerably from the present Hebrew text. As the manuscripts of this version go back more than five hundred years earlier than the oldest Hebrew, and were made from a text more than five hundred years earlier still, it contains evidence for a text at least a thousand years previous to the Hebrew text now in circulation. Hence we make much use of it in recovering the original which lies back of both. The Greek suffers from some of the same faults in transmission as the Hebrew. A single letter in Hebrew, which can easily drop out or be mistaken for another, may need a whole word in Greek (as it does in English), which is not nearly so easily taken for another. Hence the Greek is a safer witness in some ways.

LATER GREEK VERSIONS

About the second century after the coming of Christ, several fresh Greek versions, or revisions, were made, conforming to the Hebrew text of that time, which were much nearer the Masoretic text of today than that used for the Septuagint. Only fragments of these remain. They may offer slight aid in restoring the text, because the Septuagint does not always give a close rendering of the original, and is itself subject to errors of transcription. Three of these ancient versions are of special note. Each has a character of its own. But they have not nearly the weight of the earlier Septuagint because they were made from a much later Hebrew text, after a period of fierce controversy, in which the temptation to alter the Hebrew was very strong.

AQUILA'S LITERAL TRANSLATION

In the controversies of the early centuries, the Jews claimed that the Septuagint differed from the Hebrew, so they rejected it. This was partly because a new school of Jewish interpreters had formed another Hebrew text, which differed from the earlier one on which the Septuagint was based. To serve those who did not understand Hebrew, a very close, literal translation was made by Aquila. It is so crude that it can hardly be called a version. When there had been no change in the Hebrew, it sometimes gives a closer rendering than the older Septuagint.

THEODOTION'S REVISION

Another Jewish proselyte, Theodotion, revised the Septuagint to conform it to the later Hebrew text. He is not literal like Aquila, yet he actually transliterates about a hundred words. In some places his version was used instead of the Septuagint. As some of the quotations found in the inspired Greek Scriptures agree with his version, there must have been an earlier revision, at least of portions, on which he based his work.

SYMMACHUS' IDIOMATIC VERSION

A version expressing the sense in Greek idiom seems to have been the aim of Symmachus, who is said to have been a leader of the Ebionites. As a result, his version is of little help in restoring the text, except in connection with other evidence.

ORIGEN'S HEXAPLA

As the Septuagint differed from the Hebrew, Origen, who lived in the third century, sought to revise it, so as to conform it to the Hebrew text of his day. As a tool for this work he wrote the so-called "Hexapla," with six columns, as a rule. In the first column he wrote the Hebrew words or phrases, one under the other. In the second he spelled the Hebrew, as well as he could, in Greek letters. In the third he gave Aquila's literal renderings. In the fourth was Symmachus'. The fifth had the current Septuagint. The sixth gave Theodotion's version. As Origen assumed the purity of the Hebrew text and labored to conform the Septuagint to it, marking as doubtful everything which did not agree with it, his work had a false start and has little value, except as evidence of the state of the texts in his day. Only fragments of his work have come down to us.

TEXT OF THE SEPTUAGINT

The latest edition of the Septuagint, issued in 1935 by Rahlfs, is based mainly on the three most ancient manuscripts, Vaticanus (B), Sinaiticus (s), and Alexandrinus (A). These are the same as those used in compiling the Concordant Greek text. Hence it is fitting to use them in restoring the Hebrew. The margin gives their readings, so that the experience gained in compiling the former work helps us to evaluate the readings of these great witnesses, and it is not necessary to blindly follow the main text as it stands. This work is probably the most valuable aid in recovering the ancient Hebrew original. The main improvement needed is to conform its text to the Hebrew when one of the manuscripts is in agreement with it. This we do, and so have the best tool for restoring the ancient text of inspiration that has yet been found. As a result the Greek and Hebrew agree. They make good sense in translation and are in harmony with their contexts and with each other.

THE LUCIANIC READINGS

The Lucian revision of the Septuagint, made in the last quarter of the third century by an elder of the ecclesia at Antioch, contains readings not found in other manuscripts which point to a Hebrew original evidently superior to the Masoretic text. As the Rahlfs edition with which we compare the Hebrew is based on a very thorough study of this evidence and fully recognizes these in the text or footnotes, they have helped us to restore some important passages.

MISTAKES IN THE SEPTUAGINT

The Greek version suffers somewhat from the same kind of mistakes in transmission as the Hebrew. Generally, Greek words have more letters, and these are more distinct from one another, but sometimes one word is taken for another. In Mal. 1:3 the Greek reads **boundaries** where the Hebrew has **mountains.** The difference between the two is very great in Hebrew, but very small in Greek. Boundaries is [*h*]*oria*; [*h*]*orê* is mountains. Hence we reject the Septuagint reading, and use the Hebrew. In confirmation we may note the fact that Edom is mountainous, and it makes a more vigorous sense to threaten that these **mountains** are to become a desolation, than the **boundaries.**

OMISSIONS FROM THE HEBREW TEXT

Hear the word of Ieue, ye captains of Sodom!
Give ear to the law of [our] Alueim, ye people of Gomorrah! (Is. 1:10).

This is a perfect parallelism if we leave out the pronoun "our." The Greek omits the whole word [*h*]*êmōn*, (our). The Hebrew ending —nu (our) looks very much like the letter m, and was substituted for it by mistake. The ancient text probably agreed with the Greek, as this would occasion very little change in the appearance of the Hebrew, but demands the addition of a whole word in the Greek. The omission of "our" improves the parallelism. Besides, the possessive pronoun does not seem to harmonize with the place of distance given the people by the bold figure used. Here apostate Israel is compared with Sodom. As such, God is not their God.

OMISSIONS IN BOTH TEXTS

The Greek translation sometimes reads differently from the Hebrew, and concordances which connect the two are at a loss which word stands for which. Gn. 18:1, for example, ends with the phrase **as the day is warm** in Hebrew, yet has only **midday** in Greek. One cannot well represent the other. But if we take **both,** then there is quite an improvement, for it is at noon that the day is warm. Therefore we **add** "at noon," seeing that the Hebrew equivalent of the Greek calls for NOON as its standard. Combining the two, we have Abraham sitting at the opening of the tent **at noon, as the day is warm.** This gives a harmonious and satisfactory sense. The words from the Septuagint are distinguished for the reader by being enclosed by the superior figures [70] thus: [7]**at noon**[0].

The Concordant Version was started with the intention of cleaving closely to the Masoretic text. When this proved clearly impossible, we turned to the early versions, especially such as were literal in their renderings. But we found many differences in these also, because most of them were made from a text corrupted by the great controversies which followed the coming of Christ. Eventually it became clear that the safest evidence for restoring the text is found in the so-called LXX, the Septuagint, which was made before the advent of the Messiah. Our text, therefore, is based on all the worthwhile evidence at our command, but especially on the Masoretic Hebrew text as restored by the Samaritan Hebrew (in the Pentateuch) and the Septuagint. It does not necessarily agree with any, but is the result of their evidence combined with the context. Special attention was paid to parallelisms and other literary structures, for these are often decisive in establishing the ancient reading.

The procedure is as follows: The margins of Ginsburg and the readings of Davidson are transferred to our Hebrew text. Then it is compared with the Samaritan, in the Pentateuch. Then the Hebrew and Greek texts are collated, and the differences noted on the Hebrew and a record kept in the Greek by underlining all words which disagree. Greek words which do not appear in the Hebrew are put in parentheses. Omitted words are indicated by empty parentheses. Then each variation is considered from various standpoints, according to the circumstances. Often the question arises, Is there a Hebrew word corresponding to the Greek, that looks much like the Hebrew in the text? The Greek word is examined in a concordance that gives all of the Hebrew words which it translates in the LXX. Thus, in Gn. 4:7, *apostrophê*, FROM-TURNING, refuge, does not agree with the Hebrew thshqe, run about. But, if the q is changed to b (which is quite similar to it) then the Greek and Hebrew agree, and we have **restoration.**

Hebrew is the basis of the Concordant Version, even when it follows translations in other languages. Each word is first restored to Hebrew, and then turned into English in accord with our principles and standards. The versions are too loose and discordant to use in direct restoration. Usually there is sufficient evidence to fix the precise Hebrew word of the ancient original, but sometimes there is a slight question as to the exact rendering. In this case the word or phrase is followed by a small, high question mark (?). This does not indicate necessarily that we doubt its correctness. It shows only that it is not based on direct evidence, but deduced from facts, and such a deduction is always questionable among mortals. Our aim in a concordant version is to keep strictly to the facts, and to avoid the human element, but, when this intrudes, we wish our readers to be aware of it.

QUOTATIONS FROM THE HEBREW

(Ps. 8:2, 4-6, Mt. 21:16, Hb. 2:6-7)

Inspired quotations from the Hebrew in the Greek Scriptures are the best evidence for the integrity of the Hebrew text. When these agree, we may be sure that we have the real original. When they disagree, we must make sure that we have a real quotation, and not an adaptation, or a mere allusion or reference.

In the second chapter of Hebrews, verses six and seven, we have a quotation from the eighth psalm which agrees very closely with the Hebrew text as it now stands. Only two expressions really differ, so that the Hebrew text needs to be changed. There are other slight variations, but these arise from the idioms of the languages. The Hebrew Ps. 8:2 reads **found strength** where the Greek has **attune praise** (Mt. 21:16). In verses four to six, the Greek has **messengers**, where the Hebrew has **Alueim**. The phrase, "ordained strength," was changed to "**established** strength" by the English Revisers. But it seems wrong to **found strength**, as the Hebrew actually says, out of the **mouth** of sucklings. We expect something to come out of the mouth, and this is what we find in the inspired quotation, **attune praise.** Let us see if the Hebrew scribe may have slipped up in copying this, after the Septuagint was translated. The Hebrew reads: isdthoz. In the Aramaic square letters, in which Hebrew was written after the return from Babylon, these letters have many strokes in common with iklthon, which means **conclude** a **response.** Now if we will turn to the passage in Matthew (21:15), we will see that when the boys in the sanctuary cried, saying, **"Hosanna to the Son of David!"** the chief priests and scribes resented it. They did not **respond,** but the boys did. The proposed rendering fits in perfectly.

Our Authorized Version did not follow the Hebrew in rendering "Thou hast made him a little lower than the angels." The Revisers changed this to "gods," with the margin "Or, the angels, Heb. Elohim." Here again there is quite a similarity between the two renderings in Hebrew, due to the fact that the letter m (meaning **from**) stands before **God.** The Hebrew reads maleim (from God). This might easily be copied by mistake from mlakim (messengers). The letters are the same except the e and k, although two are transposed. The evidence of the inspired quotation, besides the Septuagint (which would be sufficient by itself), justifies us in restoring the text to **messengers.** This does away with a grave difficulty. Man was not made a **little lower than God!** To interpret it as meaning a little **while**, only makes matters worse, as if we would yet be the equals of the great Subjector! The argument in the epistle to the Hebrews is decisive. There the Son of God is **better** than the **messengers** (Hb. 1:2-14). In contrast to this, as the Son of Mankind, He was made a little **lower** than the messengers for the suffering of death. Mankind is made **some whit inferior** to the **messengers.** Only in Christ, and as partakers of His glories, can mankind take a place superior to messengers. Of this the Psalmist was not aware.

DEFECTIVE SPELLING

Many vowels are left out of modern Hebrew texts, principally as a result of the additions of the vowel and other signs. A comparison of parallel passages, such as 2 Sa. 22 and Ps. 18, makes it evident that this is mostly a matter of chance. The Psalm has about twenty more vowel letters, as well as mn for m (which both mean **from**) **twice.** The vowels u, i, e, and a, are often omitted because they can be replaced by signs, and are usually serviles, which do not affect the sense, but the grammar. We strive to spell all words in full.

As the Septuagint often spells Achan with an r in place of an **n**, and this means trouble, and the valley has this name, we correct Achan to Achar throughout. The Hebrew words look alike, thus: עכן okn, עכר okr.

2. THE REVISION OF THE HEBREW GRAMMAR

Grammatically, Hebrew belongs to an entirely different group of languages than English. Much confusion has been introduced by using grammatical terms which are foreign to Hebrew, and not only do not fit, but denote forms which do not even exist. The Hebrew "verb" is quite different from the English. It has no tense. It changes its form slightly to express **being** and **causing**, and has **passives** of these, as well as a **reflexive** form. All this is done without auxiliaries, by simply prefixing, inserting, or affixing a letter or two. In English we usually add an auxiliary, as **be**, **have**, or **cause** or **self**, but often our word fits one of these forms without change, as **be blest** (state), **be blest** [by] (passive), **bless self** (reflexive). The two great classes of verbs in Hebrew are called the **Complete** (Perfect) and the **Incomplete** (Imperfect).

In a concordant version the grammar must be consistent and the English equivalents have uniform and exclusive standards. This has necessitated a thorough revision of Hebrew grammar. It has been reclassified according to the facts. New names have been given which express the function of each form. Much contained in former grammars has been verified, but far-reaching changes have been made, so that this version should, under no circumstances, be used with other grammars, but compared only with the brief presentation given herewith. It is based on an exhaustive concordance of every form found in the Scriptures, and a special card index of all the branches of the verb. Only such changes have been made as were dictated by the actual evidence and the principles underlying the laws of language. It will help to point out those features in which this version differs from the usually accepted grammars.

THE ORIGINAL NATURE LANGUAGE

Hebrew, being the original, inspired tongue, not confused by the disintegration of Babel, cannot be translated into a modern language uniformly as the Concordant Version of the Greek Scriptures was done, but must use several grammatical forms for one Hebrew form to give the time, to suit the context. The very same letter combination, though having the same broad significance, may have a different usage, due to the context.

As the older Hebrew grammars referred to the "preterite" and the "future" of Hebrew verbs, we gave this a prolonged test. But we were forced to the conclusion that the Hebrew verb does not indicate the "tense" or **time** by modifying the spelling of the verb, but, as Samuel Pike said long ago, "In the Hebrew language, it is taken for granted that a person may know by the very scope, drift and currency of what he reads, whether it is the history of a thing **past**, a prophecy or promise of things **future**: or a doctrine or moral observation about what is true at **present**, or continually, and the like; so that there is no necessity to distinguish the one from the other by the use of tenses. And it is very evident that this is not the proper design of them in the Hebrew; for both the tenses, called the **preter** and the **future** are used equally and promiscuously in prophecies or promises of things long to come, and of histories of things long past. So that, when in Hebrew we are reading history, we must translate the **future** as well as the the preter tense, as if relating what is past; and in prophecy, we must explain the **preter** as well as future tense, as speaking of things to come."

God's revelation is on a higher spiritual plane than other literature. Especially in prophecy, both past and future, God sometimes speaks of things as if they are being enacted before our eyes. John, in his apocalype saw and heard what he records, although they were in the far future. So there are times when the present participial form, **—ing**, is appropriate in English (see Gen. 1:2, 3, 4, etc.)

HEBREW IDIOM

As Hebrew grammar is much simpler than later languages, the forms cover more ground than they, so exact equivalents depend on the context as well as the form. Thus it is with breath of **lives** (nshmth chiim) or of **the living**. As the Hebrew is plural, the first may be closer to the original, but, as it is not clear English and the word **living** implies the plural in this context, it may be preferable. Names, also, may be adapted to their application. Moses (Mshe), for instance, means Removed, when used of his removal from the water (Ex. 2:10). But it is more than likely that it includes his life-work as the Remover of Israel from Egypt to Canaan.

THE HEBREW VERB

Much obscurity has been introduced into the study of the first language of mankind by the use of grammatical terms, such as **past, present,** and **future** for which Hebrew has no forms. The **person** of verbs is indicated by prefixing the first part of primitive pronouns or affixing the latter part to a stem, which, by itself denotes third person, he, or it. This method divides the verb into two great classes, which we may call the **Complete** and the **Incomplete** forms. The **Complete** form calls mostly for the English Indefinite (incorrectly called the "Present"), or the Past tense, whereas the **Incomplete** form usually is rendered by the Present Participle (—ing), or Future, since this form is usually used of actions not yet completed. This agrees with the usual division into Preterite (Past), and future. In some new grammars these are called the Perfect and Imperfect states. In all cases, however, it must agree with the tenor of the context.

The Hebrew language, like living objects in nature, and unlike the lifeless angular contraptions built by man, conforms to its surroundings, and varies to suit circumstances. Occasionally there are additional letters, as **a, e, u, i, n, th,** for various reasons, such as emphasis, or ease in pronunciation. It is exceedingly condensed, and was a laborious and expensive method of writing, so we must expect brevity to be the rule.

The accompanying table, the **Chart of the Hebrew Verb,** shows the prefixes and endings of the three **Persons, singular** and **plural,** for the **Complete** and **Incomplete** forms. The three dots represent the usual three stem letters.

CHART OF THE HEBREW VERB

COMPLETE		INCOMPLETE	(FEMININE)
...*thi*	I	*a...*	
...*th*	YOU (sing.)	*th...*	*th...i*
...	HE or IT	*i...*	
...*e*	SHE	*th...*	
...***nu***	WE	*n...*	
...*thm* (masc) ...*thn* (fem)	YE	*th...u*	*th...ne*
...*u*	THEY	*i...u*	*th...ne*
Generally "I write" "I wrote"	Idiomatic English equivalents governed by the context.	"I am writing" "I will write"	

Passive of Complete form made by prefixing *n* to the stem.
Reflexive (self) form made by prefixing *eth* to the stem.
Imperative (command) form made by **prefixing** *en* to the stem.
Causative form made by prefixing *e* to the stem and inserting *i* between the second and third radicals (or stem letters).

Besides the two classes above, Hebrew verbs have two **Branches,** Causative and Reflexive, (self); two **Modes,** Indicative (I-do) and Imperative (Do); two **Voices,** Active and Passive; two **Verbals,** Infinitives (to-) and Participles (-ing). These are reflected, as nearly as possible, by the idiomatic English equivalents.

The Participles and Infinitives, being of the nature of an adjective or a noun, may be so rendered, to agree with the context.

PASSIVE VERBS

The nature of the Simple and Causative Incomplete classes of verbs is such that they cannot be inactive or **passive,** so these have **no** such form. But the Simple Complete form indicates its Passive (Niphal) by prefixing *n...* to the Indicative, or *en...* to the Imperative. In the Causative Complete branch, the Passive form (Hophal) is indicated by the **omission** of the *i* of the Causative Complete form (*e...* for *e..i.*).

The Reflexive **Self** branch (Hithpael) by its nature cannot be passive.

IDIOMATIC CAUSE FORMS

Other words must often take the place of **cause.** In place of **cause light, cause ear** and **cause alive** we must say ᶜ**give light,** ᶜ**give ear** and ᶜ**preserve alive.**

TIME OR TENSE

In Hebrew it is not necessary to change the verb to suit the time. They say simply "I go tomorrow" or "I go yesterday," not "I will go tomorrow," or "I **went** yesterday." Their simple method is just as clear, when the context indicates the time. Yet, even then, idiomatic English forces us to insert the time words or forms. As the time is indicated, to put these auxiliaries, **will** and the form **went** (which includes the word **go**) in lightface, might be misleading, so we serve this notice on the student, that these words have been added or adapted by us for the sake of English idiom, and he must consult the context for the evidence.

THE MASORETIC GRAMMAR

From the inception of this work, about a half century since, we decided that the points in the Hebrew texts are not inspired. But we supposed that some of them were used to indicate letters that had been dropped to gain space. Recent finds show that this is not the case. These letters are lacking as well as the points. This has led us to revise the grammar, omitting everything entirely dependent on points.

Before this, the grave difficulties attending an accurate and concordant rendering of these forms had led us to doubt their existence. They seem to have been an attempt of the Masorites to register varieties of usage rather than grammar. As these differ in the idioms of all languages, they vary with each word, and are explained in the lexicon. For instance, lmd **learn** is used of things, **teach** of persons, in English. This is indicated by another word in the **context**, not by a grammatical alteration in the spelling of the word **learn.** The **meaning** is the same if we say **learn others**, as in Hebrew. Modern **usage** only requires the change.

In the **noun** it is usually supposed that Hebrew has no neuter **gender**, but we name the so-called "masculine" an **indefinite**, and thus cover all genders.

The so-called "infinitive" and "participle" we call **verbals.** The former is a verbal **noun**, and belongs with the **Complete** forms; the latter is a verbal **adjective**, and belongs with the **Incomplete** forms. As these are very often the same in form as nouns and adjectives, they are often translated as such.

The so-called Hebrew "root" we call the **stem**, as this figures its function far better than a root system, out of which the main stem of a plant emerges. Instead of "radicals" we have **stem letters.** And this leads us to speak of the modifications of the stem, which spring out of it, as **branches.**

A "conjugation" of the verb we call a **branch** because it is an addition to the simple stem, and springs from it like the branch from the stem of a plant.

A special effort has been made to distinguish the various branches, as this has been largely overlooked hitherto. We differ in making the simple stem a **state**, rather than an action, as a rule, and use the auxiliaries **is** and **have** to express this in English. In this way we are able to distinguish the simple stem of the **Complete** form from the other branches, which has hitherto seemed impossible in many instances.

As so few of the Chaldee grammatical forms occur in the Scriptures, we do not publish special tables. We have compared the Chaldee with the Hebrew and used the same standards in comparable forms. In general the so-called **Peal = Kal**, the **Pael = Piel**, the Aphel = Hiphil, the Ithpeal = Hithpael.

Regularly, when the simple stem denotes a **state**, as **be resolute**, the Cause and the Self branches use these very words in the English renderings. The word **resolute** (amtz) may be rendered "**Be resolute**!" (Dt. 31:6) in the simple stem, "**cause** [your heart] to **be resolute**" (Ps. 27:14) in the Cause branch, and "[make] **themselves resolute**" (2 Chr. 13:7) in the Self branch. This simple method can be used throughout the sublinear whenever the Hebrew simple stem denotes the **state** of **being** something, as above.

HEBREW CONTEXTUAL

The context is employed by Hebrew for brevity's sake and to assure safety, far more than in the Teutonic languages into which it is mostly translated, therefore it cannot always be translated without relying on the connection to a large extent. For instance, it does not use the stem **be**, expressing mere existence, because that is self-evident. But the form **cause-be**, is often used. Even **become** must often be varied to "**come to be**," or **bcome**, or even **bec**, to accord with English idiom. But the **sense** is always the same. In the Greek Scriptures the word **be** seldom occurs, and is either emphatic or a figure of speech, as in the phrase "This **is** My body."

WORD BUILDING

The very simple structure of the language, being based on comparatively few stems, which, like trees, have branches, but unlike them each branch varies a little in its fruit, makes the various members of a word family (to change the figure), with one basic trend, yet very different in character.

THE PRONOUN

Pieces of the pronoun are added to verbs, nouns and particles in Hebrew in order to express the **person, singular**, I, you, it (or he); and **plural**, we, ye, they, with special forms for the **feminine**, you, she, ye, and they. See the table of verbs for this use. The fragments **follow** in the Complete forms, but **precede**, or are on **both** ends, of the word in the Incomplete forms.

As **suffixes**, pieces of the pronouns are largely used to point out the **object** in verbs, me, you, him, her, us, you (plural), and them. But they indicate the **genitive**, or possession, in nouns, my, your, his, her, our, your, their.

When a separate object is needed they are added to the sign of the accusative, or object, ath. See the table of Pronouns.

GRAMMAR OF THE PRONOUN

SEPARATE PRONOUN	USED WITH VERBS	SUFFIXES OF NOUNS	SUFFIXES OF VERBS	SEPARATE OBJECT
anki, anuki, ani I	I- . . . *thi*	—*i* MY	—*ni* ME	*ath i* —ME
athe YOU	YOU- . . . *th*	—*k* YOUR	—*k* YOU	*ath k* —YOU
ath YOU*f*				
eua HE	it-, he- . . .	—*eu*, —*u* HIS	—*eu*, —*u* HIM	*ath u* —HIM
eia SHE	SHE- . . . *e*	—*e* HER	—*e* HER	*ath e* —HER
anchnu, anu WE	WE- . . . *nu*	—*nu* OUR	—*nu* US	*ath nu* —US
athm YE YOU*p*	YE- . . . *thm*	—*km* YOUR*p*	—*km* YOU*p*	*ath km* —YOU*p*
athne, athn YE*f*	YE*f*- . . . *thn*	—*kn* YOUR*pf*	—*kn* YOU*pf*	
eme, em THEY	THEY- . . . *u*	—*em*, —*m* THEIR	—*em*, —*m* THEM	*ath m* —THEM
ene, en THEY*f*		—*en*, —*n* THEIR*f*	—*en*, —*n* THEM*f*	*ath n* —THEM*f*

THE HEBREW ELEMENTS

In the margin of the Concordant version the Hebrew is transliterated in *italic* type. The English transliterations use SMALL CAPITAL letters for the **stem** or central meaning, and common type for the modifications.

THE DEFINITE ARTICLE

The Hebrew definite article E corresponds somewhat in usage to the English "the." In the version a high period is used when the article cannot be expressed in English.

When the article is lacking in Hebrew we omit it, if possible, in the version. If "the" is used in the version where it fails in the Hebrew it is printed in lightface type.

Proper names of persons or cities are always without the article. Especial care is needed with such names as Adam which may mean human or humanity.

A noun with a possessive affix never has the article, as *susi*, my horse (never *Esusi*, the my horse).

THE HEBREW PLURAL

The plural, in Hebrew, denotes **two,** unless the context calls for more, so that it is necessary to add the numeral two at times, as when the Hebrew **fifty and hundreds** must be rendered two =**hundred** *a* **fifty** (Ex. 30:24). **Three** parallel lines (≡) indicate the plural in Greek, but only **two** (=) in Hebrew.

FORCE OF AUXILIARY LETTERS

In the formation of words and names, the stem is usually modified by the addition or insertion of auxiliary letters, such as the vowels **a, e, i, u,** and consonants **b, k, l, m, n.** Some seem to have a somewhat constant force, as the letter **n** for the passive, **i** for the causative, **th** for the self branch of the verb. In a few this seems quite clear. The letter **b** (in) suggests **inclusion,** the letter **m** (from) **derivation,** to form nouns from verbs, the letter **th** (give) **dispensation.** The letter **a** seems sometimes used as an **intensive.** These terms must be given their widest meaning to cover all cases.

The letters of the Name of the Deity, Ieue, are translated for us in the book of the Unveiling of Jesus Christ (1:4, 11:17, 16:5), so that we know their force when used of **time: I** (will) **e** (be) **u** (ing) **e** (was). According to this, **i** has the general sense of **causation, e of existence,** and **u of continuance.** As the letter **e** is the (unused) verb **be,** and **u** is constantly used for **and,** and the **i** is used in the pronouns **I, my,** and **me,** and to form the causative verb, it may suggest the widest sense of **causation.**

Many names of persons in the Scripture have a stem which can be determined from its usage in general. Thus **dm** denotes **like.** But why was an **a** prefixed when applied to Adam and humanity? As these are **most** like Alueim of all land life, we suggest that the **a** is **intensive,** and makes the meaning **likest.**

Three rivers of Eden have an **i** inserted in their stem, so we end all their names with —**er** to show that it is caused by their action. **Phishun** (Pison) is Diffuser, **Chuile** (Havilah) is **Travailer, Gichun** is Forth-rusher. Eve's name, however, is **Chue,** as the **u** denotes continuance we render it **living**, not liv-er. The peculiarities of modern languages, however, demand a departure from uniformity and accuracy in most cases, so the work is only suggestive and should be viewed in the light of the context.

As an important example, let us take the letter **l**. Before and distinct from a word, it has the general force of **to**. With an emphatic or nominal **a-** in front of it, it may be simply an emphatic form, or indicate a nuance which we are not able to express in English. But **a-** makes nouns, so it may mean **to-er**, one who directs or turns something or -one **to** aught else. The Septuagint translates it The-os **Plac-er**, and uses it of the Deity. There is much else that confirms this, and a study of God's consummation shows that it has the special sense of **Subjector** (1 Cor. 15:28). So we use SUBJECTOR as our standard.

3. THE COMPILATION OF THE VOCABULARY

THE ENGLISHMAN'S HEBREW CONCORDANCE

The dire need of a concordant version was first suggested to the compiler by the use of Wigram's concordances. Under the words of the original, these concordances give the passages as rendered by the Authorized Version, with their translation in italic letters. One would expect each Hebrew word to be represented by the same English term, with a few variations for the sake of idiom. This is so in some cases. Nevertheless many renderings are startlingly inconsistent. But the worst feature of such a version is the cross-wiring. Not only are many expressions used for a single word in the original, but these, in turn, serve to render other Hebrew words. This makes clarity and exactitude impossible.

To clear up this confusion, the contexts of each word were examined in order to discover the nearest English equivalent. This was underlined or entered as the exclusive term for this word only. The same was also done in the Hebrew and English indexes. To avoid being used for any other term, it was crossed out wherever it occurred elsewhere. In this way a concordant, exclusive vocabulary was built up. It was modified only when English idiom demanded it.

Word families were also studied in this way, and each stem of one, two, three or more letters was given a comprehensive STANDARD, which was distinguished by CAPITAL letters. By associating all words from the same stem together, the field of evidence for the meaning was widened. This was especially helpful when there were few occurrences, or the contexts gave no assistance.

Concordances of the Greek translation, with their indexes, which show what Greek words were used for each Hebrew expression, and the number of times, were a great help, not only in fixing the exact sense, but in adapting the version to that of the Greek Scriptures. The same things were given the same names when practicable. In collating the Greek with the Hebrew in fixing the text, the original was continually checked by the translation.

The literary form of large portions of the Hebrew, especially the numerous parallelisms, call for a close discrimination of synonyms, which helped much to refine and confirm our findings. By working with the whole vocabulary at once, it is possible to sort out the nearest English expressions much more satisfactorily than by dealing with only one word at a time. There is always a possibility that the English term fits another Hebrew word more closely and vice versa. The only drawback is a small amount of stiffness and awkwardness due to the emphasis, syllabication, or other obscure and unimportant causes, which we seek to overcome by slight adjustments in the English diction. The strangeness will disappear with use.

THOUGHT-RHYMES AS AN AID TO EXACT TRANSLATION

It is well known that the Psalms are "poetry," although only the Scotch paraphrases seem to show this in English. We think of poetry as metrical or rhyming. But, notwithstanding earnest efforts to discover some such literary features in the Hebrew Scriptures, it is questionable if they exist. Indeed, even if there were, how difficult would this be to translate closely! Instead, as everyone who reads the Bible attentively has doubtless observed, Hebrew poetry consists rather in the repetition of harmonious or nearly synonymous **ideas**, that is, in **thought-rhymes**. As an appropriate example, consider the words Hosea used to close his prophecy,

Who is wise also understands these things,
Understanding, he also knows them.

One of the chief tasks of a translator is to discover the exact thought area covered by each word, and to distinguish it from its near neighbors. Thus, in the parallel couplet just quoted, we have three words, **wise, understand, know.** It is neither easy nor practical to test these English equivalents by seeking to define them by words. A more direct and satisfactory way is to interchange them and note the effect. Suppose we render the couplet thus:

Who understands is also wise in these things,
And knowing, he also understands them.

But, alas, the understanding are not always wise, and one who understands has already gone beyond mere knowledge. The test brings out the beauty of the text as first translated, where wisdom has the highest place, understanding next and knowledge last. The wise will first understand Hosea's message, then they will make it their possession in the form of knowledge. Is it not clear that these words should never be interchanged in translation? It is one of the commendable features of our honored Authorized Version that it usually keeps them distinct. Yet, with regret, we note that it uses **wise** in place of **understanding** (Prov. 17:10, 28:7) where the distinction may not be so clear. But is it not just as good English to be consistent in these passages? We would suggest:

A rebuke is ⁷dismaying⁷ one who has understanding
More than a hundred smitings in one who is stupid.
He who preserves the law is an understanding son,
Yet an associate of prodigals confounds his father.

Our venerable version also renders another Hebrew word, which denotes **intelligent,** by means of **wise.** In these cases, to use a pardonable pun, the translation cannot be said to be **wise!** Among others we would suggest (Prov. 17:2)

An **intelligent servant** shall **rule over a son who causes shame,**
And shall **be apportioned a lot among brothers.**

THOUGHT DIVERGENCE

Unlike the poetry of sound, thought stanzas may show contrast in place of concord. They may be parallel in form, but antithetic in thought. They may give us antonyms in place of synonyms. Yet these literary forms are also valuable in fixing the thought contents and limits of the Hebrew words employed and help much in choosing the most suitable English equivalents. The following is a familiar example (Prov. 10:1):

A wise son is rejoicing a father,
Yet a stupid son is the humiliation of his mother.

4. IDIOMATIC ENGLISH, SPELLING, ETC.

CONTROLLED IDIOM

Idiom is the figure of speech which, to a large extent, renounces uniformity, and expresses a thought in accord with the peculiarities of a language. All versions are idiomatic, but the Concordant Version endeavors to keep the idiom under control, so that the translator cannot introduce his own ideas under the cover of idiomatic language. The A.V. renders the word for **hallow** as follows: proclaim (a solemn assembly 2 Ki. 10:20), prepare (war Jr. 6:4), sanctify (a fast Joel 2:15). The first two words, proclaim and prepare, do not express the sense of holy at all, and it is hardly good English to sanctify a fast, nor does it agree with the previous renderings. We have rendered it consistently: proclaim or herald a **holy war** (or **assembly,** or **fast**), thus giving a uniform rendering in accord with present day English.

The **sublinear** manuscript, as in the Greek, is **uniform** in its translations, without any regard for understandable English. It is an intermediate form, using **English words** after the **Hebrew manner.** The **version,** however, is the complement of the Hebrew, and uses the English words according to the **English** idiom. It is **not uniform,** but **consistent,** or **concordant.** Our venerable Authorized Version is supposed to be very idiomatic English, unlike the Hebrew. But a comparison of the most popular passages will show that its attractive style is not due to the pure English of the translators' day, but **because it has followed the Hebrew.** It was **not** "good" English until custom and age and associations transformed it into the best diction in the language. This has encouraged us to do likewise, even at the risk of temporary unpopularity, for only by cleaving closely to the Hebrew can we carry over the emphasis and other literary features which reveal the vivacity and force of the inspired original.

OMISSIONS OF THE PRONOUN

The pronouns, I, you, he, she, they, etc., are omitted without further notation, when English idiom does not demand it and the sense is clear, in the following cases, among others: When verbs follow one another, the later pronouns are understood in English. When Hebrew uses forms which imply the pronoun even when a noun is present, as, **And he-takes . . . Eleazar.** This we render **And Eleazar takes,** omitting the **he.** Such phrases as **which . . . in her** are resolved into **in which,** dropping the last pronoun, which is unnecessary for the sense.

THE EMPHATIC PRONOUN

Ordinary English diction has a very weakening effect on its verbs, for it usually puts the pronoun first, which is the emphatic position. The languages of the original use only one or more letters added to the stem, without affecting the emphasis. Therefore we put the pronoun **after** the verb when it is **not** emphatic. Yet if the pronoun is repeated in the inspired text, we repeat it, and put it first. In this way the point of the passage is made prominent, and the **person** is emphasized, if needed, yet the act when this is the real point.

MEANING AND USAGE

A **uniform sublinear** can give us the **meaning** of the words, but a **concordant version** must pay attention to their **usage** also. If the Hebrew connectives **in, to,** and **from** were always carried over into a version, it could no longer be understood. Usually they may be used. "**In the beginning**" is just as clear in English as in Hebrew. But we cannot say, "**sway in the fish**" (Gn. 1:26). We say sway **iover.** In this case we point out the change by putting a small **i** for **in** before **over.** This is done throughout when practicable, where English usage demands a word with quite a different **meaning.** But the Hebrew usage is retained as much as possible when it is understandable, for the Authorized Version has shown that it can readily and happily be assimilated by our tongue.

THE IDIOM OF THE ARTICLE (THE)

As there is some difference in the usage of the article in Hebrew and English, it is indicated in the Concordant Version by means of an inconspicuous dot when absent, and printed in lightface type when inserted in English. We cannot well say, "**Yet spirit of Alueim is vibrating over face of the water.**" We must insert "the" thrice. "**Yet** the **spirit of** the **Alueim** is **vibrating over** the **surface of the water.**" (Gn. 1:2). On the other hand, English idiom forbids us to say, "**And making is the Alueim two the great the luminaries.**" We must omit the two articles and say, "**And making is** the **Alueim two ·great ·luminaries.**" The two high dots show that **the** is in the original.

The so-called "indefinite" article (a or an) has the force of **one,** hence does not take the place of the missing Hebrew article. In neither Hebrew nor English has the article the force of the only one, but rather implies others, if emphasized.

THE SIGN FOR THE OBJECT

The Hebrew ath, commonly called an "article," simply points out the accusative case, or the object of the verb. There is no particle in English which has this force, so we replace it by a short stroke, like a \grave \accent, to show where it occurs in the original and to indicate the fact that the following noun is not the subject, but the object of the sentence.

SPECIAL HEBREW IDIOMS

The A.V. translates the literal Hebrew "to die you shall be dying" (Gn. 2:17), as "thou shalt surely die." Yet the event agreed perfectly with the literal Hebrew, but not with the English version. Adam became mortal and eventually died, just as his descendants do today. This idiom occurs quite often. We do not wish to follow the example of the A.V. in interpreting this form of expression. It probably is used as a figure on many occasions in order to stress a statement, but it may also be quite literal, as in the case of Adam. Figures, as a rule, need not be interpreted, but may be carried over from one language to another. Hence it seems wisest to introduce this form of expression into our version in some cases, and depend upon its context to teach the English reader its force and function. When it is used to strengthen a statement, we usually repeat the verb twice, separated by a "yea" in lightface type. In Gn. 50:24 Joseph tells his brothers, "**Yet visit,** yea **visit** will the **Alueim you.**" When this is not possible, and an adverb is supplied the initial letter of the repeated verb is affixed to it. If we used **surely** in this passage, we would put a small v, in Roman type, before it to show that it is a repetition of the word **visit** in the Hebrew text. It would read v**surely visit.**

When it was deemed necessary, we have coined a new word. Due to the theory of evolution the word **species** has lost its definite meaning of an interbreeding community, such as is indicated by the Hebrew "min" (cause-**from**), so we have used a combination of **from,** the meaning of the Hebrew, and **kind,** the familiar term of our most popular version, and separate them by a hyphen, and suggest that it be adopted into the English vocabulary (Gn. 1:11, 12, 21, 24, etc.).

THE SPELLING OF THE PROPER NAMES

In the margin we spell all Hebrew proper names as they should be pronounced, translated from the Original, so that all will have the evidence before them.

Names variously spelled in the A.V., as Hezekiah, Hizkiah, Hizkijah, are rendered uniformly **Hezekiah.** The letter **j** and its sound **dg** are unknown in Hebrew, so we avoid it when possible. Usually the A.V. ends words with **a**, when the Hebrew has it, but with **ah** when the original has **e**, so we have carried out this rule more uniformly.

By applying the two cardinal principles of a concordant version, many names had to be slightly changed, but not enough to bring in confusion in the minds of Bible readers. Thus Iddo, standing as it does for six distinct Hebrew names, has been changed, in five instances, to **Adu, Ioddu, Oddua, Oddu** and **Oddia.** These conform more closely to the Hebrew, yet are very similar to Iddo.

Many Hebrew names have the divine titles Al or Ieue as part of their composition. Thus we have Beth-el, or Beth-El, or Bethel. In order to indicate the presence of the title we would prefer to spell it Beth-Al. But it would be impracticable to carry this out uniformly, and spell Nathanael as Nathana-Al. We use Beth-El. The inscriptions found at Lachish show conclusively that, in ancient times, names ending in —ie, were changed to —ieu when the action indicated was in progress. As only part of the name Ieue Will-be-ing-was is affixed, it does not indicate the name of the Deity, but only a part of its meaning. Affixed, —ie means -will-be, —ieu, will-be-ing as in Irm-ie-u Jeremiah Exalter-will-be-ing. Prefixed, it means the same, as in Ieu-shuo Josua (Jesus) Will-be-saving.

Where there are two spellings in use, neither of which corresponds to the Hebrew, as Shealtiel and Salathiel, we have combined the two parts which are most nearly correct, as **Shalthiel.**

THE MEANING OF THE NAMES

The meaning of the names, as given in the margin, has been the subject of prolonged research. As we already knew most of the stems, we have tried to fix the force of the servile letters, but this is very difficult in English, for they cover a vast variety of words in our tongue, seeing that it, unlike Hebrew, comes from the confusion of Babel.. We have striven to come as close as we could, but often it is not satisfactory. It will be understood, therefore, that this is still under investigation and subject to further study and improvement, although anything like perfection is not to be expected.

Extra heavy vowel letters in proper names, indicate which syllable should be stressed when pronouncing these names. When an extra heavy vowel letter occurs in other words, however, it indicates that the word was the first word in the Hebrew sentence, and is therefore emphatic.

THE DIVINE NAME AND TITLES

How many gods are there? The Bible speaks of **Alueim** (To-subjectors) as "God" over two thousand times. But it also makes it plural, "gods", about one-tenth as often. It renders **Al** (Subjector) uniformly "God" over two hundred times. **Alue** (To-subjector) is also rendered the same, "God," or "god" over fifty times. Yet **Ieue** (Will-be-ing-was) is also rendered God (with small capitals) nearly three hundred times. A student would need to be very dense, mentally, if this does not confuse and confound him. Halfway measures might even make the matter worse. So the only possible way of being a real help to those who wish to know God, their Subjector, and His spirit operating in humanity, is to go back to the original, inspired titles, as is done with nearly all other names and use the inspired Hebrew pronunciation, and put the meaning in the margin.

In order to express the transcendent truth that the **one spirit** of our God (**Al**) acts through several channels, yet is the same spirit of subjection, the plural form **Alueim** or **Alueim** (without the **m** in Hebrew), take a **singular** verb. It may be incorrect grammar, but it is truth that transcends the rules of a human language.

It is practically impossible to learn, from modern translations, when the To-Subjector, the Son of Al, the Anointed, or Christ, Jesus, our Lord, appears on the pages of the Hebrew Scriptures. Of course the **spirit** of both Al and Alue appear constantly in the title Alueim. This is plural (**-im**) only in the sense that Al operates by His spirit in and through Alue, the [e]To-[Al]subject[u]or (Jn. 1:1) and others who also partake of this spirit, as prophets, including all who are energized by the holy spirit of Al, the Subjector. These are "three in one," in anticipation of the future consummation, when all are subject to Al, the Subjector, and He becomes **All** in **all** (1 Cor. 15:20-28).

5. THE FUNCTION OF THE SIGNS, TYPE FACES, ETC.

The shortcomings of our Concordant Version are publicly displayed on every page by the presence of the signs and the use of lightface and boldface type. English idiom insists on words not in the Original, so we put these in lightface type. It demands that we omit some words. These we add in very small letters, which will not interfere with the reading. Even if it forces us to place the words so as to obscure the emphasis, we preserve this by means of **extra bold** letters.

When the article (the) is omitted, a high period is placed before the word to which it belongs. When it is inserted in English, it is printed in lightface type.

If we must use a singular where the original has a plural, two horizontal lines are added if it is deemed worthwhile.

The untranslatable particle ath, which points out the object of the verb in Hebrew, is indicated by a small, slanting stroke (\) like a grave accent. If our principles did not require that we reproduce everything in the Hebrew in the English version, we might have overlooked this particle, which is sometimes mistakenly called an "article." Besides, the sign not only shows that ath is in the Hebrew, but points out the object of the verb, which is welcome in English, because the objective form is usually lacking there.

TEXTUAL SIGNS

The Concordant Hebrew Text is not based solely on the Masoretic or Traditional manuscripts, handed down by Jews, but uses the Septuagint, the Samaritan Pentateuch, and occasionally the Syriac, the Qumran and other manuscripts, in order to restore the original Hebrew text. For this reason we indicate the source of each rendering whenever it differs from the modern Hebrew. As the Septuagint is usually recognized by the number seventy, we place a tiny italic *7* before and a *0* after every passage which is based alone on this ancient Greek version. As we do not merely turn this into English, but first into Hebrew, and this into English, there may be a slight element of uncertainty, at times. In this case we put a small italic *?* in place of the *0*.

In the books of Moses the ancient copy known as the Samaritan Pentateuch has been compared with the usual text. It has preserved some readings which have fallen out. We use an italic capital *S* before such a passage and a small *n* after it. In case the Septuagint concurs, both are indicated by putting *7* before and *n* after it. When a reading is found in both of these important manuscripts, it is usually adopted.

The Syriac version is also considered. In case a reading comes from it, an italic *c* follows the passage. The Syriac is used only to confirm a Septuagint or a Samaritan reading. Then an italic *7* is placed first and an italic *c* last where the Syriac confirms the Septuagint, and an italic capital *S* and a *c* where the Syriac confirms the Samaritan reading. The *S* and *c* do not stand for Syriac alone, for we do not record such readings, but for the Samaritan and the Syriac combined.

The small italic question mark *?* is not intended to give the impression that we doubt the appropriateness of the rendering, but that it is not based on first hand evidence, hence is not as well authenticated as the rest of the text.

About the time of the return from the captivity, the ancient Hebrew characters were changed to the square Chaldean letters which are in use today. At that time some of the custodians of the text, called Sopherim, made some alterations in it. Fifteen of these are indicated in the present Hebrew text. Besides this, in 134 cases, they altered the divine name, Ieue (Jehovah) to Adon. The vowel points of Adon were always placed under Ieue, out of mistaken reverence. So arose the pronunciation Jehovah. We have always restored these passages when they affected the translation, and have marked them by placing an italic capital *S* before and small *ph* after each case.

The so-called "Severin" readings have been treated the same as other marginal notes, which are usually incorporated into the text without further comment.

HOW EMPHASIS IS INDICATED

We stress our statements, especially when our feelings are roused, by putting the most vital word first. So, in the Hebrew Scriptures, the main thought of a sentence is usually found in its leading expression. If we emphasize this, it usually gives us the point of the passage. This is often lost in a version, because the order of the words is determined by idiom in English, so that the emphatic word cannot come first. In the Concordant Version the emphasis of the original is preserved, whenever possible, by the order of the words, and, besides this, one or more letters are printed heavier and slightly larger to show which word should be stressed, even if it is not first.

Once we know the principal point in a passage, the rest of it falls into place. English idiom, we regret to say, often refuses to give the emphatic word its proper place. In most cases we may have transgressed our idiom by leading off with the verb, in order to put the stress where it belongs. This will be forgiven by all who have learned to value the correct emphasis. Those who bear with it will find it very agreeable when once accustomed to it.

The pronoun is emphatic when it repeats what is already implied in the verb. But when the objective pronoun is preceded by the sign of this case, much consideration has led us to conclude that there is no special emphasis. The particle ath does not show the weight of the word, but the direction of the thought. This we indicate by a slight stroke (\) whenever it occurs, as it cannot be translated. If it is emphatic, we ought to stress all words before which it stands, not only the pronouns.

CONCORDANT CHRONOLOGY

The Concordant Version presents to its readers a new, simplified chronology based entirely on the inspired text. It gives the number of years from the creation of the first man, Adam, to all important events up to the crucifixion of the Second Man, the last Adam, since which event time is not reckoned in the sacred scrolls. It goes from the year Adm 1 to 5498. This is the natural way. The so-called B.C. dates have a wrong end, and count backward unnaturally, so they are difficult to grasp, besides being several years astray. The **Adm** dating has a correct starting point, and is much easier to follow. This new system of dating will greatly simplify and clarify the course of events in Holy Writ.

The name Cainan (Lu. 3:36) has dropped out of the Hebrew chronology, but is found in the Septuagint, the Greek translation. This shows that the Septuagint probably has a more correct chronology, so we use this translation for the life span of the patriarchs. This makes our chronology longer than usual. Special problems about the dates will be explained in the margin, when we come to them. As the period measures the years between the creation of the first Adam and the crucifixion of the Last Adam, the two greatest events in human history, we propose to call it the **Adamic** chronology, abbreviated, when necessary by using the Hebrew spelling **Adm.** Thus the crucifixion took place in Adm 5498.

THE MARGINS

The margins of the version are placed near the center of each page opening, to make the text more readable, and to place each entry as near as possible to the part to which it refers, so that it can be seen at the same time, without shifting the eyes.

Hebrew Names. As it appears to be impracticable to revise all the Hebrew names, it seemed best to give their Hebrew spelling, with their meaning in the margin. As we already had a list of the **stems** with their meaning, we had a comparatively good basis, on which to found their main meaning. But the finer shades, due to the servile letters attached to the stem, are often difficult to express in a modern language, so we hope that our readers will at least use these findings as the basis for further research. To aid those who wish to pursue this study, the equivalent of the basic **stem** is put in SMALL CAPITAL letters, and the **serviles** in common type.

Idiom. Often English idiom for a given Hebrew word does not agree with the literal equivalent, so we use a substitute and put the Hebrew in the margin. Thus **son** is rendered **age, young, cub,** etc.

Margin Skeleton. In order to remind the reader of the vital connection of the parts to each other, the skeleton is repeated at the beginning of each section to which it refers. The connecting link (or links) which is common to both sections is repeated before each. Thus, in Genesis we have *1:1-2:4* **Annals** *2:4-50:26*, for one gives a brief history of the heavens and the earth, and the other of the patriarchs.

The Skeleton Page Headings. To further assist the reader to intelligently grasp the relation of each part to the whole, the main sections of the Skeleton are repeated above the pages of every opening, after the abbreviation of the book. The principal sections of the Skeleton are given in order to keep the reader informed of the main themes still under consideration. Thus, at the time of Abram's call we are reminded that this is in the Annals of the Patriarch Terah, then Abram was called (12:1), and promised a seed in which all the families of the ground are blessed (12:3).

6. FIGURES OF SPEECH, INCLUDING SKELETONS

The figures are indicated by small capitals, as shown on the flyleaf of the version. Further information concerning them may be found in the treatise on Figures of Speech in the Introduction to the later Greek Scriptures. Hebrew is florid with figures and has some forms which are seldom found in English, so receive individual treatment.

LITERARY CORRESPONDENCE

A concordant version should exhibit as much as possible of the concord found in the original, especially such as affects the translation and helps to recover the true text. Hence, in poetic passages, lines that are parallel in sense are indented alike when possible. Besides, groups of lines are related to each other by this means. This often reveals a marvelous method in the arrangement of the thoughts, far superior to that found in human literature.

When the same subject is dealt with in a passage more than once, that which lies between is more or less parenthetic. It sometimes helps to skip from one to the other if we wish to get another aspect of a given subject. Thus, if we wish to study the subject of light in the first chapter of Genesis, we would find its two aspects in verses *2* to *5*, and verses *14* to *19*. To connect corresponding passages, each has a reference to the other in italic numerals to distinguish them from the regular references. Themes which do not regularly affect the literary framework are covered by the regular references.

Thus all the theophanies to Abraham and Jacob may be found easily, for after each one there is a reference to connect it with the rest.

In prose this correspondence is not so readily displayed. In order to call attention to it, we have made separate paragraphs, when possible, where corresponding sections begin, and indicate their relation by means of reference numbers in the margin beside each with the general subject printed between the reference figures. Besides this, we put a little space between these sections to separate them from the rest. In the first of Genesis, the last part of verse *2* through to *5* deals with light, and corresponds with verses *14* to *19*, which treats of **luminaries.** Verses *6* to *8* refer to the atmosphere and the water, while verses *20* to *23* deal with life in these elements. In the same way verses *9* to *13* give us the dry land, and verses *24* to *31* deal with life in this sphere. It is helpful to associate these related sections and compare them with one another.

These correspondences are parts of larger sections. Thus the first verse of Genesis corresponds with the long passage including the six days, from the last part of verse *2* to chapter *2*, one giving the creation and the other describing its readjustment on earth. Verse *2* and verses *1-3* of the second chapter are complementary. The first gives the ruin, the second the restoration of God's work. See the Skeleton Index.

In poetry, correspondences abound. Often two lines form a parallelism. It would be impracticable and cumbersome to point these out by references, as in prose. They can be more clearly indicated by indentation, putting parallel lines the same distance from the left margin, with, perhaps, a correspondence reference for the larger divisions.

Short correspondences, parallel to a third, start the second with a capital letter, thus:

And ¹prostrating is the human, And abased the man,
And the eyes of the lofty are ¹lowered.

A knowledge of the literary structure of any portion of divine revelation may be helpful in understanding its message. The corresponding sections throw light upon each other. As the usual paragraphing and punctuation often hide these correspondences, and they may be found at some distance from one another, we have tried to exhibit them, not only by paragraphing, but by spacing between paragraphs and by special references printed in the margin. The word or words printed between the two references tells the general subject of both corresponding sections, although each section may show a **contrast** rather than a likeness. The hyphen in compound members ties them together consecutively, as if they were words.

7. THE SELECT REFERENCES

From the select references given in the better bibles we have selected those which are of value and rejected those which are merely superficial and may lead astray. With these and the structural correspondences and the Hebrew-English concordance which will accompany the completed work we hope to provide the student of the Scriptures with the best of all tools for finding and enjoying the infinite harmonies of God's revelation.

THE VERSE NUMBERS

The numbers of the verses of our Authorized Version do not always agree with those of the Hebrew text, or in parallel passages, as Psalms 18 and 2 Samuel 22. In such cases we give both numbers, the Hebrew slightly smaller than the A.V. figures, in order that the student may not be confused.

THE SACRED SCRIPTURES
SKELETON INDEX

The physical form of God's inspired revelation reveals its Divine origin, for it corresponds closely in its structure to His living creatures in other spheres. Therefore we call the following outline of the contents of the Scriptures "skeletons." They are always balanced, composed of two corresponding parts, like a living, organic being.

Hebrew (right to left)............**Inspired Scriptures**..............(left to right) Greek

Israel (Shadows)................**God (Alueim) Revealed**..................(Light) Christ

Animals (Shelter from Sin)............**Sacrifice**................(Sin Repudiated) Christ

The Hebrew Scriptures correspond to the Greek, the wrongly called "Old Testament" to the "New." In the former **God** is disclosed through Israel by shadows, in the latter He is revealed in Christ, the Light of the world. The principal mode of revelation is **Sacrifice.** In this we can see the same correspondence, for the animals slain could only provide a shelter from sin, but the crucifixion of Christ repudiated it altogether.

THE HEBREW SCRIPTURES

The Law (Divine)................**The Nation of Israel**...........(Human) The Writings
Joshua to Kings (Historical)........**The Prophets**......(Predictive) Isaiah to Malachi

Originally, the Hebrew Scriptures were segregated into the Law, the Prophets, and the Literature, in that order. But now the Hebrew, and especially the later versions, have altered it. We would like to restore this order, as herewith shown, putting the Law at the beginning, the Literature at the end, to balance it, and the Prophets, which are further divided, in the center. The main subject, The Nation of Israel, balances Alueim's direct revelation through Moses with man's thoughts concerning Him in the Literature. The Historical are complemented by the Predictive Prophets. The first record Israel's past, the second foretell its future.

THE HISTORICAL PROPHETS

Joshua, Judges (Theocracy)..............Rule...........(Kingdom) Samuel and Kings

Joshua (Salvation).................THEOCRACY................(Declension) Judges

Samuel (Restoration).................KINGDOM.................. (Declension) Kings

The Prophets deal with **Rule** in Israel, and are divided into **Historical** (commonly called "Former") which give us an inspired record of Israel's **past** history, and the **Predictive** (or "Latter"), which look forward largely to their **future.**

The **Historical Prophets** are divided into two corresponding groups, the first recording the rule by **Alueim,** and the second by **Man.** The **Theocracy** again falls into two parts which record the **Salvation** under Joshua, and the **Declension** under the Judges. The rule by **Kings** is divided similarly in Samuel and Kings.

THE PREDICTIVE PROPHETS

Isaiah (Salvation)....................**Restoration**..........(Salvation) Minor Prophets
Jeremiah (During) ....**Deportation**.................... (After) Ezekiel

The **Predictive Prophets** are divided into two concentric groups. The inner pair, Jeremiah and Ezekiel, are based on Israel's **Deportation,** while the outer, Isaiah and the Minor Prophets, taken as one, reveal the nation's **Restoration.**

THE MINOR PROPHETS

(Political) (Religious)

Hosea (Conjugal) Apostasy..........**Relationship**......... Apostasy (Elective) Malachi
Joel (Nations) Jehoshaphat........**Day of Ieue**.....Jerusalem (Nations) Zechariah
Amos (to Babylon) Ruin............**Temple**.......Glory (from Babylon) Haggai
Obadiah (Edom).................**Doom**..............(Babylon) Habakkuk
Jonah (Saved) ....**Nineveh**............ (Destroyed) Nahum
Micah (Samaria, Jerusalem)..**Controversy**.. (the Nations) Zephaniah

Skeleton Index

The Minor Prophets deal with two aspects of Israel's salvation, the **Political** and the **Religious,** devoting six corresponding books to each.

Hosea, the first, tells of Israel's **apostasy** in her **Conjugal Relationship** to Ieue from the **political** viewpoint, and corresponds with Malachi, the last, who deals with their apostasy from their **Elective Relationship religiously.**

Joel, the second book, corresponds with Zechariah, next to the last, in that both deal with the other **nations** in the **day of Ieue,** one **politically** in the vale of **Jehoshaphat,** the other **religiously** in **Jerusalem.**

Amos and Haggai, the third from each end, take up the **Temple** before and after the **Babylonian deportation.** The first emphasizes its **ruin,** the second its **glory.**

Obadiah and Habakkuk tell of the **doom** of **Edom** and **Babylon.**

Jonah and Nahum both denounce **Nineveh,** but the city repents and is **saved** in one case, but **destroyed** in the other.

Micah and Zephaniah reveal the **controversy** of Alueim. On the one hand it is with **Samaria** and **Jerusalem.** On the other it is with the other **nations.**

THE WRITINGS (LITERATURE)

Praises [Psalms]......................**Comments**........[Chronicles] Words of the Days
Rules [Proverbs]...................**Conduct**.........[Ecclesiastes] The Assembler
Job (Personal).......................**Evil**....................(National) Daniel
Song of Songs ....**Love**..................... Lamentations
Ruth ....**Faithfulness**..................... Esther
Ezra (Religious)...........**Restoration**........(Political) Nehemiah

The order of these books, reading down the left side and up the right, is not certain, but this arrangement seems to show that, as elsewhere, there are two treatments of every subject in the collection. In **Praises** (commonly called Psalms) we have **man's Comments** on Alueim's dealings with His people, yet in "Words of the Days" (Chronicles) Alueim says what He thinks of their doings.

Conduct is viewed from two angles in Rules (Proverbs) and The Assembler (Ecclesiastes). **Personal Evil** is the theme of Job, but Daniel traces its **national** course up to the Kingdom of Christ. **Love** leads to the joys of the Song of Songs and the tears of Lamentations. **Faithfulness** is exemplified in a foreign land by both Ruth and Esther. At the **Restoration** after the seventy years' deportation, Ezra **restores** the **temple** and Nehemiah the **walls** of **Jerusalem.**

THE LAW

The Beginning (Origin)...........**The Twelve Tribes**.........(Organization) The Words
[Genesis] [Deuteronomy]
The Names [Exodus].................**Testing**.........[Numbers] In the Wilderness
Offerings and Shelter ....**Worship**..............Offerers and Festivals
[Leviticus]

Now that we have given a **skeleton** of the whole of the Hebrew Scriptures in a general way, we will take up **each book** (as we come to it), and show the correspondence of its parts, as far as is practicable. A glance down the central column will be the quickest and best index of its contents, and help in understanding its message.

The five books of Moses, called the **Law,** are pivoted on the **Worship** of Ieue, which is their central subject, in Leviticus. It, in turn, is divided into two corresponding parts, dealing first with the **Offerings** and the **Shelter** they provided, and balancing this with the **Offerers** and the **Festivals.** On either side of Leviticus we **have** the **Testing** of the tribes, first in Exodus, then in Numbers, which is aptly named "In the Wilderness" in the Original. Beyond these, on either side, this division commences with Genesis, which gives us the **Origin** of the **Twelve Tribes** and closes with Deuteronomy, which attends to their **Organization.**

IN A BEGINNING (GENESIS)

1:1-2:3 Creation................**Heavens and Earth**................Annals *2:4-50:26*

CREATION 1:1-2:3 (=2:4-50:26)

1:1-2- Originally......................**Earth**......................Readjusted *1:-2-2:3*

THE ORIGINAL EARTH

1:1 Created to be Indwelt (Is. 45:18).........................Chaos and Vacant *1:2-*

THE READJUSTED EARTH 1:-2-2:3 (=1:1-2-)

1:2-31 The Six Days' Work....................... ...The Seventh Day's Cessation *2:1-3*

Skeleton Index

THE SIX DAYS' WORK 1:-2:31 (=2:1-3)

-2-5 Separation........................**Light**....................Luminaries *14-19*
6-8 Division..................**Waters and Atmosphere**.............Living Soul *20-23*
9-13 Fruit........................**Land**........................Living Soul *24-31*

THE ELEVEN GENEALOGIES 2:4-50:26 (=1:1-2:3)

2:4-4:26 Heavens and Earth..............................The Patriarchs *5:1-50:26*

HEAVENS AND EARTH 2:4-4:26 (=5:1-50:26)

2:4-25 Human, *3:1-24* Failure..............................Failure *4:1-24*, Sons *4:25-26*

HUMAN FORMATION 2:4-25 (=4:25-26)

2:4-7 Man Formed.....................**Sexes**..................Woman Built *2:18-25*
8 Planted—*9* Food...............**Garden—Trees**..........Serve *15*—Not Eat *16-17*
10 Four Heads ....**River**...................Four Names *11-14*

HUMAN FAILURE 3:1-24 (=4:1-24)

1-5 Serpent ....**Creatures**........................ Cherubim *-24*
6 Knowledge of Good and Evil.........**Trees**...................Tree of Lives *22:24-*
7 Man-made Girdle Skirts..........**Clothing**...........Alueim-made Tunics *20-21*
8-12 Man, *13* Woman...........**Judgment**..........Woman *16*, Man *17-19*
14 Serpent Cursed............ **Prediction**............. Seed Promised *15*

1-16 Cain and Abel......FAILURE OF SONS 4:1-24 (=3:1-24)..............Enoch *17-24*

25 Seth...............REPLACEMENT SONS 4:25-26 (=2:4-25)..............Enosh *26*

THE PATRIARCHS 5:1-50:26 (=2:4-4:26)

5:1-6:8 Adam (Mankind).............**Progenitors**.............(Israel) Jacob *37:1-50:26*
6:9-9:29 Noah—*10:1-11:9* Sons.....**Forefathers**.........Esau *36:1-8*—Sons *36:9-43*
11:10-26 Shem ....**Chosen**................. Isaac *25:19-35:29*
11:27-25:11 Terah ....**Hindrance**.............. Ishmael *25:12-18*

The bulk of the book of **The Beginning** is taken up with the lives of **The Patriarchs.** Each is introduced by Genealogical **Annals.** Except for one, these are arranged to form a reversal. The Annals of **Adam** are complemented by that of **Jacob,** the **Progenitor** of the nation of Israel, Alueim's chosen people. **Noah** and his **sons** are balanced by **Edom** and his **sons.** All mankind (adm) sprang from Noah. Edom is from the same stem, Adm, not "Edom." The two **Chosen** seeds, **Shem** and **Isaac,** counterbalance each other. So do the two **Hindrances, Terah** and **Ishmael.**

ANNALS OF THE PATRIARCH ADAM (MANKIND) 5:1-6:8 (=37:1-50:26)

5:1-5 Sons and Daughters.............**Generation**.........Daughters and Sons *6:1-3*
5-6:31 Firstborn..................**Outstanding Men**...............Distinguished *6:4-7*
5:32 Noah begets Sons..........**New Beginning**..............Noah finds Grace *6:8*

ANNALS OF NOAH 6:9-9:29 (=36:1-8)

6:9 Before the Deluge...................**Time**................After the Deluge *9:28-29*
6:10 Shem, Ham, Japheth..............**Sons**............Shem, Ham, Japheth 9:18-27
6:11-13 Corrupt ....**The Earth**............ Replenished *8:21-9:17*
6:14-22 The Ark.................**Provision**.................The Altar *8:20*
7:1-24 Enters.............**Noah and the Ark**.............Leaves *8:1-19*

THE EARTH REPLENISHED 8:21-9:17 (=6:11-13)

8:21-22 with the Earth............**Alueim's Covenant**................with Noah *9:8-17*
9:1 Blessed ....**Noah and his Sons**......................Fruitful *7*
2 over the Animals...............**Government**................ over Mankind *6*
3 Flesh Food.......................**Diet**.........................No Blood *4-5*

10:1-32 Nations Divided......ANNALS OF NOAH'S SONS......Nations Scattered *11:1-9*

THE NATIONS PARTED 10:1-32

10:1- **Shem.......................Names, Location................Sons of Shem *21-32***
-1- **Ham..........................Names, Nations................Sons of Ham *6-20***
-1 **Japheth..................Names, Coastlanders..........Sons of Japheth *2-5***

THE NATIONS SCATTERED 11:1-9

11:1 **Unity—*2* Shinar................The People..................Unity *6-7*—Babel *8-9***
3-4 **Man's Building................City and Tower....................Ieue Sees *5***

Skeleton Index

10-25 Shem................THE ANNALS OF SHEM 11:10-26..................Terah *26*

THE ANNALS OF TERAH 11:27-25:11

11:27-22:19 to Isaac's Birth.............**Abram**.............to Abraham's Death *25:5-11*
22:20-24 Nahor...................**Sons of Relatives**..................Keturah *25:1-4*
23:1-20 Sarah's Death..............**Old Age**...........**Isaac's Marriage** *24:1-67*

ABRAM TO ISAAC'S BIRTH 11:27-22:19

11:27-12:3 Call, Isaac Promised.......**The Seed**............Isaac Blessed, Trial *22:1-19*
12:4-9 Canaan ....**Sojourn**...................... Gerar *21:22-34*
12:10-20 Egypt ....**Denial of Sarai**.................. Gerar *20:1-18*
—13:1-13 Lot.............**Separation**.........—Ishmael *21:9-21*
—13:14-18 Land ....**Fulfillment**........... —Seed *21:1-8*
14:1-24 War, Rescue, Abraham..**Lot in Sodom**..Destroy, Rescue, Msgrs. *18:-16-19:38*
15:1-21 Made..............**Covenant of Faith**..........Renewed *18:1-16-*
16:1-16 Ishmael, Slavery...**The Two Seeds**...Freedom, Isaac *17:15-27*
17:1-3 Prostration.......**Abram's Seed**.....Circumcision *17:4-14*

COVENANT OF FAITH MADE 15:1-21

1-6 Seed............................**Object**.............................Land *7-21*

FREEDOM, ISAAC 17:15-27

17:15-16 Seed—*17-20* Laughter...........**Sarah**..........Seed *21-22*—Circumcision *23-27*

FAITH COVENANT RENEWED 18:1-16-

18:1-2 Appearance (Three Men)...........**Ieue**...........(Three Men) Departure *18:16-*
18:3-8 Reception......................**Abraham**..................Conference *18:9-15*

DESTRUCTION OF SODOM 18:-16-19:38

18:-16-33 Ieue.......................**Abraham**......................Ieue *19:27-29*
19:1-26 Messengers....................**Lot**..........................**Daughters** *30-38*

IEUE AND ABRAHAM 18:-16-33

-16-19 toward Abraham.............**Ieue's Attitude**...........to Sodom, Gomorrah *20-33*

LOT AND THE MESSENGERS 19:1-26

1-3 Enter Lot's House..............**Messengers**...........Warning to Leave *12-22*
4-11 After Messengers...........**People of Sodom**.................. .Destroyed *23-26*

SEPARATION OF ISHMAEL 21:9-21

9-10 In the House................**Hagar and Ishmael**........Out of the House *15*
11 Abraham ....**Suffering**........................ **Hagar** *16*
12-13 Intervenes......................**Alueim**.......................Intervenes *17-19*
14 Wilderness, Beersheba....**Hagar and Ishmael**...........Wilderness, Paran *20-21*

SOJOURN IN GERAR 21 22-34

21:22-24 At that time...................**Time**..........................**Many Days** *34*
25-26 Taken—*27* Covenant ....**The Well**........Digged *28-31*—Covenant *32-33*

ABRAHAM'S TRIAL 22:1-19

1-10 Charge and Journey................**Isaac**............................Return *19*
11-12 Charge Recalled.................**Calls**...............Blessing Promised *15-18*
13 Sacrifices Ram...............**Abraham**...............Names Ieue Jireh *14*

23:1-2 Death—*3-18* Treaty, Tomb....SARAH 23:1-20...........**Burial** *19*—Confirmed *20*

3-11 Abraham Bargains...........THE TREATY 23:3-18...........Bargain Closed *12-18*

23:3-4 Asks Tomb—*5-6* Granted.ABRAHAM BARGAINS 23:3-11.....*7-9*—Aquired *10-11*

ISAAC'S MARRIAGE 24:1-67

1-54- Mission.........................**Eleazar**.......................... Return *-54-67*

ELEAZAR'S MISSION 24:1-54-

1 Blessed in All......................**Abraham**..Blessed Exceedingly *34-36*
2-9 Oath and Commission............**Eleazar**..Oath and Commission *37-41*
10-11 Journey...Journey *42-*
12-21 Prayer......................**Worship**...............Prayer *-42-44*
22-25 ....**Rebecca**...................... *45-47*
26 ....**Ieue**....................... *48*
27-32 ....**Reception**....................... *49-53*
33 Declined........................**Entertainment**..........Accepted *54-*

Skeleton Index

ELEAZAR'S RETURN 24:-54-67

-54 Request for Departure..............**Return**............Request for Departure *56-60*
55 Hindered..........................**Departure**....................**Expedited** *61-67*

THE ANNALS OF ISHMAEL 25:12-18

12 Birth..............................**Ishmael**..............................Death *17*
13-16 Dwelling........................**His Sons**........................Dwelling *18*

THE ANNALS OF ISAAC 25:19-35:29

25:19 Birth ....**Isaac**......................... Death *35:27-29*
25:20-22 Rebecca—*23-28* 2 Sons....**Wives—Sons**..Rachel *35:16-20*—Israel's Sons *21-26*
25:29-34 Birthright ....**Esau and Jacob**............. Blessing *27:1-35:15*
26:1 Gerar—*2-5* Appearance......**Journeys**..Beersheba *23*—Appear. *24-25*
26:6-11 of Isaac................**Wives**....................of Esau *34-35*
12-22 Separation..........**Abimelech**..........Covenant with *26-33*

ESAU AND JACOB 27:1—35:15

27:1-28:5 Deception *27:1-40* Grudge *-41* Departure *42-28:5*
Reconciliation *32:3-33:17*, Deception *33:18-34:31*, Return *35:1-15*
28:6-9 Esau's Wives, *10-22* Vision, Bethel
Jacob's Wives *29:1-31:55* Vision, Mahanaim *32:1-2*

JACOB'S WIVES 29:1—31:55

29:1-14 Arrival ....**Journeys**.......................Return *31:17-55*
29:15-30:26 ....**Service**.......................*30:27-31:16*

THE RECONCILIATION OF ESAU 32:3-33:17

32:3-5 Requested ....**Grace**......................... Given *33:-1-17*
32:6 Announced.................**Esau's Approach**.....................Seen *33:1-*
32:7-8 Present—*9-12* Prayer......**Conciliation**......Present *13-23*—Prayer *24-32*

THE ANNALS OF ESAU (CANAAN) 36:1-8

1 Lives in Canaan..................**Esau (Edom)**.................Leaves Canaan *6-8*
2-3 His Wives.......................**Family**.........................His Sons *4-5*

THE ANNALS OF ESAU (MOUNT SEIR) 36:9-43

9-19 of Esau.....................**Sons and Sheiks**......................of Seir *20-43*

THE ANNALS OF JACOB 37:2-50:26

37:2-45:28 ....**Joseph and his Brethren**...................... *50:15-26*
46:1-7 to Egypt ....**Jacob Removes**...........to Canaan *46:28-50:14*
46:8-25 Severally ....**The Sons of Jacob**........... Collectively *46:26-27*

JOSEPH AND HIS BRETHREN 37:2-45:28

2-36 in Canaan ....**Joseph**..................in Egypt *39:1-41:57*
38:1-30 Judah...........................**Brethren**......................... *42:1-45:28*

JOSEPH IN CANAAN 37:2-36

2-4 ....**his Brethren**...................... Seeking *12-17*
5-11 Communicated.....................**his Dreams**.................Counteracted *18-36*

38:1-40:23 Humiliation......JOSEPH IN EGYPT 39:1-41:57..........Exaltation *41:1-57*

JOSEPH'S HUMILIATION 39:1-40:23

39:1-2 In Potiphar's House............**Place**..................In Prison *39:19-20*
3-6- of Potiphar...................**Confidence**.....................of Jailor *21-23*
-6-18 Chastity.......................**Conduct**........................Wisdom *40:1-23*

THE CHASTITY OF JOSEPH 39:-6-18

-6-7 Request.......................**Potiphar's Wife**..................Request *11-12-*
8-10 Refusal ....**Joseph**......................... Flight *-12-20*

THE WISDOM OF JOSEPH 40:1-23

1-8 The Circumstances...............**The Dreams**...................The Solution *9-23*

THE SOLUTION 40:9-23

9-11 the Cupbearer....................**Telling**...................the Baker *16-17*
12-13 ....**Interpretation**....................... *18-22*
14-15 Request Made..................**Joseph**..............Request Forgotten *23*

1-36 Foretelling...........JOSEPH'S EXALTATION 41:1-57............Fulfilled *37-57*

Skeleton Index

FORETELLING 41:1-36

1-4 Cows—*5-7* Spikes....................**Dream**..............Cows *17-21*—Spikes *22-24*
8-16 Sought..........................**Interpretation**...................Given *25-36*

FULFILLMENT 41:37-57

37-46 ....**Joseph**.................................. *-56-57*
47-49 Plenty ....**Dreams**.......................Famine *53-56-*
50-51 Manasseh ....**Fruitfulness**..................... Ephraim *52*

JOSEPH'S BRETHREN 42:1-45:28

42:1-2 Purchase Food...........**Commission**.............Purchase Food *43:1-2*
3 Journey—*4* Benjamin.........................Benjamin *3-14*—Journey *15-*
5 Egypt.......................**Arrival**...........................Joseph *-15*
6-24 in Authority..............**Meeting Joseph**..............as Brother *16-34*
25-26 Money Returned..........**Dismissal**.........Money Returned *44:1-45:24*
27-38 Jacob.....................**Return**.......................Jacob *45:25-28*

DISMISSAL OF JOSEPH'S BROTHERS 44:1-45:24

44:1-13 Feigned...True *45:17-24*
44:14-34 Brothers to Joseph........**Explanations**..........Joseph to Brothers *45:1-16*

THE FEIGNED DISMISSAL 44:1-13

1-2 Concealed.........................**The Cup**.....................Discovered *4-12*
3 Departure...Return *13*

14-15 Joseph—*16* Judah......THE CUP SOUGHT 44:14-34......Joseph *17*—Judah *18-34*

1-2- Joseph— *-2* Pharaoh....THE CUP DISCOVERED 45:1-16...Joseph *3-15*—Pharaoh *16*

3-4 to Brothers..............JOSEPH REVEALED 45:3-13................to Jacob *9-13*
5 Alueim Sent..................**Alueim's Intention**.................to Preserve *7-8*
6- Two Years......................**Famine**......................Five Years *-6*

JACOB REMOVED TO EGYPT 46:1-7

1 Departure..........................**Journey**...........................Arrival *5-7*
2 Vision........................**Alueim Speaks**.....................Promise *3-4*

8-25 Detail..............NAMES OF ISRAEL'S SONS 46:8-27..........Summary *26-27*

8-15 Leah—*16-18* Zilpah...............DETAIL.............Rachel *19-22*—Bilhah *23-25*

26 Entered, 66 ....SUMMARY.....................70 Came Out *27*

EVENTS IN EGYPT 46:28-50:13

46:28-47:12 Arrival...................**Israelites**......................Stay *47:27-50:13*
47:13-17 Sale of Cattle..............**Egyptians**..........Ground and Selves *47:18-26*

ARRIVAL OF ISRAELITES 46:28-47:12

46:28 Arrives in Goshen................**Jacob**.............Settles in Rameses *47:11-12*
46:29-30 Joseph.......................**Meets**......................Pharaoh *47:7-10*
46:31-32 Planned—*33-34* Given..**Presentation—Directions**..Made *47:1-2*—Obeyed *3-6*

STAY OF ISRAELITES 47:27-50:14

47:27 Dwells—*47:28* Lives..........**Jacob in Egypt**....Death *49:33-50:2*—Mourn *50:3-14*
47:29-31 to Joseph...................**Burial**..............to the Brothers *49:29-32*
48:1-20 Joseph and his Sons........**Blessing**............All Israel's Sons *49:1-28*
48:21 Return to Land............**Joseph**................Double Portion *22*

BLESSING OF JOSEPH AND HIS SONS 48:1-20

1-2 Brought.........................**Joseph's Sons**...................Presented *8-12*
3-4 Blessed..........................**Jacob**..........................Blesses *13-16*
5-7 United..........................**Preference**...................Reversed *17-20*

1-2 Introduction.......JACOB BLESSES ALL HIS SONS 49:1-28..........Summary *28*

3-15 Leah's Six Sons..................**Wives**..............Rachel's Two Sons *22-27*
Reuben, Simeon, Levi, Judah, Issachar, Zebulun   Joseph, Benjamin
16-18 Bilhah's Son, Dan............**Slaves**..........Bilhah's Son, Naphtali *21*
19 Gad.......................**Zilpah's Sons**......................Asher *20*

JOSEPH AND HIS BRETHREN 50:15-26

15-21 After Jacob's.....................**Death**.......................After Joseph's *-26*
22-23 Dwelling—Age...........**Joseph in Egypt**.................Died—Age *26-*
24 Restoration to the Land.........**Charges**................Bring up Bones *25*

A TEST PASSAGE

A concordant version of God's inspired revelation is the only kind which can convey a correct and consistent conception of its contents. To give practical proof of its value as compared with the venerated Authorized English Version, we will note briefly the principal variations from it in the first few chapters of "Genesis," and show why the C.V. is to be preferred. At the same time we will point out where the ancient text has been restored and how. All of this is necessarily brief. Many points are discussed at length in our other publications.

As a rule we will indicate how the Authorized Version uses one and the same English word for a number of different Hebrew stems, whereas the C.V. allows each English expression to be used for only one Hebrew word, when possible.

Conversely, the same Hebrew word is translated by several different English expressions, whereas the C.V. gives each Hebrew one standard, and uses synonyms only when forced to do so by usage and idiom.

The superior figures after many of the words indicate the number of different Hebrew stems which are so translated in the Authorized Version. For example, 14 Hebrew stems, zuo (**stir**), chphtz (**incline**), chrtz (**spike, decide**), ndd (**wander**), nuo (**rove**), nuph (**wave**), suth (**incite**), phuq (**issue**), phom (**agitate, move**), qrtz (**twitch**), rgz (**disturb**), rchph (**vibrate, hover, be tremulous**), and shrtz (**roam**) are all translated move[14] in one or more passages of the A.V. In the comment on Gen. 1:2 we condense this to move[14].

The italic figures, however, added to the **Concordant** rendering, show how often the A.V. **agrees** with the C.V. by translating the same as it. Thus (see Gen. 4:3), the C.V. renders the Hebrew mnche present*28*, like the A.V., in twenty-eight passages, including Gen. 32:13, where Jacob gave a **present** to Esau.

This will show that the **vocabulary** of the versions does not differ nearly so much as the **uniformity, consistency, concordance,** with which the words are used. The words used in the Concordant Version are in **blackface** type.

Genesis] This is not in the Hebrew, and does not agree with chapter one at all, for it deals with **creation, chaos,** and **readjustment,** not **generation,** which "Genesis" implies.
IN A BEGINNING] This is the title of the whole book, and applies to the second part (chapter 2:4 to 50) on **generation,** as well as to **creation.**

2 was] In verse 3, it is clearly evident that this verb denotes **become,** and expresses the **change** from darkness to light. Is. 45:18 says that the earth was **not** created as it became. Hence we say, **the earth became.** without form] A.V. translates this Hebrew word confusion, empty place, without form, nothing, nought, vain, vanity, waste, and wilderness. These words represent other Hebrew words, except waste. The Concordant Version uses **chaos** throughout. void][8] A.V. has emptiness in Isa. 34:11. The C.V. is always **vacant.** deep][8] The three distinct Hebrew stems rendered "deep" the C.V. differentiates as **shadow, drown,** and **submerged chaos.** The Septuagint, made about 300 B.C., almost always has it abussos. moved][14] The spirit of God **vibrated,** as a vulture **hovering** over its young (Dt. 32:11) or Jeremiah's **tremulous** bones (Jr. 23:9). The kind of motion is evident from its effect. Light is a form of vibration. This explains what follows, for light and heat separated the gases and liquids and solids.

3 Let there be . . . was] These two verbs are exactly the same in Hebrew. This form is neither imperative nor past, but may be rendered hundreds of times by **becomes.**

6 firmament] The Hebrew stem means **stamp.** Gold foil was **stamped** out in making the vestment of the chief priest (Ex. 39:3); in creation the earth was **stamped** (Is. 42:5) or solidified by **gravitation,** and so also the gaseous envelope of the earth was

stamped into a thin layer surrounding it, which we call the **atmosphere.** Without this the light would be invisible, for light disappears in a vacuum. [7]**And coming is it to be so**[0] has evidently dropped out of the Hebrew. The Septuagint supplies it.

8 [7]**And seeing is the Alueim that** it is **good**[0] has been preserved in the Greek version.

9 gather together][15] No fewer than fifteen Hebrew words are represented by this phrase in the venerable Authorized Version. As water can hardly be spoken of as **gathered,** it is better to use our idiomatic phrase, **flow together.** [7]**And flowing together is the water** *f* **under the heavens to one place, and appearing** is the **dry** land[0] is supplied from the Septuagint.

10 gathering together] We use the word **confluence** for the flowing together of waters.

11 grass][4] This Hebrew word the A.V. translates **green** and **herb** also. But other stems fit them better. Other occurrences of this word call for a much wider term, such as **verdure.** [7]**for its from-kind and for its likeness**[0] has fallen out of the Hebrew text. [7]and[nc] is found in the Septuagint, the Samaritan and the Syriac, so we are compelled to insert it. **yielding** is literally **doing** in Hebrew. See the margin.

12 12 21 21 24 24 25 25 25 after his kind] The Hebrew connective here used means **to** or **for,** but hardly **after,** even in the sense of **like. Kind,** a natural group, may denote a race, a genus, a sort, or a variety, so is too indefinite a term to represent this Hebrew word. The stem means **from,** and denotes all that descend **from** a creative original by generation. Our nearest seems to be **species.** We call it a **from**-kind.

14 lights] This is a special form of the stem which denotes **light givers** or **luminaries.** seasons][5] This word occurs over a hundred times, yet it is hardly ever translated season in the A.V., but appointed, assembly, congregation, least, solemn, synagogue, and time. But a special period of time is very often expressed by another Hebrew stem. The word does not refer to the seasons of the year. It makes the heavenly luminaries the great clock by which **appointments** are kept.

17 set][35] The Hebrew is literally **give.** It does not locate the luminaries in the atmosphere, but records the fact that their light belongs there, and is not visible outside the atmosphere. [c]**give light** indicates that the Hebrew reads **cause light.**

20 20 21 bring forth abundantly . . . moving] Both expressions have the same stem, which the A.V. also renders abundantly, breed, bring forth, or increase, as well as move and creep. The context deals with the difference between plants and animals, so all breeding is out of place. As it is applied to the weasel, the rodent, the lizard and the chamelion (Lv. 11:30), it cannot mean creep, either. The word **roam** seems to be the nearest we have in English. Plants are stationary, but animals **roam** about from place to place. 20 21 24 2:19 creature] The A.V. renders the word **soul** by any[4], appetite[2], beast[2] body[7], breath[1], creature[9], dead[8], desire[5], ghost[3], heart[15], life[119], lust[2], man[3], mind[15], one[1], own[1], person[30], pleasure[4], self[10], thing[2], will[4], fish[1], hearty[1], mortal[1], etc., the number of times indicated, in the revered Authorized Version. Here, and in verse 24, it is rendered **creatures.** In verse 30 it is **thing** (or it may stand for **life**). The phrase **living soul** is used in verses 20 21 24 of animals before it is used of a human being (2:7). It is applied to all creatures of the soil who are made alive by spirit, hence have sensation. 20 21 22 26 28 30 2:19 20 fowl] is now confined chiefly to edible birds. Here the point lies in motion through the atmosphere, and includes all with wings, **flyers,** the noun of the verb, **fly.**

21 whales] appears elsewhere as dragon, sea monster, serpent. The skeletons of these that have been found show that they probably were **monsters** of various sizes and shapes. creature] **soul.** See verse 20. brought forth abundantly] **roams.** See verse 20. 21 21 after their kind] **for their from**-kind. See verse 11. 22 fowl] **flyer.** See verse 20.

22 multiply] This weaker form denotes **increase.**

24 creature] **soul.** See verse 20. As these animals had both bodies and spirits, **Nsoul** is the figure of Near Association, as indicated by N. Literally it refers to the possession of sensation. 24 24 after his kind] **for its from**-kind. See verse 11. 24 cattle] This is also rendered behemoth, but mostly **beast,** in the A.V., which is the constant C.V. translation. 24 25 26 26 30 creeping thing] **moving** animal, which goes about seeking sustenance. 24 24 after his kind] **for its from**-kind. See verse 11. 24 25 30 2:19 20 3:1 14 beast][5] The A.V. translates five different stems by **beast**[136]. This word is simply **living,** and means any **life,** or **animal.**

25 25 25 after his kind] See verse 11. 25 that creepeth] **moving.** See verse 24.

26 [7]**and**[n] indicates that **and** is lacking in the Hebrew, but is found in both the Septuagint and Samaritan texts. have dominion] Literally, it reads [put or keep] **down.** The A.V. renders it prevail against, reign, and rule. C.V. has **sway** always. fowl] **flyer.** See verse 20. 26 26 creeping thing that creepeth] **moving** animal **moving.**

A Test Passage

28 replenish] This is the common verb **fill**, and is often so rendered in the A.V. Replenish now denotes to fill again. [7]**and [i]over the beast**[c]] is in the Septuagint and Syriac. [7]**and over all the earth**[0]] is supplied by the Greek translation. fowl] **flyer.** See verse 20.

29 bearing] This is the same stem as the noun **seed.** yielding] This is the same as bearing, above in the same verse, and means **seeding.** meat] Obsolete for **food.**

30 beast of the earth] **living** one, or **land life.** See verse 24. fowl] **flyer.** See verse 24. wherein there is life] **which has in it a living soul.** The word **soul** is omitted in the venerable Authorized Version. meat] Obsolete for **food.** No meat was eaten before the deluge (Gn. 9:3).

2:1 Thus][7] is the usual letter for **And.** It is a connective, not an adverb.

2 ended]14 Elsewhere A.V. uses **finish**[12] mostly, like the C.V. seventh] Both the Greek and Syriac versions have [7]**sixth**[c], which seems more in accord with other passages. rested][12] **ceasing**, the passage "day and night shall not **cease**" (A.V.) shows that it cannot denote rest from toil.

3 sanctified] In order to distinguish the forms of the stem **holy**, the C.V. uses **be holy** or **hallow** for the simple stem, and **sanctify** for the causative, as in Nu. 20:12 (A.V.). The A.V. also uses consecrate, prepare, proclaim, appoint, bid, dedicate, wholly, kept, etc. rested] **ceases.** See verse 2.

4 [F]generations] The A.V. uses this term for two different stems. To keep them distinct **genealogical** annals is preferable here. This is the first of the eleven annals which occupy the remainder of the book. It is used figuratively to denote the offspring of the heavens and the earth, just as in 5:1, we have Adam's descendants up to Noah. Lord] The A.V. uses this expression for seven different Hebrew ones. This one is generally called Jehovah now, although we transliterate the actual Hebrew, making it **Ieue** (pronounced Ee eh oo eh). The C.V. distinguishes all the different divine titles.

5 plant][5] A.V. also has **shrub** in Genesis 21:15. The C.V. renders it consistently. grew][12] This stem the A.V. renders bear, bring forth, branch, bud, spring up, etc., all of which are better expressed by **sprout.** till] suggests plowing and preparing for seed. The Hebrew is a much wider thought, including all needful **service.** Figuratively, [A]**serve.**

6 mist . . . watered] An ascending mist dries the earth, but **humidity** from beneath **irrigates** the surface. Five other Hebrew stems are rendered water by the A.V. This one they translate moisten and **give** or **cause**, or let or make **drink.** See the margin.

7 dust][3] The A.V. renders this stem ashes, earth, ground, mortar, powder, rubbish, as well. The human frame contains much moisture, and is continually renewed by plants that grow only in oxidized earth which contains the mineral elements of which it is composed, combined with water, that is, **soil.** breathed] This is not the verb of the following noun, breath, but another stem, **respire** or **blow**, which the A.V. renders also blow, give up, seething, snuff, etc. life] This is plural. This part of Genesis deals with generation, and the breath here spoken of has been the basis of all the **living** which have sprung from the first human. **living soul**] This identical phrase has been rendered "creature that hath life" in 1:20, living creature in 1:21 and 24, and life in 1:30, when applied to the animals. The C.V. consistently renders it **living soul,** as it registers our likeness with the lower animals, not a contrast.

9 grow] **sprout.** See verse 5. pleasant][12] This stem they render **covet**, as the C.V., besides beauty, delectable, delight, desire, goodly, lust, precious, etc. [N]**sight**] The whole man covets, not merely the [N]**sight.** It is figurative.

10 river][7] The A.V. also renders it **stream**[2], which is the constant C.V. rendering. water] **irrigate.** See verse 6.

11 compasseth]8 The stem here used is translated by about fifty variants in the A.V., meaning **surround.**

12 bdellium] This seems to be transliterated from the Hebrew bdulch. It is supposed to be the **pearl.** river] **stream.** See verse 10.

13 Ethiopia] The Hebrew is **Kush,** the same as the son of Ham (Gen. 10:6). It is not certain that it is the modern Ethiopia. compasseth] See 11.

14 Assyria] This may not coincide exactly with later Assyria, so the C.V. renders it as the Hebrew **Ashur.**

15 [7]**that He had formed**[0], Septuagint only. put][20] The stem here used means **cause stop,** or **leave.** dress] is no longer used in this sense. It is the same word as "till," in verse 5, which the C.V. renders [A]**serve.**

16 commanded][8] is used by the A.V. for say, speak, and **instruct** (C.V.). The latter they render appoint, bid, charge, order, etc., as well.

17 surely] This emphatic adverb is often necessary, but in this case, the literal **to die**

shall you be dying is an exact description of the mortality which came to Adam and **his posterity.**

18 20 meet] These are totally different from the other Hebrew words for meet. Literally they read **as-front,** which the C.V. renders idiomatically **as his complement.**

19 [7]**furthermore**[0] was preserved by the Septuagint. Lord] fits the Hebrew Adun, but not **Ieue,** Who is, and Who was, and Who is coming (Rev. 1:8). The Authorized Version uses it for Adun **(Adjudicator),** and Bol **(possessor),** and **master,** and **chieftain,** and **chief,** and **general.** beast] should be **life.** See 1:24. fowl] **flyer.** See 1:20. air] should be **heavens** as 1:1 8 9 14 15 20 26 28 30 2:1 4 4.

19 20 Adam] **the** before **a** name makes it a common noun in Hebrew. It may, of course, refer to him, yet not as an individual, but as **a** member of the race. creature] **soul.** See 1:20. gave][12] Nearly twenty words, including give, are used for **call** (C.V.) cattle] **beast.** See 1:24. fowl] **flyer.** See 1:20. [7]**every**[0] dropped out of the Hebrew text. beast] **life.** See 1:24.

21 deep sleep . . slept]. Two different words. The first is **stupor.** ribs]. This stem is rendered beam, board, chamber, corner, leaf, plank, side in the A.V. Only here is it "rib." It denotes an **angular** enclosed space. The "boards" of the tabernacle consisted of two planks, forming an angle vault. Here the female parts of humanity are severed from the male, to build the woman. The breasts of the male are a vestigial reminder that humanity was originally bisexual. instead] Literally it is **under,** as in Gen. 7:19.

22 made][14] This is a special term which the A.V. almost always translates **build.**

23 now][11] The same word the A.V. translates **once** in Gen. 18:32. [7]**her**[n] The Samaritan text and Septuagint supply this word.

24 leave][14] The A.V. has **forsake** (C.V.) 123 times, leave 67 times. cleave] This hapless word has two opposite meanings, to **cling** and to **separate,** which is unfortunate in this context, so we avoid it. [7]**two**[n] is added by both the Samaritan and the Septuagint texts.

25 were . . ashamed] **shame . . selves.** This is the only occurrence of the reflexive or **self** form. The C.V. seeks to convey all grammatical distinctions, such as this, even if, at first glance, they do not seem to be important.

3:1 subtil] The A.V. only here. Elsewhere **crafty** and prudent. beast] **living** thing, or **life.** See 1:24. [7]**serpent**[0] from the Septuagint. Yea][8] **Indeed.** No affirmation. every] English idiom demands that we say [al]**any.**

3 but] is literally **and,** which the context may give a slight negative tinge, [a]**yet.** The A.V. uses but for fifteen different Hebrew stems. die] This should be **dying,** the **incomplete form.**

4 surely die] This may be a figure, as in the A.V., but the context shows that it was literal, for they became **dying,** or mortal, to eventually **die.**

5 gods] This is exactly the same as God, in the same sentence. How could they know of other gods? See 3:22. We transliterate the divine titles, so this form is **Alueim.**

6 pleasant][12] The A.V. never uses this word for this Hebrew stem elsewhere, but lust, desire, etc. The C.V. uses **yearn** and **lust,** to suit the context. desired][12] This is the word the A.V. renders, "[Thou shalt not] **covet.**" wise] This Hebrew word, **intelligent**[11], is also rendered heart[1], wise[18] in the A.V.

7 aprons] Elsewhere the A.V. has girdle, and the verb gird. But this is usually narrow. When made of fig leaves it would be **a girdle** skirt.

8 voice] Walking makes a **sound**[39], not a voice. cool] Nowhere else so rendered. The same as **spirit** (1:2), and **wind** (8:1). trees] Only one **tree.** So Samaritan and Septuagint also.

9 [7]Adam[0] is supplied by the Septuagint.

10 [7]**walking**[0] has dropped out of the Hebrew.

11 commanded] **instruct.** See verse 2:16 not] is used for nearly a dozen Hebrew stems, which the C.V. keeps distinct. C.V. **avoid.**

13 beguiled] only here in A.V. Other places mostly deceive. **C.V. always lure.**

14 cattle] **beast.** See 1:25. beast] **life.** See 1:24. belly][5] **from five stems in A.V. torso.** Occurs only twice (Lv. 11:42). dust] **soil.** See 2:7.

15 bruise][8] This Hebrew word is also rendered break and cover in the A.V. C.V. **hurt.**

16 greatly multiply] The Hebrew figure, **Multiplying,** yea, **multiplying** seems more expressive in this case. sorrow][20] A.V. **grief,** ten times, as C.V. [7]**the groaning of**[?] is found in the Septuagint. conception] The same stem as mountain, it means **pregnancy.** desire] The Septuagint has from-turn, which shows that shb has been mistaken for shq, and that the early Hebrew read **return or restoration.**

17 [7]**alone**[0] was preserved by the Septuagint. [7]**when you ▴serve it**[0] **is from the Septuagint.**

A Test Passage

18 thistles] represents a distinct plant (2 Ki. 14:9). The word here is literally **about-about,** and it would seem to include all **weeds.** bring forth] is the same word as 2:5 grow. It should be **sprout.**

19 **face** is literally **noses,** or nostrils. See margin. dust] **soil.** See 2:7 shalt . . return] It is a present process also, **you are returning.**

21 coats] are outer, upper garments, but these were single **tunics.**

22 ever] is used by the A.V. for **permanent**[24], **further**[42], **eon**[267], **perpetuity**[2], **continual**[3]. The word oulm, here used, is in the singular, but occurs often in the plural (Is. 26:4, 45:17, 51:9). It is used of the past (Gen. 6:4). It is often followed by **and further** (Ex. 15:18). It is translated by the Greek *aiōn*, eon or age, in the Septuagint. Hence it should be **eon,** a period with a definite duration, not endless.

24 placed][8] This stem the A.V. usually renders **tabernacle.** [7]**him**[0] and [7]**And he set**[0] from the Septuagint shows that Adam **tabernacled** and the cherubim **were set.** cherubims] The ending —im is plural and needs no s. every way] the reflexive, **itself.**

4:1 conceived] **pregnant,** from the stem **prominent.** In the margin is the meaning of Cain's name. gotten][14] **acquire,** or get by one's own efforts.

2 again][7] **proceeding,** not repetition. keeper][12] **grazier,** from the stem, **graze.** sheep][6] **flock** of small cattle, as verse 4. tiller] **Jacob served** (not tilled) for Rachel (29:18).

3 process] as in "the **end** of all flesh" (6:13). time][6] as in "God called the light **day**"[1167] (1:5). offering][7] **as a present**[28] for Esau (32:13).

5 respect][8] means give **heed** in other places. wrath][9] as A.V., Ez. 3:14, "the **heat** of my anger." 5 6 **falling** is figurative to express dejection.

7 accepted][12] reverse of previous figure [N]**lift**[137]. door][5] **a tabernacle** (3:24) has no real door, like the temple (1 Ki. 6:31), which is a different word. This was an **opening.** sin][5] A.V. has sin offering, elsewhere over 100 times. Cain had offered a **present** offering without a **sin** offering. lieth][5] The firstling of the flock **reclined** (4:4). desire] [7]**restoration**[r], according to the Septuagint.

8 [7]**Go will we to the field**[n], is supplied by the Septuagint and the Samaritan. slew][12] A.V. also has **kill** in 12:12. Another word is "slay."

11 earth][5] **ground.** Same as 2:15.

12 yield][13] **give,** as in 1:29. strength][20] **vigor.** Nearly 30 Hebrew words are rendered strength in the A.V. 12 14 fugitive][4] **rover.** There is no thought of flight. vagabond][2] **wanderer,** as A.V. in Prov. 26:2.

13 punishment][9] **depravity.** Nine stems are not discriminated in the A.V.

14 earth][5] **ground**[43]. See verse 2:5. hid][16] **conceal.** Not the same as 3:8. fugitive, vagabond] **rover, wanderer.** See verse 12. slay] **kill.** See verse 8.

15 [7]**Alueim**[0] was in the ancient Hebrew text, according to the Greek Septuagint version. Therefore] [7]**Not.**[0] The letter **a** dropped out of the Hebrew text. slayeth] **killing.** As in verse 8. Lord] **Ieue.** See 2:4] set] **place.** mark][15] **sign,** as in 1:14. upon] **for.** Not like Ex. 13:16. lest][4] **to avoid.** As 3:11. kill][10] **smiting**[350]. So A.V. also translates usually.

16 went out][3] **faring forth,** as 2:10, and often. [7]**Alueim**[0] was in the ancient text.

17 conceived][4] **pregnant,** as in 4:1. after][9] **as.** So A.V. very often.

19 other][6] **second**[100]. As 1:8 and 2:13.

21 [A]**handle** Hb. **grasp.** See margin. Fig. Association. organ] Obsolete. **shepherd's pipe.**

22 also] **moreover.** See 3:6 and 4:26. instructor][8] Here only in A.V. **forger.** artificer] may also be **tool.** brass] **copper.** Brass is an alloy, not used anciently.

23 hearken][3] [C]**give ear,** causative of **ear. Hearken** belongs to hear. have slain] **killed.** As in verse 8. wounding][10] **injury.** Another word denotes **wound** (Ez. 26:15). young man][3] **boy,** as A.V. Jl. 3:3. hurt][10] **welt.** Same word as "stripes" in Is. 53:5 (A.V.)

25 [7]**Eve**[C] has been preserved in the Septuagint and Syriac. [7]**pregnant**[0] and [7]**saying**[0] have dropped out of the Hebrew. appointed][30] should be, **set,** the meaning of **Seth.** slew] **kills.** See verse 8.

26 also] **moreover.** See 3:6. Enos] **Enosh,** as A.V. has it correctly in 1 Ch. 1:1. [7]**this one**[0] was preserved by the Septuagint. began] Septuagint differs. Hebrew looks like [7]**wounded**[7]. See 23. men] Not in Hebrew. **Enosh** seems to be meant. Lord] **Ieue.** [7]**Alueim**[0] dropped out of the Hebrew.

Pleiades
Jb99 3831 Am58

Celestial
Sphere
Ph210

STARS
Gn116 155 2217 264 379
Nu2417 1Ch2723 Jb97
Jb2212 Jl 210

VIEW
OF THE
UNIVERSE
FROM THE
EARTH

SUN
Gn1512 1923 379 Is1310
Jr3135 Joel3(4)15
MOON
Gn379 Jl210 Jb392

over all of the h. Ep410
on-heavens
bodies 1C1540
seated Eph120 26
glory 1Co 1540
blessing Ep13

Terrestrial
third heaven 2C122
Ionosphere
Heavens
through the h. Hb414
Stratosphere
Water
Atmosphere
Chaos : Land
Water
Subterranean
Gn12 711 82 495 Dt3313
Lu831 Ph210 Rv91 117 201

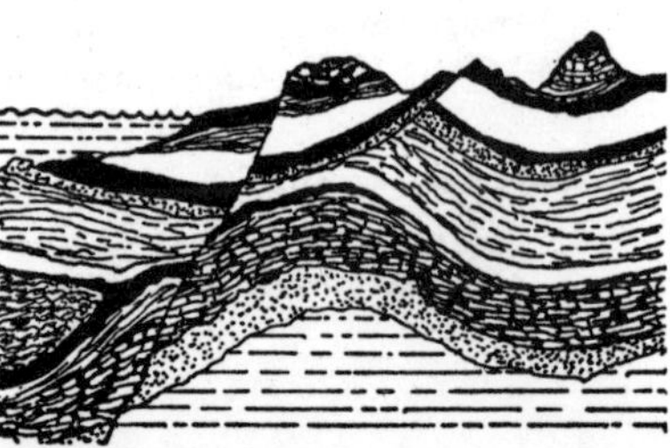

Al u e im
SUBJECT-OR-TO-S
(To-subjectors)

IN A BEGINNING

COMMONLY CALLED

"GENESIS"

1 Dt324 2S2231 Ps336 9
Pr319 Ec311 Is4512 Jr5115 11-23 Heavens and Earth=Annals 24-5026 11 Creation=Disruption 12-
Jn11 Col16 Hb110 Rv411 **Created by the Alueim were `the heavens and `the earth.**
12- Disruption=Readjustment -2-24
2 Is4518 Jer423 2Pt36 2 **[a]Yet the earth became a chaos and vacant, and darkness**
was on the surface of the submerged chaos.
1[s]one spirit in plural
1-2-31 Readjustment- **[a]Yet the spirit of the Alueim is vibrating over the surface**
Cessation 21-3 3 **of the water. And saying is the Alueim, "Become light!"**
-2-5 Light 14-19 4 **And it is becoming light. And seeing is the Alueim `the light,**
3 light *is* vibration **that it is good. And separating is the Alueim between the**
3 Ps119130 2C46 5 **light and[bt] the darkness. And calling is the Alueim [to] the light**
4 Ec311 116 **"day," and [to] the darkness He calls "night."**
5 Ps7416 922 10420 **And coming is it to be evening and coming to be morning,**
day one.

6-8 Atmosphere=Water-
souls 20-23 6 **And saying is the Alueim, "Become shall an atmosphere**
in the midst of the water, and [b]coming is a separation be-
atmosphere *rqio* STAMP 7 **tween water [t]and water." [7]And coming is it to be so.[0] And**
atm makes light visible. **making is the Alueim `the atmosphere. And separating is**
water above (descends **He between the water which is [f] under [to] the atmosphere and**
in deluge, or flood). **[bt] the water which is [f] above [to] the atmosphere. And calling is**
8 Jb3718 Ps1365 Pr828 8 **the Alueim [to] the atmosphere "heavens." [7]And seeing is the**
Alueim that it is good.[0]
And coming is it to be evening and coming to be morning,
the second day.

9-13 Land=Land- 9 **And saying is the Alueim, "Flow together shall the water**
life 24-31 **from under the heavens to one place, and appear shall the**
dry land." And coming is it to be so. [7]And flowing together
is the water [f] under the heavens to one place, and appearing
10 Jb2610 388 Ps337 10 **is the dry land.[0] And calling is the Alueim [to] the dry part**
955 1046 1366 Jr522 **"land" [or "earth"] and [to] the confluence of the water He**
Pr 829 **calls "seas." And seeing is the Alueim that it is good.**
11 **And saying is the Alueim, "Verdant shall become the land**
from-kind FROM-cause **with verdure; with herbage seeding seed [7]for its from-kind**
and for its likeness.[0] [7]and[n] with the fruit tree whose seed is
yield DOING **in it yielding fruit for its from-kind, on the land." And com-**
12 Lu644 12 **ing is it to be so. And forth is the land [c]bringing verdure;**
herbage seeding seed for its from-kind,[7]and for its likeness,[0]
yield DOING **and the [7]fruit[0] tree whose seed is in it, yielding fruit for its**
from-kind, [7]on the land.[0] And seeing is the Alueim that it is
good.
13 **And coming is it to be evening and coming to be morning,**
the third day.
-2-5 Light 14-1 14 **And saying is the Alueim, "Become shall luminaries in**
14 Ex256 2720 3514 Jr102 **the atmosphere of the heavens, [7]to [c]give light on the earth,[0]**
to separate between the day and [bt] the night. And they come
to be for signs and for appointments, and for days and
15 Ps83 7416-17 15 **years." And there come to be [to] luminaries in the atmosphere**
of the heavens to [c]give light on the earth. And coming is it
to be so.

16 And making is the **Alueim** 'two ·great ·luminaries, 'the *Al u e im*
greater ·luminary for [I]ruling the day, and 'the smaller ·lu- SUBJECT-or-to-s (To-subjectors)
17 minary for [I]ruling the night, and 'the stars. And bestowing bestow GIVE
'them is the **Alueim** in the atmosphere of the heavens to
18 [c]give light on the earth, and to [I]rule in the day and in the [I]Impersonation
night, and to separate between the light and [bt] the darkness. *18* Ps83 1367
And seeing is the **Alueim** that it is good.

19 And coming is it to be evening, and coming to be morning, the fourth day.

20 And saying is the **Alueim**, "Roam shall the water with the 6-8 Atmosphere=
roaming, living [N]soul, and the flyer shall fly over the earth Water souls 20-23
on the face of the atmosphere of the heavens." [7]And coming *20* 27 19 94 5 Lvl146
21 is it to be so.[0] And creating is the **Alueim** '·great ·monsters. *21* Ps10425
and 'every ·living ·moving [N]soul, with which the water
roams, for their from-kind, and 'every winged flyer for its f-k FROM-caused
from-kind. And seeing is the **Alueim** that it is good.
22 And blessing 'them is the **Alueim**, [to]saying, "Be [F]fruitful
and increase and fill 'the water [i]of the seas. And the flyer
is to be increasing in the earth."
23 And coming is it to be evening and coming to be morning,
the fifth day.

24 And saying is the **Alueim**, "[c]Bring forth[F] shall the earth 9-13 Land=Land-
the living [N]soul for its from-kind, beast and moving animal life 24-31
and land life for its from-kind." And coming is it to be so.

25 And making is the **Alueim** 'the land life for its from-kind,
and 'the beast for its from-kind, and 'every moving animal
of the ground for its from-kind. And seeing is the **Alueim**
that it is good.
26 And saying is the **Alueim**, "Make will We humanity in hu*Adm* LIKEST
Our image,[7]and[n] [as]according to Our likeness, and sway shall *26* 27 51 3 96 Ps86
they [i]over the fish of the sea, and [i]over the flyer of the Pr822-31 Jn114 Ac1726
heavens, and [i]over the beast, and [i]over all land [g]life[c], and 1Cl13-11 Col15 Hb13
[i]over every moving animal moving on the land." Ja39 Rv314
27 And creating is the **Alueim** '·humanity in His image. In *27* 27 18-24
the image of the **Alueim** He creates 'it. Male and female He
creates 'them. *28* 91 7 Ps85
28 And blessing 'them is the **Alueim**. And saying to them is Ac1417 Hb26-8
the **Alueim**, "Be [F]fruitful and increase and fill 'the earth,
and subdue it. And sway [i]over the fish of the sea, and [i]over
the flyer of the heavens, [7]and [i]over the beast,[c] [7]and [i]over all
the earth,[0] and [i]over all life ·moving on the land."

29 And saying is the **Alueim**, "Behold, I give to you 'all
herbage seeding seed, which is on the surface of the entire
earth, and 'every ·tree which has in it the fruit of a tree
30 seeding seed. For you it is coming to be for food. And for
all ·land life, and for every flyer of the heavens, and for
every moving animal on the land, which has in it a living
soul,'all green herbage is for food." And coming is it to be so.

31 And seeing is the **Alueim** 'all [w]that He had made, and, behold, it is very good.

And coming is it to be evening and coming to be morning,
the sixth day.

1 Dt426 Ps336 2P37
1-2-31 Readjustment-Cessation 21-3
3 122 Ex2011 Hb44

2 And finished are the heavens and the earth and all their
host.
2 And finishing is the Alueim, on the ʼsixthº day, His work
which He does. And ceasing is He ʻon the seventh day from
3 all His work which He does. And blessing is the Alueim
ʻthe seventh day, and hallowing ʻit, for in it He ceases from
all His work, which the Alueim creates to make.

Link

4 These are the genealogical annals of the heavens and the
earth, ʻwhen they were created.

I e u e
Will-be-ing-was

11-23 Heavens and Earth=Annals 24-5026 2-4-25 Human 425-26 4-7 Man-Woman 18-25

5 111 12 20 24 74
Jb3826 Ps902 10414 2P37

In the day Ieue Alueim made the earth and the heavens,
5 and every shrub of the field ere it is coming to be in the
earth, and all herbage of the field ere it is sprouting, at
that time Ieue Alueim does not ᶜbring rain on the earth,
and there was no human to ᴬserve ʻthe ᴵground.

irrigates DRINKizes
7 120 319 23 722
Ps10314 Ec127 1C1545
Adm 1 = B.C. 5465

6 ᵃYet humidity is ascending from the earth and irrigates
ʻall the surface of the ground.
7 And forming is Ieue Alueim ʻthe human of soil from the
ground, and He is blowing into his nostrils the breath of
the living, and becoming is the human ᵗᵒa living ᴺsoul.

8 Plants 15
ᴱOdn LUXURY
8 323 24 416 Is513

8 And planting is Ieue Alueim a garden in Eden, ᶠin the
east, and He is placing there ʻthe human whom He forms.

9 Food 16-17
9 322 Pr318 1130 Jn648
51 53 Rv27 222 14

9 And ʼfurthermoreʼ sprouting is Ieue Alueim from the
ground every tree coveted ᵗby the ᴺsight and good for food,
and the tree of the living in the midst of the garden, and the
tree of the knowledge of good and evil.

10 Rivers 11-14
irrigates DRINKizes

10 And a stream is faring forth from Eden to irrigate ʻthe
garden, and thence it is being parted and ᵇcomes to four
heads.

10 Rivers 11-14
ᴾ*Phish un* DIFFUSER
ᴴ*Chuil e* Travailer
11 1029 2518 1S157
ᴳ*Gich un* FORTH-RUSHER
Kush BURLY
ᴴ*Chd ql* ONE-fleet
ᴬ*Ashur* PROGRESSING
ᴱ*Phr th* FRUITS

11 The name of the one is Pison. It is ˙that surrounding ʼʻtheº
12 entire land of ˙Havilah, where there is gold, and the gold of
˙that ˙land is ˢexceedinglyⁿ good. There is the pearl and the
13 onyx stone. And the name of the second ˙stream is Gihon. It
14 is ˙that surrounding ʼʻtheº entire land of Kush. And the
name of the third ˙stream is Hiddekel. It is ˙that going east
of Ashur. And the fourth ˙stream, it is the Euphrates.

8 Plants 15
15 324

15 And taking is Ieue Alueim ʻthe human ʼthat He had
formedº and is leaving him in the garden of Eden to ᴬserve
it and to keep it.

16 32 9 Food 16-17
17 34 55 Ex1912 2112
Lv202 9 Nu1535 1K237
42 Ac530 Ro623 1P224

16 And instructing is Ieue Alueim ᵒⁿthe human, ᵗᵒ saying,
17 "From every tree of the garden, you are to eat, yea, eat. ᵃYet
from the tree of the knowledge of good and evil, you are
not to be eating from it, for in the day you eat from it, to
die shall you be dying."

4-7 Man-Woman 18-25

18 And saying is Ieue Alueim, "Not good is it for the human
for him to be alone. Make for him will I a helper as his com-
19 plement." And ʼfurthermoreº Ieue Alueim, having formed

from the ground 'all ·field life and 'every flyer of the heavens, He is also bringing it to the human to see what he will
call to it. And whatever[y] the human living [N]soul is calling to
20 it, that is its name. And calling is the human the names for
every ·beast and for 'every' flyer of the heavens, and for all
·field life. [a]Yet for the human He does not find a helper as
his complement.
21 And [F]falling is a stupor on the human, caused by Ieue
Alueim, and he is sleeping. And taking is He one [f]of his
22 angular organs and is closing the flesh under it. And Ieue
Alueim is [F]building 'the angular organ, which He takes from
the human, into a woman, and bringing her is He to the
23 human. And saying is the human, "This was ·once [M]bone [f]of
my bones and [M]flesh from my flesh. to This shall be called
24 woman, for from 'her[n] man is this taken." Therefore a man
shall forsake 'his father and 'his mother and cling [t]to his
25 wife, and they 'two[n] become to one flesh. And coming are
they two, the human and his wife, to be naked, [a]yet are not
shaming themselves.

huAdm LIKEST
20 1C119 1Ti213
I e u e Will-be-ing-was
Al u e im SUBJECT-or-to-s (To-subjectors)
ang=angle vault Ez41 (A.V.=chamber)
24 Mt195 1C616 Ep531

31-24 Failure 41-24 31-5 Living Creatures -24

3 And the serpent comes to be the craftiest [f]of all ·field
life which was made by Ieue Alueim. And saying is 'the serpent' to the woman, "Indeed! [tt]Then the Alueim says, 'Not
eat shall you from [al]any tree of the garden'?"
2 And saying is the woman to the serpent, "From the fruit
3 of the trees of the garden we are eating, [a]yet from the fruit
of the tree which is in the midst of the garden, the Alueim
says, 'Not eat [f]of it shall you, and not touch in it shall you,
lest you be dying.'"
4 And saying is the serpent to the woman, "Not to die shall
5 you be dying, for the Alueim knows that, in the day you eat
[f]of it, [a]unclosed shall be your [A]eyes, and you become as the
Alueim, knowing good and evil."

1 Nu216 9 Jb512 155
thenTHAT
anyALL
2 216 17 1Ti214

6 And seeing is the woman that the tree is good for food,
and that it brings a yearning to the [A]eyes, and is to be
coveted as the tree to [c]make one intelligent. And taking is
she [f]of its fruit and is eating, and she is giving, moreover,
to her husband with her, and 'they are[n] eating.

6 Trees 22-24
6 Mt43-10 1Jn216

7 And unclosing are their [A]eyes, they two, and knowing are
they that they are naked. And sewing are they fig 'leaves[n]
and making for themselves girdle skirts.

7 Clothing 20-21
7 Ro83

8 And hearing are they 'the sound of Ieue Alueim walking
in the garden in the windy part of the day. And hiding
themselves are the human and his wife from the [N]face of
Ieue Alueim, in the midst of a tree of the garden.
9 And calling is Ieue Alueim to the human, and He is saying to him, "'Adam!' Where are you?"
10 And saying is he 'to Him,' "'The sound of Thee 'walking'
hear I in the garden, and fearful am I, for naked am I, and I
am hiding."
11 And saying is He 'to him,' "Did anyone tell to you that you
are naked? From the tree of which 'alone' I instruct you
to avoid eating, from it did you eat?"

8-12 Man 17-19
8 2S524 1K146 Jr2324 Ep213
AAdm LIKEST

12 Dt136 Jb3133 *12* **And saying is the human, "The woman whom Thou gavest,**
withal, she gave to me from the tree and I am eating."

13 Woman 16 *13* **And saying is Ieue Alueim to the woman, "What is this**
13 2Cl13 14 **you do?"**

And saying is the woman, "The serpent lured me and I
am eating."

14 Estrangement 15 *14* **And saying is Ieue Alueim to the serpent, "[tt]As you do**
[As]THAT **this,** most cursed are you **[f]of every ·beast, and [f]of all ·field**
14 Is6525 Mi717 **life. On your torso shall you go, and soil shall you eat all**
the days of your lives.

14 Estrangement 15 *15* **"And enmity am I setting between you and [bt] the woman,**
15 177 2112 Ps419 **and between your [N]seed and [bt] her [N]seed. He shall hurt your**
Jn1318 Ro1620 Ga316 **[N]head and you shall hurt his [N]heel."**

13 Woman 16 *16* **'And" to the woman He says, "Multiplying, yea, multiply-**
16 Mt123 Lu131 Ga44 **ing am I your grief and 'the groaning of' your pregnancy. In**
1Cl13 1Ti214 15 **grief shall you bear sons.**
"[a]Yet [i]by your husband is your 'restoration,' and he shall
rule [i]over you."

8-12 Man 17-19 *17* **And to the human He says, "[tt]As you hearken to the**
[As]THAT **[N]voice of your wife, and are eating from the tree of which**
17 Ro819-23 **'alone' I instruct you,[to] saying not eat shall you from it,**
cursed shall be the **[I]ground '[i]when you [A]serve it,' [i]for your**
'sakes.' In grief shall you eat of it all the days of your lives.
18 **And thorns and weeds shall it sprout for you, and you**
19 **shall eat** 'the herbage of the field. In the [N]sweat of your
[face]NOSES **[A]face shall you eat 'your' bread, till your return to the**
19 27 Ps10314 Ec113 **ground, for from it are you taken, for [M]soil you are, and to**
127 1Cl547 2Th310 **soil are you returning."**

7 Clothing 20-21 *20* **And calling is the human his wife's name Eve, for she**
[E]*Chue* Living **becomes the [N]mother of all the living.**
20 41 2Cl13 1Ti213 *21* **And making is Ieue Alueim for Adam and for his wife**
tunics of skin, and is clothing them.

6 Trees 22-24 *22* **And saying is Ieue Alueim, "Behold! The human becomes**
as one of us,[to] knowing good and evil. And now, lest he
[stretch]SEND **stretch forth his hand, moreover, and take [f]of the tree of the**
23 **living, and eat and live for the eon—!" And Ieue Alueim is**
sending him away from the garden of Eden to [A]serve 'the
24 29 414 16 1S44 *24* **ground whence he is taken. And He is driving out 'the hu-**
Ps801 991 **man, and is causing 'him' to tabernacle [f]at the east [t]of the**
garden of Eden.

1-5 Living Creatures-24 **'And He set' 'the cherubim, and 'a flaming ·sword ·turning**
itself, to keep 'the way of the tree of the living.

31-24 Failure 41-24 1-16 Sons 17-24

[E]*Chue* Living **4** **And the human knows 'Eve, his wife, and pregnant is she**
[Q]*Qin* Acquired **and is bearing 'Cain. And saying is she, "I [F]acquire a man,**
[A]*E bl* Vanity *2* **'Ieue!" And proceeding is she to bear 'his brother 'Abel. And**
coming is Abel to be the grazier of a flock, [a]yet Cain be-
comes a [A]server of the [I]ground.
3 317 Ju11 *3* **And [b]coming is it, [f]at the end of days, [a]that bringing is**
Cain, from the fruit of the ground, a present offering to
4 Lv33 4 Ps203 Hb114 *4* **Ieue. Abel also is bringing, he, moreover, from the firstlings**
of his flock, and from their fat. And heed is Ieue giving to

Abel and to his present offering, [a]yet to Cain and to his
5 present offering He does not give heed. And [A]hot is [to]Cain's
anger exceedingly, and [F]falling is his face.
6 And saying is Ieue [7]Alueim[0] to Cain, "Why is [to] your anger
7 [A]hot? And why does your face [F]fall? Would you not, should
you be [c]doing well, [A]lift it up? And should you not be [c]doing
well, [t]at the opening a [A]sin offering is reclining, and for
you is its [7]restoration.' And you are ruler [i]over it."
8 And saying is Cain to Abel, his brother, [7]"Go will we to
the field."[n] And [b]coming is it, [t]at their coming to be in the
field,[a] [A]rising is Cain [t]against Abel, his brother, and killing
him.
9 And saying is Ieue [7]Alueim[0] to Cain, "Where is Abel, your
brother?" And saying is he, "I do not know. The keeper of
10 my brother am I?" And saying is [7]the Alueim,[0] "What have
you done? The [I]voice of your brother's [=]blood is crying to
11 Me from the ground. And now, cursed are you [f]by the
ground, which opens 'its [F]mouth wide to take your brother's
12 'blood[=] from your [A]hand. [tt]As you are [A]serving 'the [I]ground,
it will not continue to give its vigor to you. A rover and a
wanderer shall you become in the earth."
13 And saying is Cain to Ieue [7]Alueim,[0] "Too great is my
14 depravity to [F]bear. Behold, drive 'me dost Thou out 'today
off the surface of the ground, and from Thy [N]face shall I
be concealed, and become shall I a rover and a wanderer in
the earth. And it [b]comes that [al]anyone finding me will kill
me."
15 And saying to him is Ieue [7]Alueim,[0] "[7]Not[c] so. [al]Anyone
killing Cain, sevenfold shall it be avenged." And placing is
Ieue [7]Alueim[0] a sign for Cain, to avoid [al]anyone finding him
16 smiting 'him. And forth is Cain faring from before Ieue
[7]Alueim,[0] and is dwelling in the land of Nod, east of Eden.
17 And knowing is Cain 'his wife and she is pregnant and
bearing 'Enoch. And [b]coming is it that he is building a city,
and calling is he 'the name of the city as the name of his
son, Enoch.
18 And born to Enoch is 'Irad, and Irad generates 'Mehujael,
and Mehujael generates 'Methusael, and Methusael generates 'Lamech.
19 And Lamech is taking for himself two wives, the one
20 named Adah, and the second named Zillah. And Adah is
bearing 'Jabal. He becomes the forefather of the tent dweller
21 and the cattleman. And the name of his brother is Jubal. He
becomes the forefather of all who [A]handle the harp and the
22 shepherd's pipe. And Zillah, moreover, she bears 'Tubal-cain, a forger of every tool of copper and iron. And the sister of Tubal-cain is Naamah.

23 And saying is Lamech to his wives:
"Adah and Zillah, hearken to my [N]voice!
Wives of Lamech, [c]give [N]ear to my saying!
For a man killed I for my injury,
And a boy for my welt.
24 [tt]As sevenfold is the avenging of Cain,
[a]Then seventy and seven is Lamech's."

[A]*Ebl* Vanity
[C]*Qin* Acquired
I e u e Will-be-ing-was
7 Lv43 625 82 2C521 Ep52
res [H]*thushuqe*[b] RUN-ABOUT (*literally*)
8 1Jn312 Ju11
10 Mt2335 Hb1224
[As]THAT
14 38 Nu3519
[Any]ALL
[Any]ALL
15 Ex48 9 17 1213 Ez2012 20
[N]*Nud* WANDERing
[E]*Odn* LUXURY
1-16 Sons 17-24
[En]*Chnuk* DEDICATED
[Ir]*Oird* City-SUFFICES
[M]*Mch u i-Al* WIPE(*out*)-SUBJECTOR
[Mth]*Mth u shal*= Dying-ASK
[L]*L mk* To-REDUCE
[A]*Ode* Ornament
[Z]*Tzle* Shadow SHADE
[Ja]DISINTEGRATER
[Ju]*Iu bl* Jubilee
handle GRASP
22 Ru119 20
[Tu]*Thu bl-Qin* DISINTEGRATION-acquired
[Na]*Nom e* PLEASANT
[As]THAT

Adm 230 25 Sons 26 25 **And knowing is Adam 'Eve,° \his wife, again. And 'preg-**
[E]*Chue* Living **nant° is she and bearing a son. And calling is she \his name**
[S]*Shth* Set **Seth, 'saying,° "For set for me has the Alueim another**
[C]*Qin* Acquired **[N]seed instead of Abel, for Cain kills him."**

26 J1232 25 Sons 26 26 **And to Seth, moreover, to him is born a son. And calling**
[E]*Anush* Mortal **is he \his name Enosh. Then 'this° one 'is wounded.' Yet he**
calls \on the [N]name of Ieue 'Alueim.°

51-68 Progenitors 371-5026 51-5 Generation 61-3

1 Mt1 1 Lu338 5 **This is the scroll of the genealogical annals of Adam: In**
Ro514 1C1522 45 **the day the Alueim created Adam, in the likeness of the**
2 **Alueim He made \him. Male and female created He them.**
[A]*Adm* Likest **And blessing \them is He, and calling \their name Adam in**
the day they are created.

Adm 230 3 **And living is Adam 'two° hundred and thirty years. And**
3 Ps515 Ro512-19 **begetting is he one in his likeness, according to his image.**
4 **And calling is he \his name Seth. And coming are the [N]days**
Al u eim **of Adam, after his begetting \Seth, to be 'seven° =hundred**
subject-or-to-s 5 **years. And begetting is he sons and daughters. And coming**
(To-subjectors) **are all the [N]days of Adam, which he lives, to be nine =hun-**
Adm 930 **dred[yr] and thirty years. And he died.**

56-31 Distinguished 64-7 6 **And living is Seth 'two° =hundred[yr] and five years. And**
6 426 7 **begetting is he \Enosh. And living is Seth, after his beget-**
Adm 435 **ting \Enosh, 'seven° =hundred[yr] and seven years, and beget-**
8 **ting is he sons and daughters. And coming are all the [N]days**
Adm 1132 **of Seth to be nine =hundred[yr] and twelve years. And he died.**

Adm 625 9 **And living is Enosh 'a hundred[yr] and° ninety years. And**
[E]*Anush* Mortal 10 **begetting is he \Cainan. And living is Enosh, after his be-**
[C]*Quin n* Acquisition **getting \Cainan, 'seven° =hundred[yr] and fifteen years. And**
11 **begetting is he sons and daughters. And coming are all the**
[N]days of Enosh to be nine =hundred[yr] and five years. And he
Adm 1340 **died.**

Adm 795 12 **And living is Cainan 'a hundred[yr] and° seventy years. And**
[M]*M ell-Al* Praise-of- 13 **begetting is he \Malaleel. And living is Cainan, after his**
Subjector **begetting \Malaleel, 'seven° =hundred[yr] and forty years. And**
14 **begetting is he sons and daughters. And coming are all the**
[N]days of Cainan to be nine =hundred[yr] and ten years. And he
Adm 1535 **died.**

Adm 960 15 **And living is Malaleel 'a hundred°[yr] and sixty[yr] five years.**
[J]*Ird* Descended 16 **And begetting is he \Jared. And living is Malaleel, after**
his begetting \Jared, 'seven° =hundred[yr] and thirty years.
17 **And begetting is he sons and daughters. And coming are all**
the days of Malaleel to be eight =hundred[yr] and ninety-five
Adm 1690 **years. And he died.**

Adm 1122 18 **And living is Jared a hundred[yr] and sixty-two years. And**
[E]*Chnuk* Dedicator 19 **begetting is he \Enoch. And living is Jared, after his beget-**
ting \Enoch, eight =hundred years. And begetting is he sons
20 **and daughters. And coming are all the [N]days of Jared to be**
Adm 1922 **nine =hundred[yr] and sixty-two years. And he died.**

Adm 1287 21 **And living is Enoch 'a hundred[yr] and° sixty-five years.**
[M]*Mthu shlch* Die-will- 22 **And begetting is he \Methuselah. And [F]walking is Enoch**
send **\with the Alueim, after his begetting \Methuselah, 'two°**
Adm 1487 transferred **=hundred years. And begetting is he sons and daughters.**

23 **And coming 'are[n] all the [N]days of Enoch to be three =hun-** [E]*Chnuk* DEDICATOR
24 **dred[yr] and sixty-five years. And walking is Enoch \with the** *24* 2K2:11 Hb11:5 Ju14
Alueim. And not 'found[o] is he, for taken was \he by the
Alueim.
25 **And living is Methuselah a hundred[yr] and eighty-seven** Adm 1474
26 **years. And begetting is he \Lamech. And living is Methu-** [M]*Mthushlch*=
selah, after his begetting \Lamech, seven =hundred[yr] and DIE-will-SEND
eighty-two years. And begetting is he sons and daughters. [L]*Lmk* TO-REDUCE
27 **And coming are all the [N]days of Methuselah, 'which he**
lived,[o] to be nine =hundred[yr] and sixty-nine years. And he
died. Adm 2256
28 **And living is Lamech a hundred[yr] and eighty-'eight[o] years.** Adm 1662
29 **And begetting is he a son. And calling is he \his name Noah,** *29* 63 8:21
[to] **saying, "This one will console us [f]because of our 'doings,[n]** [N]*Nch* STOP
and [f]because of the grief of our [N]hands, [f]because of the
30 **ground which Ieue 'Alueim[o] makes a curse." And living is**
Lamech, after his begetting \Noah, five =hundred[yr] and 'sixty[o]-
31 **five years. And begetting is he sons and daughters. And**
coming 'are[n] all the [N]days of Lamech to be seven =hundred Adm 2227
[yr] **and 'fifty-three[o] years. And he died.**

532 New Beginning 68

32 **And coming is Noah to be five =hundred years of [s]age. And** [a]g[e]son *32* 10:1 11:10
begetting is Noah 'three sons,[o] \Shem, \Ham, and \Japheth. Adm 2164 Shem

[S]*Shm* PLACE *or* Name [H]*Chm* WARM [J]*Iphth* ENTICED

6 **And [b]coming is it that ·humanity starts to be multitudinous** 51-5 Generation 61-3
on the surface of the ground, and daughters are born to *1* 12:7 52
2 **them. And seeing are sons of the alueim \the daughters of**
the human, that they are good, and taking are they for
themselves wives [f]of all whom they choose.
3 **And saying is Ieue 'Alueim,[o] "Not 'abide[o] shall My spirit in**
the human for the eon, in [w]that moreover, he is [N]flesh. And
come shall his [N]days to be a hundred and twenty years." Adm 810

4 **'[a]Now[n] the distinguished come to be in the earth in ·those** 56-31 Distinguished 64-7
days, and, moreover, afterward, coming are those who are
sons of the alueim to the daughters of the human, and they
bear for them. They are the masters, who are from the eon,
mortals with the [N]name.
5 **And seeing is Ieue 'Alueim[o] that much is the evil of ·hu-**
manity in the earth, and every form of the devices of its *Al u e im*
6 **[F]heart is but evil all its ·days. And [C]regretting is Ieue 'Alue-** SUBJECT-or-to-S
im[o] that He made \humanity [i]on the earth, and grieving[sf] to (To-subjectors)
7 **His [F]heart. And saying is Ieue 'Alueim,[o] "[F]Wipe will I \the**
humanity, which I have created, off the surface of the
ground, from human unto beast, and unto the moving animal,
and unto the flyer of the heavens, for I [C]regret that I have
made them."

ARK

8 **[a]Yet Noah finds grace in the [A]eyes of Ieue 'Alueim.[o]** 532 New Beginning 68
69-929 Forefathers 361-8 69 Time 928-29
9 **These are the genealogical annals of Noah: Noah is a just** *9* 5:22 24 7:1
man. Flawless became he in his generations. \With the
Alueim [F]walks Noah.

10 **And begetting is Noah three sons, \Shem, \Ham, and \Ja-** 610 Sons 918-27
pheth. *10* 5:32 9:18 10:1 1Ch1:4

11-13 Condition 821-917 11 And being ruined is the [A]earth before the Alueim, and
Ieue 12 being [F]filled is the [A]earth with wrong. And seeing is [7]Ieue[0]
Will-be-ing-was Alueim ˋthe [A]earth, and behold! Ruined is it, for ruining is
13 all [N]flesh ˋits [F]way on the earth. And saying is the Alueim
[N]Nch STOP to Noah, "The [7]era of[0] the end of all [7]human[0] [N]flesh is come
before Me, for [F]full is the [A]earth with wrong [f]because of
their presence.[a]Now behold Me ruining them ˋwith the earth.

614-22 Provision 820 14 "Make for yourself an ark of sulphur [=]wood. With [F]nests
14 Ex23 Is349 shall you make ˋthe ark. And shelter ˋit from the inside and
15 from the outside [i]with a sheltering coat. And this is [w]how
Cubit=approx. 18 inches you shall make [7]ˋthe ark:[0] Three [=]hundred cubits is the
length of the ark, [7]and[n] fifty cubits its width, and thirty
16 711 86 16 cubits its rise. [7]Narrowing[r] you shall make it [t]from the [r]mid-
dle,[r] and to a cubit shall you finish it from [to] above. And the
opening of the ark you shall place in its side. With nether,
second and third decks shall you make it.
17 Ps2910 17 "And I, behold Me bringing ˋa ·deluge of water over the
earth to wreck all [N]flesh, which has in it the spirit of the
living, from under the heavens. All [w]that is in the earth
shall expire.
18 "And I set [F]up ˋMy covenant ˋwith you. And come do you
to the ark, you and your sons and your wife and your sons'
19 72 9 19 wives ˋwith you. And [7f]of every beast and [f]of every moving
animal and[0] [f]of every ·living animal [f]of all flesh, a pair from
all, are you to bring into the ark, to[c]preserve alive ˋwith you.
20 Male and female shall they be[c]. [f]Of [7]every bird of[0] the flyer
for its from-kind, and [f]of [7]every[0] ·beast for its from-kind,
[7]and[n] [f]of every moving animal [7]moving on[n] the ground for its
f-k FROM-cause from-kind. Pairs [f]of all shall come to you, to [c]preserve alive,
[7]male and female.[0]
21 "And you, take for yourselves [f]of all food which is being
eaten, and gather it to you, and it comes to be for food for
you and for them."
22 Hb117 22 And doing is Noah [as]according to all which [7]Ieue[0] Alueim
instructs ˋhim. So does he.

71-24 Enters 81-19 7 And saying is Ieue [7]Alueim[n] to Noah, "Come, you and all
your household, into the ark, for ˋyou I see righteous before
2 619 Lvl2 10 14 2 Me in ·this ·generation. [f]Of every [A]·clean ·beast you are to
[sire]MAN [dam]WOMAN take to you seven by seven, the sire and his dam, and [f]of the
beast which is not [A]clean, of it a pair, the sire and his dam.
3 [S]And,[n] moreover, [f]of the [7A]clean[n] flyer of the heavens seven
by seven, male and female, [7]and [f]of the flyer which is not
[A]clean, of it a pair, male and female,[0] to keep alive [A]seed on
4 the surface of the entire earth. For, [to]seven days further, I
will cause it to rain on the earth forty days and forty
nights, and I will [F]wipe ˋevery ·risen thing which I have
4 85 made off the surface of the [7]entire[0] ground."
5 And doing is Noah [as]according to all which Ieue [7]Alueim[0]
Adm 2262 6 instructs him. And Noah is six [=]hundred years of [S]age. And
7 the deluge of water comes to be on the earth. And coming
is Noah, and his sons, and his wife, and his sons' wives
ˋwith him, into the ark in view of the water of the deluge.
8 [f]Of the [A]clean ·beast, and [f]of the beast which is not [A]clean,
and [f]of the flyer, and [7f]of[n] every animal which is moving on

9 **the ground, pair by pair they come to Noah into the ark,** [N]*Nch* Stop
male and female, as [w]**the Alueim instructs 'Noah.** *Al u eim*
SUBJECT-or-to-S
10 **And** [b]**coming is it,** [7]**after**[0] **seven ·days,** [a]**that the waters of** (To-subjectors)
11 **the deluge come to be on the earth, in the six**[yr]**hundredth**[=] *11* 12 4925 Dt3313
year [t]**of Noah's** [=]**life, in the second ·month,** [i]**on the** [7]**twenty-** 2K72 19 Ecl23 Is2418
seventh[0] **day** [t]**of the month.** [i]**On ·this day rent are all the**
springs of the vast submerged chaos, and the [F]**crevices of the** [vast]MUCH
12 **heavens are opened, and** [b]**coming is the downpour on the**
earth forty days and forty nights. *13* 1P320

13 [i]**On ·this very ·day come Noah, and Shem,**[a]**Ham, and Japheth,** [S]*Shm* Place *or* Name
Noah's sons, and Noah's wife, and the three wives of his [H]*Chm* Warm
14 **sons, 'with them, into the ark, they and every ·living animal** [J]*Iphth* Enticed
for its from-kind, and every ·beast for its from-kind, and
every ·moving animal ·moving on the earth for its from- [f-k]FROM-cause
kind, and every ·flyer for its from-kind, every bird of every
15 [A]**wing. And coming are they to Noah into the ark, pair by**
pair, [f]**of all ·**[N]**flesh, which has in it the spirit of the living.** *15* 617
16 **And those coming, male and female** [f]**of all** [N]**flesh, come as**
[w]**the Alueim instructs 'him. And closing** [7]**the ark**[0] **is Ieue**
[7]**Alueim**[0] **about him.**

17 **And** [b]**coming is the deluge forty days** [7]**and forty nights**[0] **on**
the earth. And increasing are the waters, and lifting up 'the
18 **ark, and it is high above the earth. And having the mastery**
are the waters and they are increasing exceedingly on the
19 **earth, and going is the ark on the surface of the water. And**
the water has the mastery exceeding exceedingly on the
earth. And covered are all the lofty ·mountains which are
20 **under the entire heavens. Fifteen cubits** [to]**above has the**
water the mastery, and covered are [7]**all**[0] **the mountains.**

21 **And expiring is all** [N]**flesh ·moving on the earth,** [i]**of flyer,**
and [i]**of beast, and** [i]**of living animal, and** [i]**of every ·roaming**
22 **animal ·roaming on the earth, and every ·human. Everyone**
which has the breath of the spirit of the living in his [N]**nos-**
23 **trils,** [f]**of all** [w]**that were in the drained area, dies. And** [F]**wiped** *23* 2P25
off is 'every ·risen thing which was on the surface of [7]**all**[0]
the ground, from human [fr]**to beast,** [fr]**from moving animal** [fr]FURTHER
[fr]**to the flyer of the heavens. And being** [F]**wiped are they**
from the earth. [a]**Yea,** [7]**only**[0] **Noah is remaining, and what**
24 **is 'with him in the ark. And** [7]**lofty**[0] **are the waters on the**
earth a hundred and fifty days.

71-24 Leaves 81-19
8 [a]**Now** [C]**mindful is the Alueim of 'Noah and 'every ·living** *1* 716 *2* 711
animal and 'every ·beast [7]**and 'every ·flyer and 'every ·mov-**
ing animal[0] **which is 'with him in the ark. And the Alueim**
is causing a wind to pass over the earth, and subsiding are
2 **the waters. And being held in check are the springs of the**
submerged chaos and the [F]**crevices of the heavens, and be-**
3 **ing shut up is the downpour from the heavens, and return-**
ing are the waters off the earth, going and returning. And
abating are the waters [f]**at the end of one hundred and fifty**
days.
4 **And resting is the ark in the seventh month,** [i]**on the**
[7]**twenty-seventh**[0] **day** [t]**of the month, on the mountains of**
5 **Ararat. And the waters** [b]**came to go and abate until the** [abating]LACKING

6 1K64 Ez4016 4116 tenth ·month. In the [7]eleven month[o], [i]on day one [t]of the
7 Lv1115 Dt1414 month, appear the [A]heads of the mountains.
6 And it is [b]coming, [f]at the end of forty days, [a]that opening
7 is Noah a \porthole of the ark which he had made, and sending out is he \a ·raven [7]to see if the waters are slight[o]. And
forth is it faring, to fare forth and [7]not[o] to return till the
drying of the water off the land.

8 And sending out is he \a ·dove from \him [7]after it,[o] to see
9 if the waters are slight over the surface of the ground. [a]Yet
not find does the dove a resting place for the sole of her
foot, and she is returning to him to the ark, for the water
RAVEN is on the surface of the entire earth. And stretching forth
is he his hand and taking her, and is bringing \her to him
into the ark.

10 And waiting is he further another seven days. And pro-
11 ceeding is he to send out the\dove from the ark. And coming
is the dove to him [t]at eventide, and behold! A torn-off olive
leaf is in its beak! And knowing is Noah that the waters
are slight above the earth.

12 And waiting is he further another seven days, and [7]once
more[o] is sending out \the dove, [a]yet not any more to return
to him further.

DOVE

13 And [b]coming is it, in the year six =hundred and one [7]of
Adm 2263 Noah's life,[o] in the first month, [i]on day one [t]of the month,
9 stretch SENDING drained are the waters off the earth. And away is Noah
12 more add [c]taking the \covering of the ark, [7]which he had made,[o] and
seeing is he, and behold! Drained are [7]the waters from[o] the
14 surface of the ground. And in the second month, [i]on the
twenty-seventh day [t]of the month, the earth is dry.

15 And speaking is [7]Ieue[o] Alueim to Noah, [to]saying, [16]"Fare
16 71 16 81 16 forth from the ark, you, and your wife, and your sons, and
17 your sons' wives \with you. [7]And[n] every ·living thing which
is \with you [f]of all [N]flesh, [i]of ·flyer, and [i]of ·beast, and [i]of
every ·moving animal ·moving on the earth, [c]bring forth \with
you. They also are to roam in the earth, and to be [F]fruitful,
and increase on the earth."

18 And forth is faring Noah, and his sons, and his wife, and
19 his sons' wives \with him. [7]And[o] every ·living thing [7]and
every ·beast,[o] and every ·flyer, [8]and[n] every ·moving animal
moving on the earth, [t]by their families they fare forth
from the ark.

614-22 Provision 820 20 And building is Noah an altar to Ieue [7]Alueim,[o] and tak-
[N]Nch STOP ing is he [f]of every ·[A]clean ·beast, and [f]of every ·[A]clean ·flyer,
I e u e and is [c]offering up ascent offerings [i]on the altar.
Will-be-ing-was

821-22 Covenant 98-17 21 And [c]smelling is Ieue [7]Alueim[o] a [A]restful \smell. And say-
more add ing is Ieue [7]Alueim[o] to His [F]heart, "Not any more will I [to]
21 2S235 slight further \the ground for the sake of ·humanity, for
the form of the human [F]heart is evil from its youth. Neither
again add again will I [to] smite further \all living [7N]flesh,[o] as [w] I have
22 done. In the future, all the days of the earth, seedtime and

harvest, and cold and warmth, and summer and winter,
and day and night shall not cease."

9 **And blessing is the Alueim 'Noah and 'his sons. And say-** 91 Blessing 7
ing is He to them, "Be [F]fruitful and increase and fill 'the
earth [7]and subdue it.[0]

2 "**And the fear of you and dismay** due to **you shall [b]come** 2 Govern 6
on every living animal **of the earth, [a]even on every flyer of**
the heavens, [7]and[0] in all which is moving on **the ground,**
3 **and in all the fishes of the sea. Into your [A]hand are they**
given.

"[7]**And[0] every moving animal which [it] is living is coming to** -3 Food 4-5
be for food for you. As the green herbage **I give to you 'all.**

4 "**Yea,** only **flesh [i]with its [A]soul, its blood, you shall not eat.** -3 Food 4-5
5 **Yea, and 'your blood for your [N]souls I will require. From** 4 Hb922
the [A]**hand of every living animal will I require it, and from** require INQUIRE
the [A]**hand of 'humanity. From the [A]hand of a man's [N]brother**
I will require the [N]soul of a 'human. shed POUR-OUT

6 "The **shedder of the blood of a 'human, [i]by a human his** 2 Govern 6
blood shall be shed, for in the image of the Alueim has He 6 126
made 'humanity.

7 "**And you, be [F]fruitful and increase, [S]and[n] roam in the** 91 Blessing 7
earth and [7]sway[0] in it."

8 **And [sa]speaking is the Alueim to Noah and to his sons'with** 821-22 Covenant 98-17
9 **him,[to]saying, "And I, behold Me [F]setting up 'My covenant** set up RAISING
10 'with [=]you and 'with your seed after you and 'with every 10 121 24 219 Lvl146
'living [N]soul which is 'with you, [i]with flyer [7]and[n][i]with beast
and [i]with all land life 'with you, [f]with all faring forth from
11 **the ark, for all the land life. And I [F]set up 'My covenant 'with** set up RAISING
you, [a]that not cut off shall all [N]flesh be in the future [f]by the
waters of a 'deluge, neither will there [b]come a future deluge
[7]of water[0] to wreck the [7]entire[0] earth."

12 **And saying is [7]Ieue[0] Alueim [7]to Noah,[0] "This is the sign of** Ieue Will-be-ing-was
the covenant which I am giving between Me and [bt] you and [bt]
every living [N]soul which is 'with you for generations eonian:
13 **'My bow I [F]bestow in a cloud, and it comes to be for a sign**
14 **of the covenant between Me and [bt] the [A]earth. And it [b]comes,**
[i]when I cloud over the earth with a cloud, [a]then appears
15 **[7]My[0] [F]bow in the cloud, and I am [C]reminded of 'My covenant,**
which is between Me and [bt] you and [bt] every living [N]soul in
all [N]flesh, and there is not to [b]come a future [to]deluge of 'wa-
16 **ter to wreck all [N]flesh. And [7]My[0] [F]bow [b]comes in the cloud,**
and I see it, to be [C]reminded of the covenant eonian between
the Alueim and [bt] every living [N]soul in all [N]flesh which is
17 **on the earth." And saying is the Alueim to Noah, "This is**
the sign of the covenant which I [F]set up between Me and [bt] set up RAISING
all [N]flesh which is on the earth."

610 Sons 918-27

18 **And the sons of Noah who fare forth from the ark [b]are** N *Nch* STOP
Shem and Ham and Japheth. (And Ham, he is the father of S *Shm* PLACE *or* Name
19 **Canaan). These three are sons of Noah, and from these the** H *Chm* WARM
entire earth is scattered over. J *Iphth* ENTICED
20 **And starting is Noah as a man who [7A]serves[7] the ground,** U *Knon* SUBMITTER
21 **and planting is he a vineyard. And drinking is he [f]of the**

Al u eim SUBJECT-or-to-s (To-subjectors) [H]*Chm* WARM [S]*Shm* PLACE or Name

wine and is drunk, and is exposing himself in the midst of
22 his tent. And seeing is Ham (father of Canaan) 'the nakedness of his father, and, 'faring forth,' he is telling [to] his two
23 brothers [in] outside. And taking are Shem and Japheth 'a
'garment, and are placing it on the shoulders[b] of the two,
and they are going backward, and covering 'the nakedness
of their father. And their faces were backward, and the
nakedness of their father they did not see.

24 1S2537 Jl15 1C1534 [C]*Kno n* SUBMITTER [J]*I phth* ENTICED

24 And waking is Noah from his wine, and he knows 'what
25 his 'small son has done to him. And saying is he, "Cursed
be Canaan! A servant of servants shall he become for his
26 brothers." And saying is he, "Blest be Ieue, the Alueim of
27 Shem, and Canaan shall become his servant. Entice will the
Alueim [to] Japheth, and tabernacle shall he in the tents of
Shem. And become shall Canaan his servant."

69 Time 928-29 [N]*Nch* STOP Adm 2612

28 And living is Noah after the deluge three =hundred [yr] and
29 fifty years. And coming are all the [N]days of Noah to be
nine =hundred [yr] and fifty years. And he died.

101-119 Sons 369-43 101-32 Nations 111-9 1- Shem 21-32 -1- Ham 6-20 -1 Japheth 2-5

1 610 713 918 1021 1Ch14 5 *2* Ez382 6

10 And these are the genealogical annals of
the sons of Noah, Shem, Ham, and Japheth. And sons are being born to them
after the deluge.

-1 Japheth 2-5 [G]*Gmr* LAPSE [M]*M gug* FROM-TOP [M]*Md i* Measured [J]*Iun* ('Ionian') [E]*Al i she* Al-equalizes [Tu]*Th u bl* DISINTEGRATION [M]*Mshk* DRAW [Ti]*Thirs* ('Thrace') [A]*Ashknz* ('Armenian') [R]*Riph th* 'RELAXED' [To]*Thu grm e* 'Rib' *4* 1Ch17 *5* Rv59 79 119 [Th]*Thrshish* TOPAZ [K]*Kth i im* POUNDERS [R]*Rd n im* DOWNED-ones

2 The sons of Japheth: Gomer and Ma-
gog and Media and Javan 'and Elisha,'
and Tubal and Meshech and Tiras.
3 And the sons of Gomer: Ashkenaz and
Riphath and Togarmah.
4 And the sons of Javan: Elishah and
5 Tharshish, Kittim and 'Rodanim.' From
these are parted the coastlanders of the
nations 'among their lands, each man to
his [A]tongue, to their families, in their nations.

-1- Ham 6-20 *6* Jr469 Ez2710 305 385 Na39 [H]*Chm* WARM [C]*Cush* BURLY [M]*M tzr im* Narrows [P]*Phut* (Lybia) [Ca]*Kno n* SUBMITTER [S]*Sba* Arouse [H]*Chuil e* Travailer [S]*Sbth a* 'Cease' [R]*Rom e* THUNDER *Sb thk a* [S]*Shb a* RETURN [D]*Ddn* FONDED [N]*Nm rud* 'Revolter' [C]*Cush* BURLY *9* Jr1616 *10* 119 Is1111

6 And the sons of Ham: Cush and Mizraim
and Phut and Canaan.
7 And the sons of Cush: Sebah and Havilah and Sabtah and Raamah and Sabtechah.
And the sons of Raamah: Sheba and
Dedan.
8 And Cush generates 'Nimrod. He starts
9 to become a master in the earth. He becomes a master hunter before Ieue 'Alueim.' Therefore is it being said, "As Nim-
10 rod, the master hunter before Ieue." And
coming is the beginning of his kingdom
to be Babel and Erech and Accad and
11 Calneh, in the land of Shinar. (From 'that
'land fares forth Ashur, and building is
he 'Nineveh and 'Rehoboth city, and 'Ca-
12 lah, and ''Desen' between Nineveh and [bt]
Calah. That 'city is 'great.)
13 And Mizraim generates 'Ludim and
'Anamim and 'Lehabim and 'Naphtuhim

[B]*B bl* IN-DISINTEGRATION [E]*Ark* LONG [A]*A kd* Dart [C]*K ln e* AS-LODGE-is [S]*Shn or* Double-city [A]*Ashur* PROGRESSING [N]*Nin u e* PROPAGATERESS [R]*Rchb uth* WIDE-will-be [C]*Klch* MATURITY [L]*Ludi im* GENERATORS [Le]*Leb im* BLAZES [N]*N phthch im* OPENEDS

14 and 'Pathrusim and 'Casluhim, whence
fare forth the Philistim and 'Caphthorim.
15 And Canaan generates 'Sidon, his first-
16 born, and 'Heth and 'the Jebusite and 'the
17 Amorite and 'the Girgashite and 'the Hi-
18 vite and 'Arkite and 'the Sinite and 'the
Arvadite and 'the Zemarite and 'the Ha-
mathite. And afterwards the families of
19 the Canaanite are scattered. And coming
is the boundary of the Canaanite to be
from Sidon, as you come toward Gerar
unto Gaza, as you come toward Sodom
and Gomorrah and Admah and Zeboiim,
unto Lasha.
20 These are the sons of Ham, [t]by their
families, [t]by their [A]tongues, in their lands,
in their nations.

PPhthrs im OKs lch im COVER-SMOOTHS PhPhl shth im Distinguished-SET-ites CKph thr im 'Spheres' SiTzid un PROVISION HChth Dismay JI bus i TRAMPLER-ite AAmr i SAYITE GGr gsh i Sojourn-CLOSE-ite HiChu i LIVING-ite AOrq i GNAWITE SSin i THORN-BUSH-ite AArud i 'Sway-over-ite' ZTzmr i WOOL-ite HChm th i WARM-th-ite CKno n SUBMITTER
14 Dt223 Jr474 Am97 16 2S56-9 Ez163 45
STzid n Provision GGrr Chew GaOze STRENGTH SSd m FOUNDED GOmr e OMER AAdm e LIKEST ZTzbo im STREAKS LLsho SAFE
HChm WARM

21 And to Shem sons are born. Moreover,
he is the forefather of all the sons of
Eber. He is a brother of Japheth, the
22 eldest. The sons of Shem: Elam and
Ashur, and Arphaxad and Lud and Aram
'and Cainan.°
23 And the sons of Aram: Uz and Hul and
Gether and Mash.
24 And Arphaxad 'generates Cainan and
Cainan° generates 'Shelach, and Shelach
generates 'Eber.
25 And to Eber two sons are born. The
name of 'one is Peleg, for in his days the
[N]land was distributed. And the name of
his brother is Joktan.
26 And Joktan generates 'Almodad and
'Sheleph and 'Hazarmaveth and 'Jerah,
27 and 'Hadoram and 'Uzal and 'Diklah,
28 and 'Obal and 'Abimael and 'Sheba,[29]and
29 'Ophir and 'Havilah and 'Jobab. All these
30 are sons of Joktan. And coming is their
dwelling to be from Mesha, 'till° you come
toward Sephar, a mountain of the east.
31 These are the sons of Shem, [t]by their
families, [t]by their [A]tongues, in their lands,
[t]by their nations.
32 These are the families of the sons of
Noah [t]by their genealogical annals, in
their nations. And from these the 'coast-
land[n] nations are parted in the earth after
the deluge.

1- Shem 21-32 SShm PLACE or Name
21 532 924 101
EObr PASS JI phth ENTICED eldest GREATEST EOilm OBSCURITY AAshur PROGRESSING AAr phk shd 'Lion-SPOUT DEPRIVE' LLud GENERATOR AArm HEIGHT CQin n NESTER or Acquirer UUz FIX or Counsel HChul Sand MMsh REMOVE
23 Jb115 17 211
AAr phk shd 'Lion-SPOUT-DEPRIVE' CQin n NESTER or Acquirer EObr PASS
24 1413
PPhlg DISTRIBUTE
JI qtn SMALLED
AAlm u dd COMPRESSING-FOND SShlph PULL HChtzr muth ENVIRON-of-DEATH JIrch Spirited HEd u rm OBTRUDING-HIGH UAuzl DEPARTING AbAb im al FATHERS-SUBJECTOR ShShb a RETURN OAuphir ASH HChuil e 'Travailer' JI u bb Interior MM i sha SALVATION SSphr e NUMBERER
NNch STOP

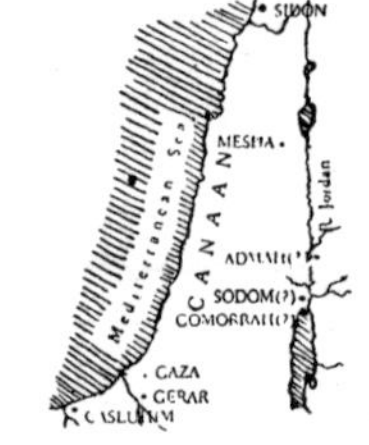

11 [a]Now coming is the entire [A]earth to be of one [A]lip, 'all° of
one [=]speech.
2 And [b]coming is it in their journey from the east, [a]that
they are finding a valley in the land of Shinar, and dwelling
there are they.

111 Unity 6-7
2 People 8-9
SShn or Double-city

3-4 Building 5 3 And saying are they, each man to his associate, "Prithee!
[mold]brick Let us mold bricks and burn them [t]with a burning." And
[asph]clay (TURBIDITY) coming is the brick to be their [to] stone, and asphalt becomes
3 2S1231 their [to] mortar.

4 108-10 122 4 And saying are they, "Prithee! Build will we for our-
Al u eim selves a city and a tower [a]with its [A]head in the heavens, and
SUBJECT-or-to-s (To-subjectors) make for ourselves a [N]name, lest we are scattering over
I e u e the surface of the entire earth."
Will-be-ing-was

3-4 Building 5 5 And descending is Ieue to see 'the city and 'the tower
which the [A]sons of ·humanity build.

1 Unity 6-7 6 And saying is Ieue, "Behold! One people is it. And one [A]lip
is for them all. And this they started to do! And now nothing
will be defended from them of all [w]that they will plan to do.
7 1821 Ex38 7 Prithee! Descend will We, and there disintegrate their [A]lip,
[w]that they may not [A]hear each man 'the [A]lip of his associate."

2 People 8-9 8 And scattering 'them is Ieue thence on the surface of the
8 Ac81 entire earth. And leaving off are they building 'the city [7]and
[B]B bl IN-DISINTEGRATION 9 'the tower.[n] Therefore its name is called Babel, for there
9 Jb512 Ac24 Rv79 Ieue disintegrates 'the [A]lip of the entire [A]earth. And thence
See map page 53. Ieue [7]Alueim[0] scatters them over the surface of the entire
earth.

1110-26 Chosen 2519-3529 10-25 Progenitor 26 [S]Shm PLACE or Name [A]Ar phk shd [f]Lion-SPOUT-DEPRIVE[f]

Adm 2264 10 [7]And[0] these are the genealogical annals of Shem: Shem is a
[age]son hundred years of [s]age, and begetting is he 'Arphaxad two
11 532 1Ch118 Lu336 11 years after the deluge. And living is Shem after his begetting 'Arphaxad five [=]hundred years. And begetting is he
Adm 2764 sons and daughters. [7]And he died.[0]

Adm 2399 12 And Arphaxad lives [7]a hundred and[0] thirty-five years, and
13 he is begetting [7]'Cainan.[0] And living is Arphaxad after his
begetting [7]'Cainan[0] four [=]hundred [yr] and three years. And
Adm 2802 begetting is he sons and daughters. [7]And he died.[n]

Adm 2529 [7]And living is Cainan a hundred and thirty years, and
[S]Shlch SEND begetting is he Shelach. And living is Cainan after his be-
getting Shelach three [=]hundred [yr] and thirty years, and be-
Adm 2859 getting is he sons and daughters. And he died.[0]

Adm 2659 14 And living is Shelach [7]a hundred and[n] thirty years, and
[E]Obr PASS 15 begetting is he 'Eber. And living is Shelach after his beget-
ting 'Eber [7]three[n] [=]hundred [yr] and [7]thirty[n] years, and beget-
Adm 2989 ting is he sons and daughters. [7]And he died.[n]

Adm 2793 16 And living is Eber [7]a hundred and[n] thirty-four years and
[P]Phlg DISTRIBUTOR 17 begetting is he 'Peleg. And living is Eber after his beget-
16 1024 25 17 Lu335 ting 'Peleg [7]two [=]hundred [yr] and seventy[0] years, and beget-
Adm 3063 ting is he sons and daughters. [7]And he died.[n]

Adm 2923 18 And living is Peleg [7]a hundred and[n] thirty years. and
[R]Rou GRAZER 19 begetting is he 'Reu. And living is Peleg after his begetting
'Reu two [=]hundred [yr] and nine years, and begetting is he
Adm 3132 sons and daughters. [7]And he died.[n]

Adm 3055 20 And living is Reu [7]a hundred and[n] thirty-two years, and
[S]Shrug INTERTWINER 21 begetting is he 'Serug. And living is Reu after his begetting
20 Lu335 'Serug two [=]hundred [yr] and seven years, and begetting is he
Adm 3262 sons and daughters. [7]And he died.[n]

22 And living is Serug 'a hundred and[n] thirty years, and Adm 3185
23 begetting is he 'Nahor. And living is Serug after his beget- [S]Shrug INTERTWINER
ting 'Nahor two "hundred years, and begetting is he sons [N]Nchur SNORTER
and daughters. 'And he died.[n] Adm 3385

24 And living is Nahor 'seventy[n]-nine years, and begetting Adm 3264
25 is he 'Terah. And living is Nahor after his begetting 'Terah [T]Th rch GIVE-spirit
a hundred[yr] and 'twenty-nine[o] years. And begetting is he
sons and daughters. 'And he died.[n] Adm 3393

26 And living is Terah seventy years, and begetting is he 10-25 Progenitor 26
'Abram, 'Nahor, and 'Haran. Adm 3334

1127-2511 Hindrance 2512-18 1127-2219 Isaac Birth 255-11 1127-123 Seed 221-19

27 And these are the genealogical annals of Terah: Terah be- [A]Abrm FATHER-HIGH
gets 'Abram, 'Nahor, and 'Haran; and Haran begets 'Lot. [H]Ern PROMINENT
28 And Haran died [on]in the presence of Terah, his father, in [L]Lut WRAPPER
the land of his birth, in Ur of the Chaldeans. [U]Aur LIGHT
29 And taking are Abram and Nahor to themselves wives. [Ch]Kshd im ?Demoniacal?
The name of Abram's wife is Sarai, and the name of Na- [S]Shri My-REGARDED-one
hor's wife is Milcah, the daughter of Haran, the father of [M]Mlke Queen
30 Milcah and the father of Iscah. [a]Yet coming is Sarai to be [I]Iske OVERSHADOWER
barren. No child is hers.
31 And taking is Terah 'Abram, his son, and 'Lot, the son of 31 Ac71-5
Haran, his son's son, and 'Sarai, his daughter-in-law, wife
of Abram, his son, and faring forth is 'he[n] 'with them from [C]Knon SUBMITTER
Ur of the Chaldeans, to go to the land of Canaan. And [U]Aur LIGHT
coming are they as far as Charan, and dwelling there are [far]FURTHER
they. [Ch]Chrn HEATED
32 And coming are 'all[o] the [N]days of Terah to be two "hun- Adm 3469
dred[yr] and five years. And dying is Terah in Charan.

12 [a]Now saying is Ieue to Abram, "Go[to] you from your land 1 244 Js242 Hb118
and from your kindred and from your father's house to the I e u e
2 land which I shall show you. And make you will I into a Will-be-ing-was
great nation, and bless you will I and make 'your [N]name 2 Ex64-8
3 great, and become must you a blessing. And bless those will 3 5024
I who bless you, and those making light of you will I curse.
And blest in you [S]and in your [A]seed[c] are all the families of
the ground." Adm 3469 124-9 Sojourn 2122-34
4 And going is Abram as[w] Ieue speaks to him. And going
'with him is Lot. And Abram was seventy-five[yr] years of
5 [s]age[t] when he fares forth from Charan. And taking is Abram
'Sarai, his wife, and 'Lot, his brother's son, and 'all their
goods which they got, and 'every[o] ''soul[N] which they make
their own in Charan, and forth are they faring to go toward
the land of Canaan. And coming are they to[d] the land of
Canaan.
6 And passing is Abram into the land as far as the place [far]FURTHER
of Shechem, as far as the 'high[o] oak. And the Canaanite [Sh]Shkm BACK
is then 'dwelling[o] in the land. 6 137 3320
7 And appearing is Ieue to Abram and is saying 'to him,[n] See map page 57.
"To your [A]seed am I giving 'this ''land." And building is 8 2819 356 483 Js162
8 'Abram[o] there an altar to Ieue, Who 'appeared to him. And 1813 Jd123 26
shifting is he thence toward the mountain [f]on the east [t]of [B]Bith-Al House-
Beth-El, and 'there[o] is stretching out his tent, with Beth-El of-SUBJECTOR
[f]on the seaward side, and Ai [f]on the east, and building is he [A]Oi Rubbish-heap

[A]Abrm FATHER-HIGH there an altar to Ieue. And calling is he [i]on the [N]name of
9 131 3 9 Ieue. And journeying goes Abram. And the journey is
toward the south-rim.

1210-20 Denial 201-18 10 And [b]coming is a famine in the land. And down is Abram
[E]M tzr im Narrows going to[d] Egypt to sojourn there, for [F]heavy is the famine
10 261 4154 Ru11 in the land.
2S211 1K182 11 And [b]coming is it, as [w 7]Abram[0] nears to come to[d] Egypt,
[S]Shr i My-REGARDED-one [a]that saying is [7]Abram[0] to Sarai, his wife, "Behold, pray!
12 I know that a woman of lovely appearance are you, and
[E]M tzr i Narrows-ites when it [b]comes that the Egyptians see 'you and say, 'His
wife is this,' [a]then they will kill 'me, [a]yet 'you they will keep
13 2012 13 alive. Say, pray, that my sister are you, that it may be
well [t]with me [i]for your sake, and [in] live may my [N]soul due to
you."

14 And [b]coming is it, as Abram comes to[d] Egypt, [a]that the
15 Egyptians see 'the woman, that very lovely is she. Seeing
[P]Phro e(Hb. UNCOVERED) 'her also are the chiefs of Pharaoh, and they praise 'her to
Pharaoh, and the woman is [c]being taken to Pharaoh's house.
16 And to Abram is he good [i]for her sake. And [b]coming is he
Al u eim to have a flock [s]and a very [F]heavy[n] herd of [s]cattle[n] and asses
SUBJECT-or-to-s and menservants and maids and jenny-asses and camels.
(To-subjectors;
matterword 17 And touching is Ieue [7]Alueim[0] 'Pharaoh with contagions,
great [7]and evil,[0] also 'his household, [on]in the matter of Sarai,
18 Abram's wife. And calling is Pharaoh to Abram and is
saying, "What is this you do to me? Why did you not tell[to]
19 me that she is your wife? Why did you say, 'My sister is
she'? And I am taking 'her to me for a wife! And now, behold your wife [7]before you.[0] Take her and go."
20 And instructing is Pharaoh the mortals [on]concerning
[7]Abram.[0] And sending 'him away are they, 'his wife and 'all
[w]that is his, [7]and Lot with him.[n]

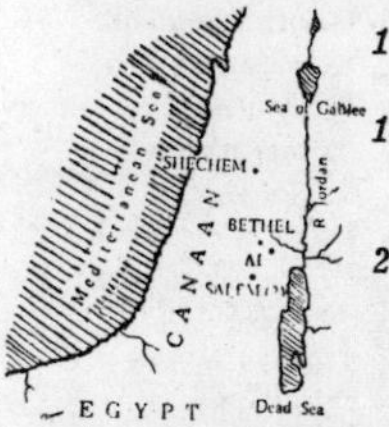

131-13 Separation 219-21 13 And up is Abram going from Egypt, he and his wife and
1 129 3 128 all [w]that is his, and Lot with him, to[d] the south-rim.
[B]Bith-Al House- 2 And Abram is very [F]heavy in ·cattle, in ·silver, and in
of-SUBJECTOR 3 ·gold. And going is he, [t]in his journeyings from the south-
[far]FURTHER rim, [a] as far as Beth-El, as far as the place where his tent
[bt]between 4 came to be [i]at the start, between Beth-El and [bt] Ai, to the
[A]Oi Rubbish-heap place of the altar which he made there [i]at the first. And
there calling is Abram [i]on the [N]name of Ieue.
5 And, moreover, Lot, who is ·going 'with Abram, [b]comes
6 to [t]have a flock and a herd and tents. And not [F]bearing is
the land 'their [to]dwelling together, for coming are their
7 1412 7 goods to be many and they cannot [to]dwell together. And
[b]coming is a contention between the graziers of Abram's
[C]Kno n i SUBMITTER cattle and [bt] the graziers of Lot's cattle. And the Canaanite
[P]Phrz i VILLAGE-ite and the Perizzite are then dwelling in the land.
[L]Lut WRAPPER 8 And saying is Abram to Lot, "There must not, pray,
come to be contention between me and [bt] you, and between
my graziers and [bt] your graziers, for mortals, brethren are
9 we. Is not the entire land before you? Be parted, pray,
from [on] me. If to the left, [a] to the right will I [c]go. And if to
the right, [a] to the left will I [c]go."
[basin]DISK 10 And lifting is Lot 'his eyes and is seeing 'all the basin of

the Jordan, for all of it was irrigated before Ieue wrecked
'Sodom and 'Gomorrah, as the garden of Ieue [7]Alueim,[0] as
11 the land of Egypt as you come to[d] Zoar. And choosing is
Lot for his 'all the basin of the Jordan. And journeying is
Lot[f] east. And being parted are they, each man from[on] his
12 [N]brother. Abram dwells in the land of Canaan, and Lot
dwells in the cities of the basin. And tenting is he as far as
13 Sodom. [a]Now the mortals of Sodom are [=]evil and sinners
[t]against Ieue [7]Alueim[0] exceedingly. See map page 54.

[J]Ird n Descender
irrigate DRINKIZED
[Z]Tzuor INFERIOR
basin DISK [G]Omr e OMER
[L]Lut WRAPPER
[C]Kno n SUBMITTER
far FURTHER
[S]Sd m FOUNDED

1314-18 Fulfillment 211-8

14 And Ieue [7]Alueim[0] says to Abram after Lot was parted
from[wi] him, "Lift your eyes, pray, and see. From the place
where you [7]now[0] are, northward and toward the south-rim
15 and eastward and seaward, for 'all the land which you are
seeing, to you am I giving it, and to your [A]seed, till the eon.
16 And I make 'your [A]seed as the soil of the land. [w]Could a
man[to] count 'the soil of the land, moreover, then your [A]seed
17 shall be counted. Rise, walk in the land,[to] its length and[to] its
width, for to you am I giving it, [7]and to your [A]seed, for the
18 eon.[0]" And tenting is Abram, and coming and dwelling
among the oaks of Mamre, which are in Hebron. And building is he there an altar to Ieue.

[A]Ab rm FATHER-HIGH
14 155 182 2217
15 263 2813 3512 5024
16 155 Hb31 119-12
Al u eim
SUBJECT-or-to-S
(To-subjectors)
18 1413 232 Nu1322
[M]M mr a [f]Bitterness[f]
[H]Chbr un JOINED

1 1922 5 1520 Dt211 20 311 13 Js124 1312 141-24 Sodom, Lot 18-16-1938

14 And [b]coming is it in the days of [7]the reign of[0] Amraphel,
king of Shinar,[S]and[n] Arioch, king of Ellasar, [7]and[0] Chedor-
2 laomer, king of Elam, and Tidal, king of nations, that they
make war 'with Bera, king of Sodom, and 'with Birsha,
king of Gomorrah, [7]and[n] Shinab, king of Admah, and Shem-
eber, king of Zeboiim, and the king of Bela. (It is now Zoar.)
3 All these are joined[to] at the vale of the [7]salt[0] fields. (It is now
4 the salt sea.) Twelve years they serve 'Chedorlaomer, and
5 [S]in[n] the thirteenth year they revolt. And in the fourteenth
year comes Chedorlaomer and the kings which are 'with
him, and smiting are they 'the Rephaim in Ashteroth Kar-
naim, and 'the [7]strong nations [i]with them[0] and 'the Emim
6 in the Shaveh towns, and 'the Horites in the [7]mountains[n] of
Seir, as far as [7]the terebinth of[0] Paran, which is[on] at the
wilderness. See map page 60. 6 Dt212
7 And returning are they and coming to En-Mishphat (It
is now Kadesh). And smiting are they 'all the [7]chiefs[0] of
the Amalekites and, moreover, 'the Amorites 'dwelling in
Hazezon-tamar.
8 And forth is faring the king of Sodom and the king of
Gomorrah, and the king of Admah and the king of Zeboiim
and the king of Bela (It is now Zoar). And arranging 'themselves are they for battle in the vale of the [7]salt[0] fields,
9 'with Chedorlaomer, king of Elam, and Tidal, king of nations, and Amraphel, king of Shinar, and Arioch, king of
Ellasar—four kings 'with 'five.
10 And the vale of [7]'salt[0] fields had wells, asphalt wells. And
fleeing are the king of Sodom and [7]the king of[0] Gomorrah,
and falling are they there, and the [=]remainder flee toward
11 the mountain. And taking are they 'all the goods of Sodom
12 and Gomorrah and 'all their food, and are going. And tak-

[Ar]Ar iu k Lion-like
[E]Al sr Al-stubborn
[Ch]Kdr lo mr [f]ONSLAUGHT-SWALLOW-bitter[f]
[E]O i lm OBSCURITY
[Be]B ro IN-GRAZE
[Bi]Br sho PURE-SAVE
[Shi]Shn ab= REPEAT-FATHER
[A]A dm e Ground
[S]Shm abr PLACE-STURDY
[B]B lo IN-SWALLOW
[R]Rph a im HEALERS
far FURTHER
[A]Oshth r uth = [f]REFLECT-AIMS[f]
[K]Qrn im HORNS
[E]Aim im FAITHFULS
[Sh]Shue Compensator
[H]Ch uri Pale-ites
[S]Shoir HAIRY
[P]Phar n Beautiful
[E]Oin Spring
[M]M shpht JUDGMENT
[K]Qdsh HOLY
[A]Amr i SAYITE
[Haz]Chtz tz un thmr= DIVISION-PALM
[Sh]Shn or Double-city
asph clay TURBIDITY
See map page 60.
12 1312

[L]*Lut* WRAPPER **ing are they 'Lot, Abram's brother's son, and [s]all[n] 'his**
[A]*Ab rm* FATHER-HIGH **goods, [a]for he was dwelling in Sodom, and they are going.**
13 3914 4112 Nu2424 *13* **And coming is one who was ·delivered, and he is telling [to]**
[H]*Obr i* PASSER **Abram, the Hebrew. [a]Now he is tabernacling among the**
[M]*M mra* 'Bitterness' **oaks of Mamre, the Amorite, brother of Eshcol and brother**
[Am]*Amr i* SAYITE **of Aner. And they are possessors of a covenant with Abram.**
[E]*Ashk u l* Cluster *14* **And hearing is Abram that [7]Lot,[o] his [N]brother, is captured.**
14 125 **And [7]numbering[o] is he 'those dedicated to him, born in his**
household, three-hundred and eighteen, and is pursuing
[far]FURTHER *15* **[7]them[o] as far as Dan. And, being apportioned, [7]falling is[o]**
[D]*Dn* ADJUDICATE **his force on them by night, he and his servants. And smit-**
[H]*Chub e* FONDLER **ing them is he, and pursuing them as far as Hobah, which is**
[D]*Dum shq* SUFFICE- RUN-ABOUT *16* **[f]to the left [t]of Damascus. And restoring is he 'all the goods**
[7]of Sodom,[o] and, moreover, he restored 'Lot, his [N]brother,
See map page 60. **and his goods, and moreover, 'the women and 'the people.**
17 2S1818 *17* **And forth is faring the king of Sodom to meet him, after**
[O]*Kdr lo mr* 'ONSLAUGHT- **his return from smiting Chedorlaomer and 'the kings who**
SWALLOW-bitter' **were 'with him, [to]at the vale Shaveh (It is now the vale of**
[Sh]*Shue* Compensate **the king).**
[M]*Mlk i tzdq* KING-JUST *18* **And Melchizedek, king of Salem, [c]brings forth bread and**
[S]*Shlm* Welfare *19* **wine. And he is a priest for the Al Supreme. And blessing**
18 Nu2416 Dt328 Ps92 **is he [7]Abram,[n] and is saying, "Blest is Abram [t]by the Al**
8318 Lu176 Hb71-4 *20* **Supreme, Owner of the heavens and the earth. And blest is**
the Al Supreme, Who awards your foes into your [7A]hands.[o]"
And giving is he to him tithes from all.
[S]*Sd m* FOUNDED *21* **And saying is the king of Sodom to Abram, "Give to me**
the [N]souls, [a]yet the goods [to]you take."
22 **And saying is Abram to the king of Sodom, "High [c]hold I**
'my hand to swear to Ieue, **the Al Supreme,** Owner of the
[even]FURTHER *23* **heavens and the earth.** If it be more [f]than a thread [a]**or even**
a sandal lacing, [a]or if taking am I from anything which is
I e u e Will-be-ing-was *24* **yours, [a]then will you not say, 'I enrich 'Abram'? But, apart**
is this from what the lads eat, and the portion of the mor-
tals who went 'with me: **Aner, Eshcol, and Mamre. They**
See map page 60. **shall take their portion."**

151-21 Faith Covenant 181-16- 1-6 Object, Seed 7-21

[matters]words **15** **After ·these ·matters [b]came** the **word of Ieue to Abram**
1 Nu244 16 Ez137 Jn856 **in a vision, [to] saying, "You must not fear, Abram! I am your**
[M]Shield, your exceedingly increased [M]Hire."
[D]*Dum shq* SUFFICE-RUN-ABOUT *2* **And saying is Abram, "My Lord Ieue, what art Thou**
giving to me, [a]when I am going heirless, and the [A]son [r]run-
[E]*Al i ozr* MY-SUBJECTOR-HELPS **ning about[r] my house, he is Damascus Eliezer?"**
3 **And saying is Abram, "Behold! To me no seed have You**
given. And behold! A [A]son of my household is to enjoy 'my
tenancy."
4 **And, behold!** The **word of Ieue comes to him, [to]saying,**
"Not this one is to enjoy your tenancy, but rather one who
shall fare forth from your [A]bowels, he is to enjoy your ten-
5 Hb31 119-12 *5* **ancy." And forth is He [c]bringing 'him ·outside and saying,**
"Look, pray, toward the heavens and number the stars, if
you can [to]number 'them." And saying is He to him, "Thus
shall your [A]seed become."
6 69 71 Ro1017 *6* **And [7]Abram[o] believes in Ieue [7]Alueim,[o] and reckoning it**
is He to him for righteousness.

7 **And saying is He to him, "I am Ieue [7]Alueim[0] Who**
[·]brought you forth from Ur of the **Chaldeans, to give to**
you ['·]this ·land to tenant it." See map page 56.
8 **And saying is he, " My Lord Ieue, whereby am I** to **know**
that I am to enjoy its **tenancy?"**
9 And saying is He to him, "**Take for Me a heifer** in her
third year, and a **goat** in **her third** year, and a **ram** in his
third year, and a **turtledove**, and a **fledgling.**"
10 **And taking is he for Him 'all these and sundering 'them**
is he in the **midst**, and **is putting each sundered part to**
11 **meet its** associate. [a]**Yet 'the [7]birds[n]** he did **not sunder. And**
descending are the birds of prey on the [7]severed[0] cadavers,
[a]**yet Abram [7]is sitting by[0] and turning 'them back.**
12 **And, at the [b]coming of the setting [t]of the sun, a stupor**
[F]**falls on Abram. And, behold! The dread of a great darkness**
is [F]falling on him. [set]ING, coming
13 **And saying is He to Abram, "Knowing, yea, knowing are**
you that a sojourner is your [A]seed to become in a land not
theirs, and they are to serve them. [a]**Yet [7]evil shall they do to**
14 **them[0] and humiliate 'them four [=]hundred years. Moreover,**
also,'the nation which they are serving will I adjudicate. And
afterward they are to fare forth [7]hither[0] [i]with great goods.
15 [a]**Yet you shall come to your forefathers in peace, [S]and[n] be**
16 **entombed [i]at a good grey-haired age. And in the fourth**
generation they shall return hither, for the depravity of the
Amorites has not been repaid hitherto." [A]Amr i SAYite
17 [a]**When the sun [b]comes to set, and twilight [b]comes, [a]then,**
behold, a smoking stove, and a torch of fire which passes
between ·these ·severed parts.
18 **In ·that ·day Ieue [A]contracted a covenant 'with Abram,[to]**
saying, "To your [A]seed I give 'this ·land, from the stream of
Egypt as far as the great ·stream, the stream Euphrates,
19 **the Cainite and 'the Kenizite and 'the Kadmonite [20]and the**
21 **Hittite and 'the Perizzite and 'the Rephaim and 'the Amor-**
ite and 'the Canaanite [7]and 'the Hivite[n] and 'the Girgashite
and 'the Jebusite."

161-16 Two Seeds 1715-27

16 [a]**Now Sarai, the wife of Abram, does not bear for him.**
[a]**Yet an Egyptian maid [t]has she and her name is Hagar.**
2 **And saying is Sarai to Abram,"Behold, pray! Ieue restrains**
me from bearing. Come, pray, to my maid. Perhaps I will
be built [f]by her." And hearkening is Abram to the [N]voice of
Sarai.
3 **And taking is Sarai, the wife of Abram, 'Hagar, the**
Egyptian, her maid, [f]at the end of ten years [t]of Abram's
dwelling in the land of Canaan, and giving 'her is she to
4 **Abram, her husband, for his[to]wife. And coming is he to**
Hagar, and pregnant is she becoming. And seeing is she
that she is pregnant, and lightly esteemed is her mistress in
her [A]eyes.
5 **And saying is Sarai to Abram, "My wrong comes on you.**
I, I gave my maid into your [N]bosom. And seeing is she that
she is pregnant, and lightly esteemed am I in her [A]eyes.
Judging is Ieue [7]Alueim[0] between me and [bt] [S]her.[ph]"
6 **And saying is Abram to Sarai, "Behold, your maid is in**

1-6 Object, Land 7-21
[U]Aur LIGHT
[C]K shd im [f]Demoniacal[f]
Al u e im
SUBJECT-or-to-s
(To-subjectors)
10 Jr3418 20
[put]GIVING [each]MAN
12 2127 Ga320
13 2112 Ex1240 Ac76 
[set]ING, coming
17 Dt420 1K851 Is621
18 Ga317
20 137 145 Ex332 Js310
[far]FURTHER
[E]M tzr im NARROWS
[Eu]Phrth FRUITS
[Ka]Qdmn i Easternite
[Hit]Chth i Dismay-ite
[Can]Kno n i SUBMITTerite
[G]Gr gsh i Sojourn-close-ite
[J]I bus i TRAMPLERite
1 1S2541
Adm 3479
[S]Shr i My-REGARDed-one
[H]E gr THE-STIR(er)
[E]M tzr i NARROWS-ite
[C]Kno n SUBMITTER
[A]Ab rm FATHER-HIGH

your [7A]hands.[o] Do to her what is ·good in your [A]eyes." And
Sarai is humiliating her, and away is she running from her
I e u e **[N]face.**
Will-be-ing-was 7 **And finding her is a messenger of Ieue [on]at a spring of**
·water in the wilderness, [on]at a spring [i]on the way of the
barricade.
[S]*Shr i* My-REGARDED-one 8 **And saying [7]to her[o] is [7]the messenger of Ieue,[o] "Hagar,**
maid of Sarai, whence come you and whither are you
going?"
And saying is she, "From the [N]face of Sarai, my mistress,
am I running away."
9 **And saying to her is the messenger of Ieue, "Return to**
your mistress and humble yourself under her [A]hands."
10 **And saying to her is the messenger of Ieue, "[1]Verily, I**
am increasing \`your [A]seed, and not shall it be numbered [f]for
multitude."
11 **And saying to her is the messenger of Ieue, "Behold!**
Pregnant are you, [a]bearing a son, and you are to call \`his
[I]*Ishmo-Al* HEARING- 12 **name Ishmael, for Ieue hears [to]of your humiliation. And**
is-SUBJECTOR **becoming is he a wild ass of a human, his [A]hand [i]against all,**
12 2120 2518 3728 **and the [A]hand of all [i]against him. And adjoining all his**
Jd822 24 **brethren will he tabernacle."**
13 3230 Jd1322 13 **And calling is [7]Hagar[o] the name of Ieue ·Who spoke to**
See map page 66. **her, "Thou-Al-seest me." For she says, "Moreover, hither**
[B]*Bar lch irai* [f]WELL- 14 **see I, after my seeing?" Therefore [s]she[n] calls [to] the well**
to-LIVE-mirror[f] **"Bar-lechi-rai." Behold! It is between Kadesh and [bt] Bered.**
[K]*Qdsh* HOLY 15 **And bearing is Hagar for Abram a son, and Abram is**
[B]*Brd* Dapple **calling \`the name of his son which Hagar bears [7]for him,[c]**
15 Ga319 41-5 19 31 **Ishmael.**
[H]*E gr* THE-STIR(er) 16 **And Abram is [yr] eighty [a]six years of [s]age [i]when Hagar**
Adm 3480 **bears \`Ishmael for Abram.**

171-3 Abram's Seed 4-14 17 **And coming is Abram to be [yr] ninety [a]nine years of [s]age.**
[age]son Adm 3493 **And appearing is Ieue to Abram and is saying to him, "I**
1 2C617 18 **am the Al-Who-Suffices. [F]Walk before Me and become flaw-**
less.
2 **"And giving am I My covenant between Me and [bt] you, and**
increasing am I \`you [in] exceedingly exceedingly."
3 Hb1112 3 **And falling is Abram on his face.**

171-3 Abram's Seed 4-14 4 **And speaking \`with him is the Alueim, [to] saying, "I, be-**
hold! My covenant is \`with you. And you are to become [to]
[A]*Ab rm* FATHER-HIGH 5 **the forefather of a throng of nations. And no further shall**
[A]*Ab r e m* FATHER- **your name be called \`Abram. [a]Yet your name becomes**
HIGH-throng **Abraham, for the forefather of a throng of nations have**
[made]GAVE 6 **I made you. And [F]fruitful I cause \`you to be [in] exceedingly**
[make]GIVE **exceedingly. And I make of you [to] nations, and kings from**
7 2112 Is447 7 **you shall fare forth. And I [F]set up \`My covenant between**
Me and [bt] you, and [bt] your [A]seed after you, for their genera-
tions, for a covenant eonian, to become your [to] Alueim and
8 **your [A]seed's after you. And I give to you and to your [A]seed**
after you \`the land of your sojournings, \`all the land of
[O]*Kno n* SUBMITTER **Canaan, for a holding eonian. And I become their [to] Alueim."**
9 **And saying is the Alueim to Abraham, "And you shall**
[F]keep \`My covenant, you and your [A]seed after you for their

10 generations. This is My covenant, which you shall [F]keep be- *I e u e*
tween Me and[bt] you and[bt] your [A]seed after you [7]for their Will-be-ing-was
11 generations:[0] Circumcise to yourselves every male. And circumcised shall you be in ˋthe flesh of your foreskin. And it
comes to be for a sign of the covenant between Me and[bt]
12 you. And a son of eight days shall be circumcised [t]by you,
every male of [t]your generations, homeborn [a]or acquired
with money from any[son] foreigner, he who is not [f]of your
13 [N]seed. With circumcision shall be circumcised the home-
born and the one acquired with your money. And My cove-
14 nant comes to be in your flesh for a covenant eonian. And
the uncircumcised male, ˋthe flesh of whose foreskin was not
circumcised [S]in the eighth day,[n] ˙that ˙[N]soul also shall be
cut off from his people. ˋMy covenant he annuls."

161-16 Two Seeds 1715-27 15-16 Sarah 21-22

15 And saying is the Alueim to Abraham, "Sarai, your wife [A]*Abrem* FATHER-
16 —you shall not call ˋher name Sarai, for Sarah is her name. HIGH-throng
And I bless ˋher, and, moreover, I give[to] you a son [f]of her. -[ai]*Shri* My-REGARDED-one
And bless[S] him[n] will I and [7]he[0] comes to be for nations, [7]and[n] -[ah]*Shre* Chiefess
kings of peoples shall [b]come from [7]him.[0]"

17 And falling is Abraham on his face. And laughing is he 17-20 Laughter 23-27
and saying in his [F]heart, "To one a hundred years of [s]age *17* Jn856 Ro419 Hb1112
shall [7]a son[0] be born? And should Sarah, ninety years of
[dt]age, be bearing?" [age]daughter
18 And saying is Abraham to the Alueim, "O that Ishmael [I]*Ishmo-Al* HEARING-
should live before Thee!" is-SUBJECTOR
19 And saying is the Alueim [7]to Abraham,[0] "Nevertheless,
[7]behold,[n] Sarah, your wife is bearing you a son, and you
shall call ˋhis name Isaac. And I [F]set up ˋMy covenant ˋwith [I]*Itzchq* LAUGH-causer
him for a covenant eonian, [7]and[n] [t]with his [A]seed after him.
20 "And as to Ishmael, [7]behold![0] I hear you. Behold! Bless
ˋhim do I, and [F]fruitful do I [c]make him, and increase him[in]
exceedingly exceedingly. Twelve princes shall he beget, and
I make [t]of him a great nation. [make]GIVE

21 "[a]Yet ˋMy covenant will I [F]set up ˋwith Isaac, whom 15-16 Sarah 21-22
Sarah will bear for you [t]at ˙this, the appointed time[in]
another ˙year."
22 And finishing is He[to] speaking ˋwith him, and ascending
is the Alueim from[on] Abraham.

23 And taking is Abraham Ishmael, his son, and ˋall who are 17-20 Circum-
born in his household, and ˋall acquired with his money, cision 23-27
every male among the mortals of Abraham's household, and
he is circumcising ˋthe flesh of their foreskin [i]on ˙this very
˙day, as[w] the Alueim had spoken ˋto him.
24 And Abraham is ninety[a] nine years of [s]age [i]at his circum- [age]son
25 cision in ˋthe flesh of his foreskin. And Ishmael, his son, is Adm 3493
thirteen years of [s]age [i]at his circumcision in ˋthe flesh of
26 his foreskin. [i]On ˙this very ˙day is Abraham circumcised,
27 and Ishmael, his son. And all the mortals of his household,
home-born [a]or acquired with money from ˋa[son] foreigner [7]of
the nations,[0] are circumcised ˋwith him.

151-21 Faith Covenant 181-16- 181-2 Appearance 16-

18 And appearing to him is Ieue [7]Alueim[0] among the oaks of *1* 1318 1413 188

[M]*Mmra* 'Bitterness' Mamre. And sitting is he at the opening of the tent at
Al u eim 2 noon, as the day is warm. And lifting is he his eyes and
SUBJECT-or-to-s (To-subjectors) seeing, and behold! Three mortals are stationed [on]by him.
2 1314 191 15 And seeing is he and running to meet them from the open-
See map page 60. ing of the tent, and is prostrating to[d] the earth.

3-8 Reception 9-15 3 And saying is he, "My lord, pray, should I find grace in
your [A]eyes, pray, you must not pass on from your [F]servant.
4 2432 4324 4 Let a little water, pray, be taken, and they will wash your
5 feet. And lean back under the tree. And I will take a morsel
of bread and you shall eat and [F]brace your [F]hearts. And
afterward shall you pass on your way, for therefore you
pass [on]by your [F]servant."
And saying are they, "So be doing as [w]you speak."
6 And hastening is Abraham toward the tent to Sarah. And
saying is he to her, "Hasten! Three seahs of meal flour
7 knead, and make ember cakes." And to the herd runs Abra-
[young]son ham, and is taking a [s]young one of the herd, tender and
good, and is giving it to the lad. And hastening is he to
8 Ac1041 8 make 'it ready. And taking is he clotted cream and milk,
and the [s]young one of the herd which he had made ready,
[put]GIVING and he is putting it before them. And he is standing [on]by
them under the tree, and eating are they.

3-8 Conference 9-15 9 And saying are they to him, "Where is Sarah, your wife?"
And answering, he is saying, "Behold! In the tent."
10 And saying is He, "Return, yea, return will I to you [as]accord-
[S]*Shre* Chiefess ing to this season of life, and, behold! A son [t]has Sarah, your
[A]*Abrem* FATHER- wife." And Sarah is hearing at the opening of the tent,
HIGH-throng 11 [a]for she was behind him. [a]Now Abraham and Sarah are
old, coming into [N]days. It had left off to [b]come to Sarah,
12 1717 1P36 12 [as]according to the path of 'women. And laughing is Sarah
within herself [to]saying, "After my decadence shall luxury
[b]come to me? 'It has not come to me till now.' My lord also
is old."
13 And saying is Ieue to Abraham, "Why this? Sarah
laughs, [to]saying, 'Indeed, truly, shall I bear [a]when I am
[matter]word 14 old?' Is it a matter too marvelous [f]for Ieue Alueim? [t]At
14 Lu137 the appointed time will I return to you [as]according to the
season of life, and Sarah [t]has a son."
15 And dissimulating is Sarah, [to]saying, "Not laugh did I,"
for she is fearful. And saying is He, "No! For laugh did you."

18[1]-2 Departure 16- 16 And rising are the mortals thence, and they are gazing
[S]*Sdm* FOUNDED on the [A]face of Sodom and Gomorrah.

14[1]-24 Sodom, Lot 18-16-19[38] 18-16-33 Abraham 19[27-29] -16-19 Ieue, Abraham 20-33

See map page 66. And Abraham is going with them to send them away.
17 Am37 17 And Ieue says, "Shall I cover from Abraham, My serv-
18 2218 18 ant, what I am doing, [a]when Abraham shall become, yea
become [to] a nation, great and staunch, and blest in him are
19 Ps781-8 19 all the nations of the earth? For I know him, [w]that, responding, he will instruct 'his sons and 'his household after him,
and [F]keep will they the [F]way of Ieue to do justice and judgment, that Ieue may bring on Abraham all '[w]that He speaks
[on]concerning him."

-16-19 Ieue, Sodom 20-33 20 And saying is Ieue, "Seeing that the outcry of Sodom and

20 Ieue and
Gomorrah is much, and that their sin is exceedingly [r]heavy, [G]*Omre* OMER
21 descend will I, pray, and see, do they [as]according to all the *21* 117 Ex38
cry which is coming to Me? And if not, I will know." See map page 66.
22 And facing thence are the mortals, and they are going *22* 191
to[d] Sodom. And [S]Ieue[ph] still is standing before [S]Abraham.[ph]
23 And close is Abraham coming and saying, "Indeed, [A]*Abrem* FATHER-
[r]sweeping up art Thou the righteous with the wicked? [7a]So HIGH-throng
24 become the righteous as the wicked.[o] Perhaps, forsooth, *I e u e*
fifty righteous are there in the midst of the city. Indeed, Will-be-ing-was
[r]sweeping them up art Thou and not bearing [t]with [7]the
entire[o] place on account of the fifty righteous who are with- within IN NEAR
25 in it? Far be it from [to]Thee [f]to do [as]according to ·this word,
to [c]put to death the righteous with the wicked, and [as]so
come the righteous to be as the wicked. Far be it from [to]
Thee! The Judge of the entire [A]earth, will He not [do]execute
judgment?"
26 And saying is Ieue, "If finding am I in Sodom fifty [S]*Sdm* FOUNDED
righteous in the midst of the city, [a]then bear will I [t]with
the entire place [in]for their sake."
27 And answering is Abraham and saying, "Behold, pray!
Disposed am I to speak to [7]Ieue,[ph] and I am but [M]soil and
28 [M]ashes. Perhaps lacking are of the fifty righteous, five.
Ruin wilt Thou, [t]for five, ·the entire city?"
And saying is He, "Not ruin it will I if I shall find there
forty [a]five."
29 And proceeding is he further to speak to Him and saying,
"Perhaps will be found there forty."
And saying is He, "Not do it will I for the sake of the
forty."
30 And saying is he, "My Lord must not, pray, be hot [a]when I
speak. Perhaps will be found there thirty."
And saying is He, "Not do it will I if I shall find there
thirty."
31 And saying is he, "Behold, pray! Disposed am I to speak
to my Lord. Perhaps will be found there twenty."
And saying is He, "Not ruin it will I, for the sake of the
twenty."
32 And saying is he, "My Lord must not, pray, be hot, [a]when I
shall speak, yea, ·once more. Perhaps will be found there ten."
And saying is He, "Not ruin it will I, for the sake of the
ten."
33 And going is Ieue, as [w] He finishes [to] speaking to Abraham. And Abraham returns to his place.

191-26 Lot, Daughters 30-38

19 And coming are two of the messengers to[d] Sodom in the **1-8** Messengers 12-22
evening. And Lot is sitting in the gateway of Sodom. And [L]*Lut* WRAPPER
seeing them is Lot, and rising is he to meet them. And *1* 1816
prostrating is he, nostrils to[d] the earth. See map page 66.
2 And saying is he, "Behold, pray, my lords! Withdraw,
pray, to the house of your servant and lodge and wash your
feet, and [c]rise early and go [t]on your way."
And saying are they, "No, for in the square will we
lodge."
3 And urging [in]them is he exceedingly. And withdrawing *3* 188
are they to him, and coming to his house. And making is he

Al u eim SUBJECT-or-to-s (To-subjectors) for them a feast, and he bakes unleavened bread, and they
are eating.

4-11 People, Sodom 24-26 4 Ere they are lying down, [a]then mortals of the city, mor-
[S]Sdm FOUNDED tals of Sodom, surround [on] the house, from the lad [a]even un-
5 [L]Lut WRAPPER to the elder, the entire people, from the outmost parts. And
calling are they to Lot, and saying to him, "Where are the
mortals who came to you tonight? [c]Bring them forth to us,
and we will know them."
6 And forth to them is Lot faring, to[d] the portal, [a]yet the
7 door he closes after him. And saying is he to them, "Pray,
8 you must not, my brethren, [c]do evil! Behold, pray, my two
daughters who have not [A]known a man. Pray, forth will I
[c]bring them to you, and do you to them as is good in your
thing word [A]eyes. But to these mortals you must not do anything
evil, for therefore come they into the [A]shadow of my
rafters."
9 [a]Yet saying are they, "Come close you, beyond." And
saying are they, "The one who came to sojourn [a] is judging,
[S]even as a judge! Now we will [c]do more evil to you [f]than
to them." And urging are they [in] the man [in] Lot exceedingly,
and close are they coming to break the door.
stretch SENDING 10 And stretching forth are the mortals their hands and
bringing Lot to them into the house, and the door they
11 Jd1621 2K618 Ac1311 11 close. And the mortals who are at the portal of the house
[fr]FURTHER they smite [t]with dazzlings, from the small [a fr]to the great,
[a]so they are tiring themselves trying to find the portal.

1-3 Messengers 12-22 12 And saying are the mortals to Lot, "Still any [t]of yours
here, sons-in-law, [a]or your sons [a]or your daughters, [a] all
who are yours in the city, [c]bring forth from this place,
13 for ruining are we this place, for great is the cry concerning them before the [c]face of Ieue, and sending us is Ieue to
wreck it."
14 137 11 12 14 And forth is Lot faring, and is speaking to his sons-in-
law, who took his daughters, and is saying, "Rise! Forth
from this place, for ruining is Ieue the city!" And becoming is he as one making fun, in the [A]eyes of his sons-in-law.
[wt]what 15 And as [wt] dawn [A]ascends, [a]then rushing are the messengers [in] Lot, [to] saying, "Rise! Take your wife and your two
daughters, who are found, and come out, lest you be [F]swept
up in the depravity of the city."
16 [a]Yet dallying is he, and fast hold are the mortals taking
of his hand and [in] the hand of his wife and [in] the hands of
his two daughters, [t]at Ieue's sparing [on] him. And forth are
they [c]bringing him, and leaving him [f] outside [to] the city.
17 And [b]coming is it, as they [c]bring them forth outside,
they are saying also, "Be sure to escape [on] with your [N]soul!
behind AFTER You must not look behind you, and you must not stand in
basin DISK any part of the basin. Escape to the mountain, lest you be
[F]swept up!"
18 And saying is Lot to them, "It must not be, pray, [S]Ieue![ph]
19 Behold, pray! Thy servant finds grace in Thine [A]eyes, and
magnifying art Thou Thy kindness which Thou doest to me
[f]in [c]preserving alive my [N]soul. [a]Yet I, I cannot [to] escape to
20 the mountain, lest evil [F]cling to me and I die. Behold, pray!
This city is near to flee there, and it is inferior. Pray,

escape shall I there—Is it not inferior?—and live shall — *I e u e* Will-be-ing-was
my [N]soul."
21 And saying is He to him, "Behold! Lifted up have I your — 22 142 8
[N]face, even as to ·this matter, to avoid My overturning — [even]moreover
22 ʼthe city of which you speak. Hasten! Escape there, for not — [matter]word
a thing can I [to]do till you come there." Therefore he calls — [thing]word
23 the name of the city Zoar. The sun comes forth over the — [Z]*Tzu or* INFERIOR
earth [a]when Lot comes to[d] Zoar. — [L]*Lut* WRAPPER

24 And Ieue rains on Sodom and on Gomorrah sulphur and — 4-11People, Sodom24-26
25 fire from ʼIeue, from the heavens. And overturning is He — 24 Dt2923 Is1319 Jr4918
·these ʼ·cities and ʼthe entire basin, and ʼall dwelling in the — Mt1015
cities and [7]everything[0] sprouting from the ground. — [basin]DISK
26 [a]Yet looking back is his wife from behind him, and be- — [behind]AFTER
coming is she a monument of salt. — 26 Lu1732

27 And early is Abraham [c]rising in the morning to go to the — 18-16-33 Abraham 27-29
28 place where he had stood before the [c]face of Ieue. And — 27 1822
gazing is he on the surface of Sodom and Gomorrah and on — [S]*Sdm* FOUNDED
all the surface of the land of the basin, and is seeing, and — [G]*Omre* OMER
behold! Up go the fumes of the land as the fumes of a ·lime- — [basin]DISK
kiln.
29 And [b]coming is it, [i]as [7]Ieue[0] Alueim wrecks [7]all[0] ʼthe cities
of the basin, [c]remembering also is the Alueim ʼAbraham — [A]*Abrem* FATHER-
and is sending ʼLot from the midst of the overturning [i]when — HIGH-throng
[7]Ieue[0] overturns ʼthe cities in which Lot dwelt. — 29 2Pt26-9

30 And up is Lot going from Zoar, and dwelling in the — 1-26Lot, Daughters30-38
mountain, and his two daughters with him, for he fears to
dwell in Zoar. And dwelling is he in a ·cave, he and his two
31 daughters [7]with him.[n] And saying is the firstborn to the
inferior in station, "Our father is old, and man there is
none in the earth to come on us as is the [r]way of the entire
32 [A]earth. Go! [c]Give will we ʼour father wine to drink, and lie
with him and keep alive [A]seed from our father."

33 And [c]giving are they ʼtheir father wine to drink in ·that
night. And coming is the firstborn, and lying ʼwith her
father [7]in that night[0], and he knows not [in]her lying [a]nor [in]
34 her rising. And [b]coming is it [f]on the morrow [a]that the
firstborn is saying to the inferior in station, "Behold! I lay
yesternight ʼwith [7]our[0] father. We will [c]give him wine to
drink ·tonight, moreover. And you come, lie with him, and
we will keep alive [A]seed from our father."
35 And, moreover, they are [c]giving ʼtheir father wine to
drink in ·that night, and rising is the inferior in station,
and is lying with [7]her father.[0] And he knows not [in]her lying
36 [a]nor [in]her rising. And pregnant are the two daughters of — PARAN Red Sea (gulf)
Lot [f]by their father.
37 And bearing is the firstborn a son, and is calling ʼhis
name Moab, [7]saying, "From my father."[0] He is the fore- — [M]*Muab* FROM-FATHER
38 father of Moab till ·this day. And the inferior in station, — 38 Nu2129 Dt219 20 233
she, moreover, bears a son, and is calling ʼhis name Ben- — Jd109 11 2Ch201
Ammi. He is the forefather of the sons of Ammon till ·this — [B]*Bnomi* SON-(of)-
day. — my-people

1210-20 Denial 201-18 20 **And journeying thence is Abraham** to[d] **the south-rim.**
KQdsh Holy **And dwelling is he between Kadesh and**[bt] **Shur, and is so-**
SShur Barricade **journing in Gerar.**
SShr e Chiefess 2 **And saying is Abraham** ⁷**concerning**° **Sarah, his wife,**
1 129 131 **"My sister is she,"** ⁷**for he feared to say, "My wife is she,"**
2 261 **lest he be killed by the men of the city because of her.**° **And**
GGr r Chew or Saw **sending is Abimelech, king of Gerar, and taking 'Sarah.**
AAb i mlk My-father- 3 **And coming is the Alueim to Abimelech in a dream in**
is-king **the night, and is saying to him, "Behold yourself dying on**
3 3124 375 9 **account of the woman whom you take,** [a]**when she is 'pos-**
sessed by a possessor."
4 **And Abimelech comes not near to her. And saying is he,**
"[S]**Ieue,**[ph] **A nation, moreover,** ⁷**unknowing and**° **just, are you**
5 **killing? Said not he to me, 'My sister is she'? And she,**
moreover, said, 'My brother is he.' In the sincerity of my
[F]**heart and in the innocency of my** [A]**palms, I did this."**
Al u eim 6 **And saying is the Alueim to him in the dream, "More-**
subject-or-to-s **over, I know that, in the sincerity of your** [F]**heart you did**
(To-subjectors) **this, and I, moreover, am keeping 'you back from sinning**
allowGIVE [t]**against Me. Therefore, I did not allow you to touch**[to] **her.**
7 Ex416 71 7 **And now restore the man's 'wife, for a prophet is he, and**
pray will he about you, and live shall you. And should you
not restore her, know that you shall die, yea, die, you and all
who are yours."
8 **And early is Abimelech** [c]**rising in the morning, and call-**
ing is he[to] **all his servants, and is speaking 'all 'these 'words**
in their [A]**ears. And fearing are** ⁷**all**[n] **the mortals exceedingly.**
AAbr e m Father- 9 **And calling is Abimelech to Abraham, and saying to him,**
high-throng **"What have you done to us? And in what have I sinned**
[t]**against you, that you bring on me and on my kingdom a**
great sin? Deeds which are not being done you do ⁷**to me.**°**"**
10 **And saying is Abimelech to Abraham, "What do you see**
thingword **that you have done 'this '-thing?"**
11 **And saying is Abraham, "**[S]**For I feared**[n] **seeing that I**
say, 'But no fear of the Alueim is in 'this place, and they
matterword 12 **will kill me over the matter of my wife.' And, moreover,**
truly, my sister is ⁷**she**[n]**, the daughter of my father is she,**
yea, but not the daughter of my mother, and she becomes
13 **my**[to] **wife. And it** [b]**comes, as**[w] **the Alueim** ⁷**causes**[n] **'me to**
stray from my father's house [S]**and from the land of my**
kindred,[n] [a]**that I am saying to her, 'This is your kindness**
which you shall do ⁷**for me.**°[to] **At every 'place where we are**
coming, say as to me, "My brother is he".'"
14 **And taking is Abimelech** ⁷**a thousand silverlings**[n] **and a**
flock and a herd, and servants and maids, and is giving
them to Abraham. And he is restoring to him 'Sarah his
15 **wife. And saying is Abimelech** ⁷**to Abraham,**° **"Behold! My**
land is before you. In 'that which is good in your [A]**eyes,**
dwell."
16 **And to Sarah he says, "Behold! I gave a thousand silver-**
lings to your brother. Behold! It is for you a [M]**covering of**
the eyes [S]**and**[n] **for all who are 'with you. 'All is being cor-**
rected also."
17 **And praying is Abraham to the Alueim and healing is**

the **Alueim** ˋAbimelech and his wife and his maidservants, *Al u e im*
18 and they are bearing, for Ieue restrains, yea restrains all the SUBJECT-or-to-s (To-subjectors)
wombs [t]of the house of Abimelech over the matter of Sarah, [matter]word
Abraham's wife.

1314-18 Fulfillment 211-8

21 And Ieue visits ˋSarah, as [w] He had said, and doing is Ieue [S]*Shr e* Chiefess
2 to Sarah as [w]He had spoken. And pregnant is Sarah and is
bearing for Abraham a son for his old age, [t]at the appointed *3* 1717 21 1812 13 15
3 time of which the **Alueim** had spoken ˋto him. And Abraham [A]*Abr e m* FATHER-HIGH-throng
is calling ˋthe name of his son ˙who is born to him, whom
Sarah bears for him, Isaac. [I]*I tzchq* LAUGH-causer
4 And circumcising is Abraham ˋIsaac, his son, at eight
5 days of [s]age as [w]the **Alueim** had instructed ˋhim. And Abra- [age]son
ham is a hundred years of [s]age [i]when his son ˋIsaac is born Adm 3494
to him.
6 And saying is Sarah, "Laughter the **Alueim** makes for
7 me. Everyone ˙hearing is laughing for me." And saying is *7* Lu154 55
she, "Who declared to Abraham, 'Sarah suckles sons'? For [Who]ANY
I bear [S]him[n] a son [7]in my[o] old age."
8 And growing up is the boy and being weaned. And making [grow up]GREATEN
is Abraham a great feast [i]on the day of the weaning of *8* Lu240
ˋIsaac, [7]his son.[n]

131-13 Separation 219-21

9 And seeing is Sarah ˋthe son of Hagar, the Egyptian, 9-10 House, in 15
whom she bore for Abraham, making fun [7]of Isaac her son.[n] [E]*M tzr i* Narrows-ite
10 And saying is she to Abraham, "Drive out ˙this ˙maidser- *10* Ga422-31
vant and ˋher son, for not shall he enjoy the tenancy—the
son of ˙this ˙maidservant—with my son, with Isaac!"

11 [a]Yet evil is this ˙word exceedingly in the [A]eyes of Abra- 11 Suffering 16
ham, on account of his son's [=]case.

12 And saying is the **Alueim** to Abraham, "Let it not be evil 12-13 Intervention 17-19
in your [A]eyes on account of the lad, and on account of your *12* Ro97 Ga316 Hb1118
maidservant. In all [w]that Sarah is saying to you, hearken
13 [i]to her [N]voice, for in Isaac your [A]seed shall be called. And,
moreover, ˋthe son of [7]˙this[n] ˙maidservant, a [7]great[n] nation I
will constitute him, for your [M]seed is he."

14 And early in the morning Abraham is [c]rising, and taking 14 Wilderness 20-21
bread and a flask of water and is giving it to Hagar, and [H]*E gr* THE STIR(er)
places it on her shoulder[b], [a]with ˋthe boy, and is sending her [sh]shoulder blade
away. And going is she and straying in the wilderness of See map page 66.
Beer-sheba. [B]*Bar shbo* WELL-oath

15 And finishing are they the water from the flask. And 9-10 House, out 15
flinging is she ˋthe boy under one of the shrubs.

16 And going is she and sitting [t]by herself, aloof from [7]him,[o] 11 Suffering 16
far off as a bow shot, for, she says, "I must not see [in]the
death of [7]my[o] ˙boy." And sitting is she aloof from [7]him.[o] And
[7]the lad[o] is lifting up [7]his[o] ˋvoice and lamenting.

17 And hearing is the **Alueim** ˋthe voice of the lad [7]from 12-13 Intervention 17-19
the place where he is.[o] And calling is a messenger of the
Alueim to Hagar from the heavens and is saying to her,
"What is the [S]matter[n] [t]with you, Hagar? You must not [matter]declaration
fear, for the **Alueim** hears ˋthe voice of [7]your[o] lad [7]from the

I e u Will-be-ing-was

18 **place**[o] [in] **where he is. Rise! Lift up** 'the **lad, and encourage**
'**your hand in him, for** [to] **a great nation will I constitute**
him."

19 **And unclosing is** the **Alueim** '**her eyes, and seeing is she**
a well of '**living**[o] **water, and is going and filling** '**the flask**
with water, and giving '**the lad a drink.**

14 Wilderness 20-21 · grow up GREATening · great MANY · PPhar n BEAUTIFUL · EM tzr im Narrows

20 **And** [b]**coming is it that the Alueim is** '**with the lad, and he**
is growing up. And dwelling is he in the wilderness, and is
21 **becoming great with his bow. And dwelling is he in** the
wilderness of Paran. And his mother is taking a wife for
him from the land of Egypt.

124-9 Sojourn 2122-34 · 22-24 Time 34 · speak SAYING · AhAchzth 'HOLD-GIVE' · PPhl kl MOUTH-ALL · 23 2013 · AAb r e m FATHER-HIGH-throng

22 **And** [b]**coming is it** [i]**at** ·**that** ·**season** [a]**that Abimelech** '[a]**with**
Ahuzzath, his associate,[o] '**and Phicol,**' **the chief of his host,**
is speaking to Abraham, [to] **saying, "The Alueim is with you**
23 **in all** [w]**that you are doing. And now, swear to me** [i]**by the**
Alueim. Behold! Should you be false to me and to my pro-
pagator and to my progeny—! [as]**According to the kindness**
which I do [wi]**to you shall you do** '**with me,**[o] **and with the**
land in which you sojourn."
24 **And saying is Abraham, "I will swear."**

25-26 Well 28-31 · 25 2619 20 Ex217 Jd511

25 [a]**Yet Abraham corrected** '**Abimelech on account of the**
=**case of a well of** ·**water which had been snatched** 'by **the**
servants of Abimelech.

thing word

26 **And saying is Abimelech** '**to him,**[o] **"Not know do I** [an]**who**
did ·**this** '·**thing. And, moreover, you did not tell** [to] **me. More-**
over, also I did not hear, barring ·**today."**

27 Covenant 32-33 · 27 1510-18 Jr3418-20 Ga320

27 **And taking is Abraham a flock and a herd, and is giving**
them to Abimelech. And they two are contracting a cove-
nant.

25-26 Well 28-31

28 **And stationing is Abraham** '**seven ewe lambs of the flock**
29 [to] **alone. And saying is Abimelech to Abraham, "What are**
they, ·**these seven ewe lambs** '**of the flock**[o] **which you station**
[to] **alone?"**

30 **And saying is** '**Abraham,**[o] **that "**[S]**The**[n] '**seven ewe lambs**
are you taking from my [A]**hand in order to become** [to] **a testi-**
31 **mony to me that I delved** '·**this** ·**well." Therefore he called**
'**the name of**[o] ·**that** [to] ·**place Beer-sheba, for there they swore,**
they two.

27 Covenant 32-33 · BBar-shbo WELL-oath · PPhl shth Distinguished-SET-ite · 33 223 Ps902

32 **And contracting are they a covenant in Beer-sheba. And**
rising is Abimelech '**and Ahuzzath, his associate,**[o] **and**
Phicol, the chief of his host, and returning are they to the
33 **land of the Philistines. And planting is** '**Abraham**[n] **a tama-**
risk in Beer-sheba, and is calling there [i]**on the** [N]**name of**
Ieue, the Al eonian.

22-24 Time 34

34 **And sojourning is Abraham in the land of the Philistines**
many days.

1127-123 Seed 221-19

1-10 Abraham's Trial, Isaac, Journey 19

things words · 1 Ex1525 164 2020 Dt82 16 Ec21 723

22 **And it is** [b]**coming, after** ·**these** ·**things,** [a]**that the Alueim**
probes '**Abraham and is saying to him, "Abraham!** '**Abra-**
ham![o]**"**
And saying is he, "Behold me!"

2 **And saying is He, "Take, pray, 'your son, 'your only one,** [I]*Itzchq* LAUGH-causer
whom you love, 'Isaac, and go[to]**you to the land of ·Moriah,** [M]*Murie* 'Bitter-ness'
and [c]**offer him up there for an ascent offering on one of** [apprize]SAY
the mountains of which I will apprize [to] **you."** 2 1Ch21[22] 22[1] 2Ch3[1]
Mt27[33]
3 **And early in the morning is Abraham** [c]**rising, and is sad-**
dling 'his ass, and is taking 'two of his lads 'with him, and [A]*Abrem* FATHER-
'Isaac, his son, and is rending the =wood for the ascent HIGH-throng
offering. **And rising is he and going,** [7]**and came**[0] **to the place** See map page 72.
4 **of which the Alueim apprized** [to] **him** [i]**on the third ·day. And** [apprize]SAY
lifting up 'his eyes is Abraham and seeing 'the place from *I e u e*
afar. Will-be-ing-was

5 **And saying is Abraham to his lads, "Sit** [to] **you here with**
the ass, and I and the lad will go, meanwhile, and we will
worship and return to you."

6 **And taking is Abraham 'the =wood for the ascent offer-** 6 12[7] 13[4] 18 21[33]
ing and is placing it on Isaac, his son. And taking is he in Jn10[30] 14[10] 11 16[32]
his hand 'the fire and 'the knife. And going are they two Ro8[32] 2C5[19]
together.

7 **And speaking is Isaac to Abraham, his father, and say-** [speak]SAYING
ing, "My father!"
And saying is he, "Behold me, my son."
And saying is he, "Behold the fire and the =wood, [a]**yet**
where is the flockling for the ascent offering?"
8 **And saying is Abraham, "The Alueim will see for Him-**
self as to the flockling for the ascent offering, my son."
9 **And going are they, they two, together. And coming are**
they to the place of which the Alueim had **apprized** [to] **him.** [apprize]SAY
And building is Abraham 'the altar there, and is arranging
'the =wood. And trussing is he 'Isaac, his son, and placing
10 **'him on**[to]**the altar, above**[to]**the =wood. And stretching** out [stretch]SENDING
is Abraham 'his hand and taking 'the knife to slay 'his son.

11 **And calling is the messenger of Ieue to him from the** 11-12 Calls 15-18
heavens and saying, "Abraham! Abraham!" 11 46[2] Ex3[4]
And saying is he, "Behold me!"
12 **And saying is he, "You must not stretch out your hand** [stretch]SEND
[7]**on**[n] **the lad, and you must not do aught to him, for now I**
know that you fear the Alueim, [a]**for you have not kept back**
'your son, 'your only one from Me."

13 **And lifting is Abraham 'his eyes and seeing, and, behold!** 13 Sacrifice 14
[7]**One**[n] **ram is** [af]**behind him, held in a thicket** [i]**by its horns.** [behind]AFTER
And going is Abraham and taking 'the ram, and [c]**offering**
it up for an ascent offering instead of [7]**Isaac,**[0] **his son.**

14 **And calling is Abraham the name of ·that ·place Ieue-** 13 Sacrifice 14
jireh, which is being said ·today, "In the mount of Ieue it is [I]*Ieue-irae* Ieue-
being seen." 14 1Ch21[26] 2Ch7[1-3] is-See-er

15 **And calling is the messenger of Ieue to Abraham a second** 11-12 Calls 15-18
16 **time from the heavens, and saying, "**[i]**By Myself I swear,**
averring is Ieue, that, because[w]**you have done '·this ·thing** [thing]word
and have not kept back 'your son, 'your only one, [7]**from Me,**[n] 16 24[7] 26[3] 50[24] Ex13[5]
17 **that, blessing, yea, blessing you am I, and increasing, yea,** 11 33[1] Psl32[11] Lu1[73]
increasing your [A]**seed am I as the stars of the heavens and** 17 13[16]
as the sand which is on the sea shore. And your [A]**seed shall**

Al u eim SUBJECT or-to-s (To-subjectors) 18 **tenant ˋthe gateway of its enemies, and blessed, in your**
[A]seed, shall be **all the nations of the earth, inasmuch as you**
hearken [i]**to My voice."**

1-10 Abraham's Trial, Isaac, Return 19 [A]*Ab r e m* FATHER- HIGH-throng [B]*Bar-shbo* WELL-oath

See map page 72. 19 **And returning is Abraham to his lads. And rising are**
[M]*Mlk e* Queen **they and going together to Beer-sheba. And dwelling is**
[N]*Nchur* SNORTER **Abraham in Beer-sheba.**

[U]*Outz* Counsel 22 20-24 Son of Relative 25 1-4 [thing]word

[B]*Buz* Despiser 20 **And** [b]**coming is it, after ˙these ˙things,** [a]**that it is being**
[K]*Qm u Al* RISING (is) Al **told to Abraham,**[to]**saying, "Behold! Milcah, she, moreover,**
[A]*Ar m* HEIGHT 21 **bears sons for Nahor, your brother, ˋUz, his firstborn, and**
[C]*K shd* As-DEPRIVED 22 **ˋBuz, his brother, and ˋKemuel,** the **father of Aram, and**
[H]*Chz u* PERCEIVER **ˋChesed and ˋHazu and ˋPildash and ˋJidlaph and ˋBethuel.**
[P]*Phl dsh* Bean-THRESHER 23 **And Bethuel generates ˋRebecca. These eight** [7]**sons**[0] **Milcah**
[I]*I dlph* LEAKER **bears for Nahor,** the **brother of Abraham.**
[B]*Bth u-Al* House-of-Al 24 **"And his concubine, and her name is Reumah, she more-**
[Reb]*Rbq e* Enthraller **over, also is bearing ˋTebah and ˋGaham and ˋThahash and**
[T]*Tbch* SLAUGHTER **ˋMaachah."**

[T]*Thchsh* AZURE Adm 35 31 23 1-20 Sarah's Death 24 1-67 1-2 Death, Burial 19

[M]*Mok e* SQUASH **23** **And coming is the** [=]**life of Sarah to be a hundred** [yr] **and**
24 Dt31 4 Js12 5 2S10 6 2 **twenty** [yr] **seven years**—the **years of** the [=]**life of Sarah. And**
[S]*Shr e* Chiefess **dying is Sarah in the town of Arba,** [7]**in the vale.**[n] **(It is**
[H]*Chbr un* JOINED **Hebron, in** the **land of Canaan.) And coming is Abraham**
[C]*Kno n* SUBMITTER to **wail** [t]**over Sarah and to lament for her.** See map page 72.

3-18 Tomb 20 3 **And rising is Abraham from over the face of his dead.**
3-11 Bargain 12-18 4 **And speaking is he to** the **sons of Heth,**[to]**saying, "A so-**
3-4 Asked 7-9 **journer and a settler am I with you. Give**[to]**me a holding**
[H]*Chth* Dismay **for a tomb with you, and I will entomb my dead from**[to]**my**
2 Nu13 22 4 Ps39 12 1P2 11 [N]**face."**

5-6 Granted 10-11 5 **And the sons of Heth are answering ˋAbraham,**[to]**saying,**
6 **"**[7]**No!**[n] **Hear us, my lord! A prince of** the **Alueim are you**
in our midst. In the choice of our tombs entomb your ˋdead.
Not a man [f]**of us will forbid** the **use of his tomb from you**
[f]**to entomb your dead** [7]**there.**[0]**"**

3-4 Asked 7-9 7 **And rising is Abraham and bowing down to the people**
8 **of the land, to the sons of Heth. And speaking is** [7]**Abraham**[0]
ˋ**with them,**[to]**saying, "Should it forsooth,** please **your** [N]**soul**
to entomb ˋmy dead from [to] **my** [N]**face, hear me, and inter-**
[E]*Ophr u n* SOILER **cede for me**[i]**with Ephron, the son of Zohar,**[S]**the Hittite**[n]**,**[a]**that**
[Z]*Tzchr* GREY 9 **he shall give to me ˋthe double cave which is his, which is**
[H]*Chth i* Dismay-ite [i]**at the end of his field.** [i]**For silver, in full, shall he give it to**
me for **a holding** for **a tomb in your midst."**

5-6 Acquired 10-11 10 **And Ephron is sitting in the midst of the sons of Heth.**
And answering is Ephron, the Hittite, ˋAbraham in the
[A]**ears of the sons of Heth, to all entering the gateway of his**
11 **city,**[to]**saying, "No, my lord! Hear me! The field I give to**
you. And the cave which is in it, to you I give it. [t]**Before**
the [A]**eyes of the sons of** [7]**all**[0] **my people I give it to you.**
Entomb your dead."

3-11 Bargain 12-18 12 **And bowing down is Abraham before the people of the**
13 **land. And speaking is he to Ephron in the** [A]**ears of the**
people of the land,[to]**saying, "Yea, should you be for** [7]**me,**[n]
hear me! Give will I silver for the **field. Take it from me**
and I will entomb ˋmy dead there."

14 And answering is Ephron 'Abraham,[to]saying, "[7]No,[0] lord! *Al u e im*
15 Hear me. The land is four -hundred shekels of silver. What SUBJECT-or-to-S
is that between me and[bt]you? 'Your dead entomb." (To-subjectors)
16 And hearkening is Abraham to Ephron. And weighing is [A]*Abrem* FATHER-
Abraham for Ephron 'the silver of which he spoke in the HIGH-throng
[A]ears of the sons of Heth, four -hundred shekels of silver, [H]*Chth* Dismay
17 passing [t]with the merchant. And confirmed is the field of [conf]RISEN
Ephron in which is[in]the double [7]cave,[0] which is adjoining [E]*Ophrun* SOILER
Mamre, the field and the cave which is in it, and all the
trees which are in the field, which are in all its boundary
18 around, to Abraham [t]by acquisition, [t]before the [A]eyes of the
sons of Heth [i]to all entering the gateway of his city.

19 And afterward Abraham entombs 'Sarah, his wife, [to]at 1-2 Death, Burial 19
the [7]double[0] cave of the field adjoining Mamre. (It is Heb- [S]*Shre* Chiefess
ron, in the land of Canaan.) [C]*Knon* SUBMITTER

20 And confirmed is the field and the cave which is in it to 3-18 Tomb 20
Abraham for a holding for a tomb from 'the sons of Heth. [conf]RISEN

231-20 Isaac's Marriage 241-67 1-54- Eleazar Mission -54-67 1 Abraham Blessed 34-36

24 And Abraham is old, come [i]to [N]days. And Ieue blesses
'Abraham in all things.

2 And saying is Abraham to his servant, the oldest of his 2-9 Eleazar 37-41
household, the ruler [i]over all [w]that is his, "Pray place your *2* 152
3 hand under my thigh, and adjure you will I [i]by Ieue, the
Alueim of the heavens and the Alueim of the earth, [w]that
you will not take a wife for my son [7]Isaac[0] from the daugh-
4 ters of the Canaanite[in]near whom I am dwelling, for to my *4* 2635 2746 281 8
land [7]whence I [b]came,[f] and to my kindred [S]should[n] you go,
and take a wife for my son, for Isaac, [7]thence[0]." [I]*I tzchq* LAUGH-causer
5 And saying to him is the servant, "Perhaps the woman
will not be willing to go after me to 'this 'land. Shall I
restore, yea restore 'your son to the land whence you fared
forth?" *6* Hbl115
6 And saying to him is Abraham, "Beware[to]you, lest you [Bew]KEEP
7 restore 'my son thither! Ieue, the Alueim of the heavens
[7]and the Alueim of the earth,[0] Who took me from my father's household and from the land of my kindred, [7]whence
I [b]came,[0] and Who spoke to me, and Who swore to me,[to]say-
ing, 'To [7]you and[0] your [N]seed will I give ''this 'land,' He will
send His messenger before you, and you take a wife for my
8 son, [7]Isaac,[0] thence. And should the woman not be willing to
go after you [7]to this land[0], innocent are you [f]of this my oath,
but 'my son you shall not restore thither."
9 And placing is the servant 'his hand under the thigh of
Abraham, his -lord, and is swearing to him on account of
'this 'matter. [matter]word

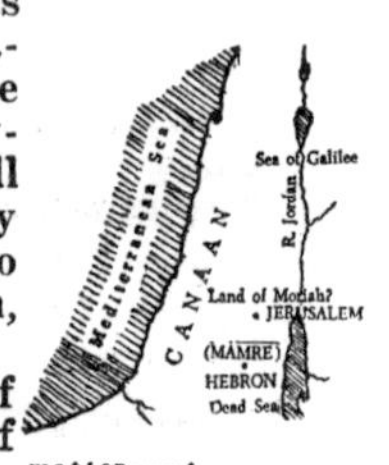

10 And taking is the servant ten camels from the camels of 10-11 Journey 42-
his -lord, and is going. And all manner of good things of *10* 1131
his -lord are in his [A]hand. And rising is he and going to
11 Syria of the streams, to the city of Nahor. And causing is [N]*Nchur* SNORTER
he the camels to kneel[f]outside[to]the city[to]at a well of 'water See map page 56.
[t]at eventide,[to]the time the women fare forth to 'bail it. [time]SEASON

12 And saying is he, "Ieue, Alueim of my lord Abraham, 12-21 Prayer -42-44
pray, cause a meeting before me today, and do a kindness

I e u e 13 [wi]to my lord Abraham. Behold! I am stationed [on]at this
Will-be-ing-was spring of ·water, and the daughters of the mortals of the
14 Jn428 14 city will fare forth to bail water. And [b]comes it that the
maiden to whom I will say, 'Pray stretch out your jar and
give me a drink,' [a]says [7]to me[0], 'Drink. And, moreover, ·your
camels also will I give to drink [7]till they should finish
drinking'[0], that ·her Thou dost find correct for Thy servant,
[I]Itzchq LAUGH-causer for Isaac, and [i]by it will I know that Thou doest a kindness
[wi]to my lord [7]Abraham.""

15 Is6524 15 And [b]coming is it, ere he finishes [to]speaking [7]in his
[Reb]Rbqe Enthraller [A]heart,[0] [a]that behold! Rebecca is faring forth, who was
[B]Bthu-Al House-of-Al born to Bethuel, the son of Milcah, the wife of Nahor,
[M]Mlke Queen 16 Abraham's brother, and her jar is on her shoulder[b]. And
[N]Nchur SNORTER the maiden is of exceedingly good appearance, a virgin,
[A]Abrem FATHER- and not a man had [A]known her. And down is she going to
HIGH-throng the spring, and is filling her jar and is coming up.
17 And running is the servant to meet her, and is saying,
"Pray, [c]let me sup a little water from your jar."
18 And saying is she, "Drink, my lord." And hastening is she
and is [c]letting down her jar on her hand and [c]giving him to
19 drink. And finishing is she [c]giving him to drink and is saying,
"Moreover, for your camels will I bail till they should finish
[empty]NAKEDing 20 [to]drinking." And hastening is she and emptying her jar into
the drinking basin, and running again to the well to bail.
21 And bailing is she for all his camels. And the man is in a
tumult [t]over her, [7]and[n] silent, to know if Ieue prospers his
[or]IF [F]way or not?

22-25 Rebecca 45-47 22 And [b]coming is it, as[w] the camels finish [to]drinking, taking is the man a pendant of gold, its weight a bekah, [S]and is
placing it on her nose,[n] and two bracelets on her hands of
23 ten gold shekels' weight. And he [7]inquires of her and[0] is say-
[whose]ANY ing, "Whose daughter are you? Tell [to]me, pray. Forsooth,
[S]in[n] the house of your father, is there place for us to lodge?"
24 1811 12 2436 24 And saying is she to him, "A daughter am I of Bethuel,
25 the son of Milcah, whom she bore for Nahor." And saying
is she to him, "Moreover, crushed straw [mr]and provender
there is much with us, [S]and,[n] moreover, a place to lodge."

26 Ieue 48 26 And bowing is the man his head and worshiping [to]Ieue.

27-32 Reception 49-53 27 And saying is he, "Blest be Ieue, Alueim of my lord
Abraham, Who does not forsake His kindness and His
truth [f]with my lord [S]Abraham.[n] I am [i]on the right way.
Guided me has Ieue to the house of my lord's brothers."
28 And running is the maiden and telling [to]her mother's
[matter]word household as to ·these ·matters.
[L]Lbn WHITE 29 And Rebecca [t]has a brother, and his name is Laban. And
30 running is Laban to the man ·outside [to]at the spring. And
[b]coming is it, as [S]he[n] sees ·the pendant, and ·the bracelets
on his sister's hands, and as he hears ·the words of Rebecca,
his sister, [to]saying, "Thus spoke the man to me," [a]that
coming is he to the man. And, behold! Standing is he [on]with
31 the camels [on]at the spring. And saying is he [7]to him,[0] "Come,
blest of Ieue! Why are you standing [in] outside [a]when I
[7]have prepared[0] a surface in the house and a place for the
camels?"

32 **And coming is the man into the house. ^a^Yet, unloosening** *I e u e*
is he the camels' girths and giving crushed straw and pro- Will-be-ing-was
vender to the camels, and water to wash his feet and the
feet of the mortals who are ˋwith him.

33 **And placing is he ⁷ᴺbread⁰ before him to eat.** 33 Entertainment 54-

^a^Yet saying is he, "Not eat will I till I should speak my ᴺword."

And saying is he, "Speak."

1 Abraham Blessed 34-36

34 **And saying is he, "A servant of Abraham am I. And** ᴬ*Abrem* FATHER-
35 **Ieue has blessed ˋmy lord exceedingly, and he is growing** HIGH-throng
great, and He is giving to him a flock and a herd and silver
and gold and servants and maids and camels and asses.
36 **And Sarah, the wife of my lord, bore ⁷one⁰ son for my lord** ˢ*Shre* Chiefess
after she was old. And give will he to him ˋall ʷthat he
ᵗhas.

37 **"And adjuring me is my lord ᵗᵒsaying, 'You shall not** 2-9 Eleazar 37-41
take a wife for my son from the daughters of the Canaan- ᴷ*Knoni* SUBMITite
38 **ite, in whose land I dwell, ˢforⁿ you should go to the house-**
hold of my father, and to my family, and take a wife for my
39 **son ⁷thence.'⁰ And saying am I to my lord, 'Perhaps the**
40 **woman will not go after me.' And saying is he to me,**
'Ieue ⁷Alueim⁰, before Whom I ᶠwalk, ⁷Heᶜ will send His
messenger ˋwith you and prosper your ᶠway. And take shall
you a wife for my son from my family, and from the house-
41 **hold of my father. Then you shall be innocent from my**
oath of imprecation. For come shall you to my family, and
should they not give to you, ^a^then you shall beᶜ innocent
from my oath of imprecation.'

42 **"And coming am I ˙today to the spring.** 10-11 Journey 42-

"And saying am I, 'Ieue, Alueim of my lord Abraham, 12-21 Prayer -42-44
pray, shouldst Thou, forsooth, be prospering my ᶠway on
43 **which I am ⁷now⁰ going, behold! I am stationed ᵒⁿat the** *43* Ex28 Ps6825 Is714
spring of ˙water ⁷ᵃwhere the daughters of the mortals of
he city will fare forth to bail water.⁰ And ᵇcomes it that
the damsel is ˙faring forth to bail, and I say to her, "Pray
44 **give me a little water to drink from your jar," and she says**
to me, "ᵐʳYou drink, and, moreover, for your camels will
I bail," she is the woman whom Ieue finds correct for
⁷Isaac,⁰ the son of my lord, ⁷and ⁱby this will I know that
Thou doest a kindness to my lord Abraham.'ʳ

45 **"Ere I am finishing ᵗᵒspeaking ᵗin my heart, ^a^ behold!** 22-25 Rebecca 45-47
Rebecca is faring forth, and her jar is on her shoulderᵇ, ᴿᵉᵇ*Rbqe* Enthraller
and down is she going to the spring and is bailing. ˢʰshoulder blade

46 **"And saying am I to her, 'ᶜGive me a ˢlittle waterⁿ to**
drink, pray, ˢfrom your jar.ⁿ' And hastening is she and
ᶜletting down her jar ᶠ on her ⁷hand⁰ and is saying, 'Drink.
And, moreover, your camels will I ᶜgive a drink.' And
drinking am I, and, moreover, she ᶜgives the camels a drink.

47 **"And asking ˋher am I and saying, 'Whose daughter are** ᵂʰᵒˢᵉANY
you?' And saying is she, 'A daughter of Bethuel, son of ᴮ*Bthu-Al* House-of-Al

[N]*Nchur* SNORTER Nahor, whom Milcah bore for him.' And placing am I the
[M]*Mlke* Queen pendant on her nose and the bracelets on her hands.
26 Ieue 48
48 Ps1077 48 "And bowing my head am I and worshiping[to] Ieue, and
Al u eim blessing 'Ieue, Alueim of my lord Abraham, Who guides
SUBJECT-or-to-S me in the [F]way of truth, to take 'the daughter of my lord's
(To-subjectors) brother for his son.

27-32 Reception 49-53 49 "And now, if you, forsooth, [do]deal in kindness and truth
'with my lord, tell[to] me. And if not, tell[to] me, and I will [F]face
[on]to [S]the[n] right or [on]to [S]the[n] left."
50 And answering are Laban and Bethuel and saying,
[matter]word "From Ieue fares forth [7]this[o] 'matter. We cannot speak to
[Reb]*Rbqe* Enthraller 51 you evil or good. Behold! Rebecca is before you. Take her
and go, and she shall become the wife of your lord's[to] son,
as[w] Ieue speaks."
[A]*Abrem* FATHER- 52 And [b]coming is it, as[w] Abraham's servant hears 'their
HIGH-throng 53 words, [a]that he is prostrating to[d] the earth to Ieue. And
forth is the servant [c]bringing articles of silver and articles
of gold and clothes, and is giving them to Rebecca. And
token presents he gives to her brother and[to] her mother.

33 Entertainment **54-** 54 And eating are they and drinking, he and the mortals
who are with him, and lodging.
1-54- Eleazer, Mission **-54-67**
-54 Return **56-60**
And rising are they in the morning, and saying is he,
"Send me, [7]and I will go[o] to my lord."

55 Departure 61-67 55 And saying are her [7]brothers[n] and her mother, "The
maiden shall dwell 'with us two [=]days or ten. [7]And[n] afterward she shall go."

-54 Return **56-60** 56 And saying is he to them, "You must not delay 'me [a]when
Ieue prospers my [F]way. Send me, and I will go to my lord."
57 And saying are they, "We will call[to] the maiden and ask
at 'her [N]mouth."
58 And calling are they[to] Rebecca and saying to her, "Will
you go with 'this 'man?" And saying is she, "I will go."
59 And sending are they 'Rebecca, their sister, and 'her wet-
60 nurse, and Abraham's 'servant and 'his mortals. And blessing are they 'Rebecca, [7]their sister,[c] and saying to her, "Our
sister are 'you. May you become thousands of myriads, and
may your [A]seed tenant 'the gateway of those hating them."

55 Departure **61-67** 61 And rising is Rebecca and her maidens, and they are
riding on the camels, and are going after the man. And
taking is the servant 'Rebecca and is going.
[L]*Lchirai* To- 62 [a]Now Isaac comes [7]into the wilderness,[n] to the well Lehi-
LIVE-mirror 63 rai. And dwelling is he in the land of the south-rim. And
63 Ps4425 La320 forth is Isaac faring to worship in the field before the evening. And lifting is he his eyes and seeing. And behold!
Camels are coming.
[I]*Itzchq* LAUGH-causer 64 And lifting is Rebecca 'her eyes and is seeing 'Isaac and
[alight]COMING-DOWN 65 is alighting off the camel. And saying is she to the servant,
[What]ANY "What 'man is 'this 'going in the field to meet us?"
And saying is the servant, "He is my lord."
And taking is she a 'veil and covering herself.
[thing]word 66 And relating is the servant to Isaac 'all the things which
he had done.

67 And bringing her is Isaac to[d] the tent of Sarah, his
mother. And taking is he 'Rebecca, and becoming is she his
[to]wife, and he is loving her. And [7]comforted[0] is Isaac after
the loss of his mother, [7]Sarah.[0]

2220-24 Son of Relative 251-4

25 And continuing is Abraham, and taking is he a wife, and
2 her name is Keturah. And bearing is she for him 'Zimran
and 'Jokshan and 'Medan and 'Midian and 'Ishbak and 'Shuch.
3 And Jokshan generates 'Sheba [7]and 'Thumun[r] and 'Dedan.
And the sons of Dedan come to be [7]Raguel and Nabdeel and[c]
Ashurim, and Letushim and Leummim.
4 And the sons of Midian are Ephah and Apher and Enoch
and Abida and Eldaah. All these are sons of Keturah.

1127-2219 Abraham's Death 255-11

5 And giving is Abraham 'all which is his to [7]his son[n]
6 Isaac. And to the sons of the concubines which are Abraham's, Abraham gives gifts. And sending them is he away
from [on]Isaac, his son,[in] while he is still living, eastward to
the land of the East.
7 And these are the [N]days of the years of the [=]life of Abraham, which he lives—a hundred [yr] and seventy [yr a] five years.
8 And expiring is Abraham, and dying in a good [N]grey-haired
9 age, old and satisfied [7]with [N]days.[n] And gathered is he to
his [=]people. And entombing 'him are his sons, Isaac and
Ishmael, [to]in the [7]double[0] cave [to]in the field of Ephron, the
10 son of Zohar, the Hittite, which is adjoining Mamre, the
field [7]and the cave[0] which Abraham bought from 'the sons
of Heth. There is made a tomb for Abraham, and Sarah,
his wife.
11 And [b]coming is it, after the death of Abraham, [a]that the
Alueim is blessing 'Isaac, his son. And dwelling is Isaac
[wi]by the well Lehi-rai.

1127-2511 Hindrance 2512-18

12 And these are the genealogical annals of Ishmael, son of
Abraham, whom Hagar, the Egyptian, Sarah's maid, bore
for Abraham: [I]Ishmo-Al HEARING-is-SUBJECTOR
13 And these are the names of the sons of Ishmael, [i]by their
names, for their [=]genealogical annals: The firstborn of
14 Ishmael, Nebaioth; and Kedar and Adbeel and Mibsam and
15 Mishma and Dumah and Massa [7]and[0] Chador and Tema
16 [7]and[0] Jetur [7]and[n] Naphish and Kedemah. These, they are
the sons of Ishmael, and these are their names, in their
environs and in their domiciles—twelve princes for their
[to]clans.

17 And these are the years of the [=]life of Ishmael: a hundred
[yr] and thirty [yr a] seven years. And expiring is he, and died,
and is gathered to his people.

18 And tabernacling are they from Havilah unto Shur,
which is adjoining Egypt, as you come to[d] Assyria. It falls
to him to be adjoining all his brothers. See map page 78.

1110-26 Chosen 2519-3529 2519 Birth-Death 3527-29

19 And these are the genealogical annals of Isaac, son of
Abraham: Abraham begets 'Isaac.

[I]Itzchq LAUGH-causer
[S]Shr e Chiefess
[Reb]Rbq e Enthraller
2 1612 1720 3725 28
[K]Qtur e FUMER (incense)
[Z]Zmr n Musician
[J]Iqsh n STIFF
[Me]Mdn MEASURER-an
[Mi]Md in Quarreler
[I]Ishbq LEAVE-BE-er
[S]Shuch Prostrator
[S]Shb a RETURN
[T]Thum un Amazement
[D]Dd n FOND
[A]Ashuri PROGRESSIVES
[L]Ltushm FORGE
[Leu]Lam im FOLKSTEMS
4 [E]Oiph e Faint
[A]Ophr SOIL
[En]Chnuk DEDICATED
Abido MY-FATHER-KNOWS
[E]Al do e AL-KNOWS
7 124 Adm 3569
[E]Ophr un SOILER
[Z]Tzchr GREY
[H]Chth i Dismay-ite
[M]M mr a [r]Bitterness[r]
8 Js242 9 239
10 2316
See map page 72.
11 1614 2119 2462
[L]L chi rai TO-LIVE-mirror
12 Ishmael, Birth 17
13-16 Sons, Ishmael 18
[N]Nb iuth PRODUCTIONS
[K]Qdr SOMBER
[Mib]M bshm AROMATIC
[Mis]M shmo HEARING
[D]Dum e LIKENESS
[M]M sha Load
[Ch]Chdr CHAMBER
[N]Nphish SOULISH
[K]Qdm e PRECEDENCE
12 Ishmael, Death 17
(born Adm 3480)
Adm 3617
13-16 Sons, Ishmael 18
[H]Chuile PERFORATED
[S]Shur Barricade
[E]M tzr im Narrows
[A]Ashur PROGRESSING
18 1612 391 Jd824
[A]Abr e m FATHER-HIGH-throng

2520-22 Rebecca 3516-20 20 **And coming is Isaac to be forty years of [s]age [t]at his**
Adm 3534 **taking 'Rebecca, the daughter of Bethuel, the Syrian [f]of**
[B]*Bth u-Al* House-of-Al **Padan, [7]Syria,[0] the sister of Laban the Syrian, for his wife.**
[S]*Arm* HEIGHT 21 **And Isaac is entreating Ieue for the invigorating of**
[L]*Lbn* WHITE **[7]Rebecca,[0] his wife, for barren is she. And Ieue is being**
See map page 83. 22 **entreated [t]by him, and pregnant is Rebecca, his wife. And**
bruising themselves are the sons within her. And saying
is she, "Should it be so? Why have I this?" And going is
she to inquire of 'Ieue.

2523-28 Sons 3521-26

I e u e Will-be-ing-was 23 **And saying is Ieue to her,**
Al u eim **"Two [N]nations are in your belly,**
SUBJECT-or-to-s **And two [N]folkstems shall be parted from your bowels.**
(To-subjectors) **And one folkstem shall be more resolute [f]than the other**
[great]MANY **And the greater shall serve [S]the[n] inferior." [folkstem.**

24 **And fulfilled are the days of her bearing. And behold!**
25 **Twins are in her belly. And forth is faring the first, ruddy,**
Adm 3554 **all of him as a fur robe of hair. And calling are they his**
[E]*Oshu* Doer 26 **name Esau. And afterward his brother fares forth. And**
[J]*I oqb* HEEL **his hand is holding [in] the heel of Esau. And [S]calling are they[n]**
[I]*I tzchq* LAUGH-causer **his name Jacob. And Isaac is sixty years of [s]age [t]when**
[Reb]*Rbq e* Enthraller **[7]Rebecca[0] bears 'them.**
[grow]GREATING 27 **And growing up are the lads. And becoming is Esau a**
27 Jb11 8 23 **man, a knowing hunter, a man of the field. [a]Yet Jacob is a**
28 273 4 Hb1120 28 **flawless man, dwelling in tents. And loving is Isaac 'Esau,**
for his game is in his mouth. [a]Yet Rebecca is loving 'Jacob.

2529-34 Birthright 271-3515

29 **And stewing is Jacob a stew. And coming is Esau from**
30 **the field and is faint. And saying is Esau to Jacob, "Glut**
me, pray, [f]with the [N]red—'this 'red stew, for faint am I."
[Ed]*A dum* Red **Therefore called is his name Edom also.**
31 Nu36 12 1Ch51 2 31 **And saying is Jacob [7]to Esau,[0] "Sell, as of 'today, 'your**
birthright to me."
32 **And saying is Esau, "Behold! I am [A]going to die, and [to]**
what is this birthright to me?"
33 **And saying is Jacob [7]to him,[0] "Swear to me as of 'today."**
And swearing is he to him. And selling is [7]Esau[0] 'his birth-
right to Jacob.
34 Hb1216 34 **And Jacob gives [to] Esau bread and stewed lentils. And**
1 1210 **eating is he and drinking, and rising and going. And**
261 Gerar 23 **despising is Esau 'the birthright.**
[P]*Phl shth* Distinguished-SET-ite 26 **And [b]coming is a famine in the land, aside from the first**
[G]*Grr* Chew or Saw **'famine which [b]came in the days of Abraham. And going**
See map page 78. **is Isaac to Abimelech, king of the Philistines, to[d] Gerar.**

2-5 Appearance 24-25 2 **And appearing to him is Ieue and saying, "You must not**
[apprize]SAY **go down to[d] Egypt. Tabernacle in the land of which I apprize**
3 1315 2813 5024 Ex36 3 **[to] you. Sojourn in 'this 'land, and I will come to be with you**
Mt2223-33 **and will bless you. For to you and to your [N]seed will I give**
[carry out]RISE **'all 'these 'lands, and carry out will I 'the oath which I swore**
4 **to Abraham, your father. And increase will I 'your [N]seed as**
the stars of the heavens, and give will I to your [A]seed 'all
'these 'lands. And blessed, in your [A]seed, are all the nations
5 Jn117 Ro1017 5 **of the earth, inasmuch as hearken did Abraham, [7]your**
father,[n] [t]to My [N]voice and kept My charge, My instructions,
My statutes, and My laws."

6 **And dwelling is Isaac in Gerar. [7]And asking are the mor-** 26 6-11 Wives 34-35
7 **tals of the place as to [7]Rebecca,[0] his wife. And saying is he,** 7 12 13 20 2 12
"My sister is she." For he fears to say, "My wife [S]is she,"[n] Reb *Rbq e* Enthraller
lest the mortals of the place kill [7]him[0] on account of Rebecca,
8 **for a good appearance has she. And [b]coming is it that his** A *Ab i mlk* MY-
·days there are long. And gazing is Abimelech, king [7]of FATHER (is) KING
Gerar[0] of the Philistines, through a ·window, and is seeing, through about
and behold! Isaac is having fun \with Rebecca, his wife. P *Phl shth* Distinguished-
9 **And calling is Abimelech [to] Isaac and saying [7]to him,[0] "Yea,** SET-ite
behold! Your wife is she! And how say you, 'My sister is how WHERE-AS
she'?"

And saying to him is Isaac, that, "I say it lest I die on her I *I tzchq* LAUGH-causer
account."

10 **And saying is Abimelech [7]to him,[0] "What is this you do**
to us? As if it were a little thing if one of [7]my[0] ·people lie
with \your wife and you bring the guilt upon us!"

11 **And instructing is Abimelech \all [7]his[n] ·people [to] saying,**
"[7]Everyone[0] ·touching ·this [in]·man [a]or [in] his wife shall [d]surely H die yea die[b]
be [c]put to death."

12 **And sowing is Isaac in ·that ·land and is finding in ·that** 12-22 Abimelech 26-33
·year a hundredfold of =barley. And blessing him is Ieue.
13 **And great is growing the man. And going is he to go on**
14 **and grow greater, till [tt] he is great exceedingly. And it is** tt THAT
[b]coming at his acquiring flocks and acquiring herds and
many to serve, [a]that jealous are the Philistines of \him.
15 **And all the wells which his father's servants had delved in**
the days of Abraham, his father, the Philistines stop them
up, and are filling them with soil.
16 **And saying is Abimelech to Isaac, "Go from our people,**
17 **for you are very much stauncher [f]than we." And going is**
Isaac thence, and is camping in the watercourse of Gerar,
and is dwelling there.
18 **And returning is Isaac and delving \the wells of ·water**
which were delved by [7]servants[n] of Abraham, his father, and
the Philistines had stopped them up after the death of
Abraham, [7]his father.[0] And calling is he [to] them by names
[as] according to the names which [7]Abraham,[0] his father, called
[to] them. 
19 **And delving are the servants of Isaac in the watercourse**
[7]of Gerar,[0] and finding are they there a well of =living water. 19 21 19
20 **And contending are the graziers of Gerar with Isaac's** G *Gr r* Chew or Saw
graziers [to] saying, "Ours is the water." And calling is he
the name of the well Esek, for extortionate show they E *Oshq* EXTORTION
21 **themselves with him. [7]And shifting is Isaac thence,[0] and**
delving are they another well. [a]Yet contending are they,
moreover, over it. And calling is he its name Sitnah. S *Shtn e* Accusation
22 **And shifting is he thence, and delving [8]are they[c] another**
well. And they do not contend over it. And calling is he its
name Rehoboth. And saying is he, "For now Ieue widens R *Rchb uth* WIDE
for us, and [F]fruitful are we in the land." B *Bar-shbo* WELL-oath
23 **And up is he going thence to Beer-sheba.** 26 1 Beer-sheba 23

24 **And appearing to him is Ieue in ·that \night, and saying,** 2-5 Appearance 24-25
"I am the Alueim of Abraham your father. You must not *I e u e*
fear, for \with you am I. And bless you will I, and increase Will-be-ing-was
will I \your [A]seed for the sake of Abraham [7]your father,[0]

Al u eim SUBJECT-or-to-s (To-subjectors)
25 My servant." And building is he an altar there. And calling
is he [i]on the [N]name of Ieue. And stretching out is he his
tent there. And digging are the servants of Isaac a well.

26 2122
12-22 Abimelech 26-33
[A]*Ab i mlk* MY-FATHER-is-KING
[G]*Gr r* Chew or saw
[Ah]*Achz th* 'HOLD-GIVE'
[P]*Phi kl* MOUTH-ALL

26 And Abimelech goes to him from Gerar [a]with Ahuzzath,
27 his associate, and Phicol, the chief of his host. And saying
to them is Isaac, "For what reason do you come to me,
[a]when you hate 'me and you are sending me away from
'you?"
28 And saying are they, "We see, yea, see that Ieue has
come to be with you, and we are saying, 'Let there [b]come,
pray, an oath of imprecation between us, between us and
29 [bt]you, and contract will we a covenant with you. Should
you do [wi]to us evil, [as]when [w]we do not touch you, and [as]when
[w]we do [wi]to you but good, and send you away in peace?'
You are now the blest of Ieue."
30 And making is he for them a feast, and eating are they
31 and drinking. And [c]rising early are they in the morning,
and swearing are they, a man to his [F]brother. And sending
them away is Isaac. And they are going from 'him in peace.

[I]*I tzchq* LAUGH-causer

32 And [b]coming is it [i]on 'that 'day, coming also are servants
of Isaac. And telling are they [to] him concerning the [=]case of
the well which they delve, and are saying to him, "We found
33 water." And calling is he 'it Sheba. Therefore the name of
the city is Beer-sheba till 'this 'day.

[S]*Shbo e* SATISFACTION
[B]*Bar-Shbo* WELL-oath
33 2131
6-11 Wives 34-35
[J]*I eud ith* Acclaimer-ess
[B]*Bar i* WELL-ite
[H]*Chth i* Dismay-ite
[B]*Bsh m th* 'AROMATICS'
[E]*A i lun* Oak

[E]*Osh u* Doer *34* 362 5 14 24 25 1K1029 Adm 3594

34 And [b]coming is Esau to be forty years [s]old [a]when he is
taking as wife 'Judith, the daughter of Beeri, the Hittite,
35 and 'Bashemath, the daughter of Elon, the '[7]Hivite.[o] And
coming are they to be a [M]bitterness of spirit to Isaac and
[to]Rebecca.

2529-34 Birthright 271-3515

271-40 Deception-Reconciliation 323-3317

1 3528
[eld]GREATER

27 And [b]coming it is that old is Isaac, dim-sighted are his
eyes. And calling is he 'Esau, his 'elder son, and is saying
to him, "My son!" And saying is he to him, "Behold me!"
2 And saying is he, "Behold, pray! Old am I, [7]and[c] not know
3 do I the day of my death. And now, pray, lift up your gear,
your hanger and your bow, and fare forth to the field and
4 hunt game for me, and make for me tasties, such as [w]I love,
and bring them to me, and eat will I, in order that my
[N]soul may bless you [in] ere I die."

3 2529
4 2528 Hb1120
[Reb]*Rbq e* Enthraller
[E]*Osh u* Doer
[spoke]SAY
[J]*I oqb* HEEL

5 And Rebecca is hearing Isaac [in] speaking to Esau, his son.
And going is Esau to the field to hunt game [7]for his father.[o]
6 And Rebecca spoke to Jacob, her son, [7]the inferior in
station[o], [to]saying, "Behold! I heard 'your father speaking
7 to Esau, your brother, [to]saying, 'Bring [to] me game and
make for me tasties, and eat will I and bless you will I
8 before Ieue before my death.' And now, my son, hearken [t]to
9 my [N]voice [t]in that which I am instructing 'you. Go, pray, to
the flock, and take for me thence two kids of the goats,
[7]tender and[o] good, and I will make of 'them tasties for your
10 father, such as [w]he loves, and you shall bring them to your
father, and eat will he, in order [w]that [7]your father[o] may
bless you before his death."
11 And saying is Jacob to Rebecca, his mother, "Behold!

Esau, my brother, is a hairy man, and I am a slick man. *Al u e im*
12 **Perhaps my father will feel me, and become will I in his** SUBJECT-or-to-s (To-subjectors)
ᴬeyes as one who leads him astray, and I bring on me a
slight and not a blessing."
13 **And saying to him is his mother,** "On me be your slight,
my son. Yea, hearken ᵗto my ᴺvoice and go. Take them for
me."
14 **And going is he and taking and bringing them to his**
mother. And making is his mother tasties, such as ʷ his
father loves.
15 **And taking is Rebecca the ˋcoveted garments of Esau,** 15 Hb1216
her ·elder son, which are ˋwith her in the house, and is eldGREATER
16 **putting them on ˋJacob, her ·smaller son. And ˋthe skins of** RebRbqe Enthraller
the kids of the goats she puts on ᵒⁿ his hands and on the EOshu Doer
17 **slick of his neck. And giving is she ˋthe tasties and ˋthe** JIoqb HEEL
bread which she made into the hand of Jacob, her son.
18 **And coming is he to his father and saying, "My father!"**
And saying is he, "Behold me! Who are you, my son?" WhoANY
19 **And saying is Jacob to his father, "I am Esau, your first-**
born. I did as ʷ you spoke to me. Rise, pray! Sit and eat ᶠof
my game, in order that your ᴺsoul may be blessing me."
20 **And saying is Isaac to his son, "What is this? You hasted** IItzchq LAUGH-causer
to find it, my son!"
And saying is he, "For Ieue, your Alueim, caused it to
happen before me."
21 **And saying is Isaac to Jacob, "Come close, pray, and I**
will feel you, my son. Is this you, my son Esau, or not?" orIF
22 **And close is Jacob coming to Isaac, his father. And feeling**
him is he and saying, "The voice is the voice of Jacob, ᵃyet
the hands are the hands of Esau."
23 **ᵃYet he did not identify him, for his hands are become as** idenRECOGNIZE
the hands of Esau, his brother, hairy. And blessing him is
he.
24 **And saying is he, "This is you, my son Esau?"**
And saying is he, "I am."
25 **And saying is he, "ᶜBring it close to me, and I will eat**
ᶠof my son's game, that my ᴺsoul may be blessing you."
And close is he ᶜbringing it to him, and he is eating. And
he is bringing ᵗᵒ him wine, and he is drinking.
26 **And saying to him is Isaac, his father, "Come close, pray,**
and kiss ᵗᵒ me, my son."
27 **And close is he coming and kissing ᵗᵒ him. And smelling is**
he ˋthe smell of his garments and is blessing him, ᵃ saying,

"See! The smell of my son
Is as the smell of the ʼfullⁿ field ʷ blessed by Ieue. 28 La212
28 **And give ᵗᵒ you will the Alueim ᶠ the night mist of the heavens.**
And the ᶠ oil of the earth, and much grain and grape juice.
29 **Serve you shall peoples,**
And down shall bow to you the folkstems.
Master be you ᵗover your brothers,
And down to you shall bow the sons of your mother,
One cursing you is accursed.
And one blessing you is blessed!"

30 **And ᵇcoming is it, as ʷ Isaac finishes ᵗᵒ blessing ˋJacob,**

[H]forth, yea forth[b] [7]his son,[0] and [b]coming, yea [f]barely forth, is Jacob from 'the
[I]*I tzchq* LAUGH-causer [N]face of Isaac, his father, [a]when Esau, his brother, comes
I e u e 31 from his hunting. And making tasties is he, moreover, and
Will-be-ing-was is bringing them to his father. And saying is he to his
father, "Rise will my father and eat [f]of his son's game, in
order that bless me will your [N]soul."
[Who]ANY 32 And saying to him is Isaac, his father, "Who are you?"
[E]*Osh u* Doer And saying is he, "I am your son, your firstborn, Esau."
33 2526 3228 Hb1217 33 And trembling is Isaac, a trembling, great unto excess.
[Who]ANY And saying is he, "Who, indeed, was he, the hunter of
game [a] who brought it to me, and I ate [f]of all [in] ere you
came, and bless him did I? [S]And,[n] moreover, blest shall he
be[c]!"
34 [7]And [b]coming is it,[n] as Esau hears 'the words of his father
[7]Isaac,[0] [a]that crying is he a cry great and bitter unto excess.
And saying is he to his father, "Bless me, me moreover, my
father!"
35 And saying is he [7]to him[0], "Your brother came [i]with
deceit, and he has taken 'your blessing."
[Because]THAT 36 And saying is he, "Because he calls his name Jacob, is it
[J]*I oqb* HEEL [a]that he is circumventing me [7]already[7] this twice? 'My
birthright took he. And, behold! Now he takes my blessing!"
And saying is [7]Esau to his father,[0] "Have you not besides
a blessing for me?"
37 2S814 37 And answering is Isaac and saying to Esau, "Behold! As
master have I placed him [t]over you, and 'all of his brothers
have I given to him for servants, and with grain and grape
juice I support him. And for you, indeed, what shall I do,
my son?"
38 And saying is Esau to his father, "Your one blessing is it,
my father? Bless me, me moreover, my father!" [7a]Yet silent
is Isaac,[7] and lifting is Esau his voice and is lamenting.
39 And answering is Isaac, his father, and saying to him,

"Behold! Away from the=oil of the earth is coming to be your
And from the night mist of the heavens above. [dwelling,
40 1S1447 2S814 1K2247 40 And [on]by your [A]sword shall you live,
2K820 22 And your brother shall you serve.
[a]Yet it [b]comes, as [w] you are caused to sway,
You also break off his [F]yoke off your neck."

2741 Grudge 3318-3431 41 And a grudge is Esau holding against 'Jacob on account
of the blessing with which his father blesses him. And
saying is Esau in his [A]heart, "Approaching are the days of
mourning for my father, [a]when I will kill 'Jacob, my
brother."

2742-285 Departure, Return 351-15

[eld]GREATER 42 And told to Rebecca are 'the words of Esau, her 'elder
[Reb]*Rbq e* Enthraller son. And sending is she, and calling for Jacob, her 'smaller
son, and saying is she to him, "Behold! Esau, your brother,
43 1131 43 is consoling himself as to you, intending to kill you. And
See map page 83. now, my son, hearken [i]to my [N]voice, and rise, run away [t]by
[S]*Arm* HEIGHT 44 yourself [7]to Syria,[0] to Laban, my brother, to[d] Charan. And
[L]*Lbn* WHITE dwell with him several days, till [w]back is turning your
[O]*Chr n* HEATED 45 brother's fury, till [w]back turns your brother's anger from
you, and forgotten has he 'what you did to him, and I send

and take you thence. Why shall I be bereaved, moreover, of *I e u e*
you two in one day?" Will-be-ing-was
46 And saying is Rebecca to Isaac, "Irritated am I in my *46* 2634 35
"life [f]because of the presence of the daughters of [7]the sons [Reb]*Rbq e* Enthraller
of[o] Heth. Should Jacob take a wife such as these from the [I]*I tzchq* LAUGH-causer
daughters of Heth, from the daughters of the [A]land,[to] what [J]*I oqb* HEEL
has "life for me?" [H]*Chth* Dismay

28 And calling is Isaac to Jacob, and is blessing 'him and *1* 243
instructing him. And saying is he to him, "Not take shall [C]*Kno n* SUBMITTER
2 you a wife from the daughters of Canaan. Rise, go to[d]
Padan, Syria, the home of Bethuel, your mother's father. [S]*Arm* HEIGHT
and take for yourself thence a wife, from the daughters of [B]*Bth u-Al* House-of-Al
3 Laban, the brother of your mother. And Al-Who-Suffices [L]*Lbn* WHITE
will bless 'you and [c]make you [f]fruitful and increase you, and
4 you shall become [to] an assembly of peoples. And give to you *4* 126
will He 'the blessing of Abraham, [7]my father,[o] to you and [A]*Ab r e m* FATHER-
to your [A]seed 'with you, for you to tenant 'the land of your HIGH-throng
sojournings, [w] given by the Alueim to Abraham."
5 And Isaac is sending 'Jacob away. And going is he to[d]
Padan, Syria, to Laban, son of Bethuel the Syrian, brother [P]*Phd n* RANSOM
of Rebecca, the mother of Jacob and Esau. [Reb]*Rbq e* Enthraller

28[6-9] Esau's Wives-Jacob's 29[1]-31[55]

6 And seeing is Esau that Isaac blesses 'Jacob and sends [Es]*Osh u* Doer
'him to[d] Padan, Syria, to take thence a wife for himself,
and, in his blessing 'him, he is also instructing [on] him,[to] saying, "You shall not take a wife from the daughters of Ca-
7 naan," and that Jacob is hearkening to his father and to *8* 2634 35
8 his mother, and is going to[d] Padan, Syria. And seeing is *9* 363
Esau that evil are the daughters of Canaan in the [A]eyes of [I]*I shmo-Al* HEARING-
9 Isaac, his father. And going is Esau to Ishmael, and taking is-SUBJECTOR
'Mahalath, a daughter of Ishmael, Abraham's son, sister of [M]*M chl th* Illnesses
Nebaioth, [on] to his wives, for his wife. [N]*Nb i uth* PRODUCTIONS

28[10-22] Bethel 32[1-2]

10 And forth is Jacob faring from Beer-sheba, and going [B]*Bar-Shbo* WELL-oath
11 toward Charan. And coming is he upon [in] a place and is [C]*Chr n* HEATED
lodging there, for the sun has set. And taking is he one [f]of [set]INed
the stones of the place, and is placing it for his "pillow, and
12 lying down is he in 'that place. And dreaming is he, and, *12* Jn1[51]
behold! [v]A stairway set up earthward, [a]with its head touch- [set up]STATIONED
ing the heavens. And behold! Messengers of the Alueim are
ascending and descending [i]on it.
13 And behold! Ieue is stationed on it. And saying is He. *13* 13[15] 26[3] 50[24]
"I am Ieue, the Alueim of Abraham, your forefather, and
the Alueim of Isaac. [7]Do not fear.[o] The land on which you
14 are lying, to you will I give it, and to your [A]seed. And *14* 15[5] 17[7]
become shall your [A]seed as the soil of the land. And breach
forth will you seaward and eastward and northward and
toward the south-rim. And blest, in you, are all the families
15 of the [A]ground, and in your [A]seed. And, behold! I am with
you, and keep you in every [7f]way[o] which you shall go, and *15* Dt31[6] Js1[5 8]
will restore you to 'this 'ground, for not forsake you will I, 1Ch28[20] Hb13[5 6]
till [w] I should do [7]all[o] 'which I have spoken to you."[v]
16 And waking is Jacob from his sleep and saying, "Surely,
17 forsooth, Ieue is in 'this place, and I knew it not." And *17* 1Ch22[1] Ps146[5]
fearing is he and saying, "What a fearful 'place is 'this! But

Al u eim is not this rather the [M]house of the Alueim, and this the
SUBJECT-or-to-s (To-subjectors) [M]gateway of the heavens?"
18 Lv261 Dt1622 18 And early is Jacob [c]rising in the morning, and taking is
he 'the stone which he had placed ⁷there° for his =pillow,
topHEAD and is placing 'it for a monument, and pouring oil on its top.
[B]Bith-Al House-of-Al 19 And calling is ⁷Jacob° 'the name of 'that 'place Beth-El. [a]
[L]Luz DEVIATOR Howbeit, Luz was the name of the city [t]at first.
[J]Ioqb HEEL 20 And vowing is Jacob a vow,[to]saying, "Should it be coming
See map page 78. that Ieue Alueim stands by me, and [F]keeps me in 'this
[F]way which I am going, and gives to me [N]bread to eat and
21 a [N]garment to put on, and I return in peace to my father's
22 1420 22 household,[a]then Ieue becomes my[to]Alueim, and 'this 'stone,
which I place for a monument, shall become the house of
Alueim ⁷for me.° And of all [w]that Thou art giving to me,
tithe, yea, tithe it will I for Thee."

291-14 Arrival 3117-55 29 And [N]lifting is Jacob his feet and is going toward the
2 2119 land of the [A]sons of the [A]east, ⁷to Laban, the son of Bethuel,
the Syrian, brother of Rebecca, the mother of Jacob and
2 Esau.° And seeing is he, and, behold! A well in the field.
And, behold! There are three droves of small cattle reclin-
givcause ing [on]at it, for from 'that 'well are they [c]giving the droves
a drink. And the stone on the [F]mouth of the well is great.
3 And gathered there are all the droves. And they roll 'the
givcause stone off the [F]mouth of the well and [c]give 'the small cattle
a drink. [a]Then they restore 'the stone on the [F]mouth of the
well to its place.
4 And saying to them is Jacob, "My [F]brethen, whence are
you?"
[U]Chr n HEATED And saying are they, "From Charan are we."
5 2415 5 And saying is he to them, "Do you know 'Laban, the son
[N]Nch u r SNORTER of Nahor?"
And saying are they, "We know him."
fare wellpeace 6 And saying is he to them, "Fares he well?"
[R]Rchl EWE And saying are they, "Well fares he. And, behold! Rachel,
his daughter, is coming with the flock."
7 And saying is ⁷Jacob° [S]to them,[n] "Behold! Still is the day
givcause great. It is not seasonable to gather the cattle. [c]Give a drink
to the flock, and go, graze them."
8 And saying are they, "We cannot till [w]gathering are all
9 Ex216 17 1S1713-15 the ⁷herds,[n] and they roll 'the stone off the [F]mouth of the
givcause well and [c]give a drink to the flocks."
9 At his still speaking with them, Rachel, ⁷the daughter of
Laban,° comes with the flock which is her father's, for
10 the grazier is she of ⁷her father's flock.° And [b]coming is it,
as [w]Jacob sees 'Rachel, the daughter of Laban, his mother's
brother, and 'the flock of Laban, his mother's brother, [a]then
close is coming Jacob, and he is rolling 'the stone off the
[F]mouth of the well, and is [c]giving a drink to the flock of
11 Laban, his mother's brother. And Jacob is kissing[to]Rachel,
12 and is [F]lifting up 'his voice and lamenting. And telling is
Jacob to Rachel that he is her father's brother, and that the
RebRbq e Enthraller son of Rebecca is he. And running is she and telling[to]her
thingwords father ⁷these things.°
13 And [b]coming is it, as Laban hears 'the report of Jacob,
his sister's son, running is he also to meet him. And em-

bracing[to]him is he and kissing[to]him, and bringing him to *Al u e im*
his house. And relating is he to Laban 'all 'these 'things. SUBJECT-or-to-s (To-subjectors)
14 And saying to him is Laban, "Yea, my [N]bone and my thingword
[N]flesh are you." And dwelling with him is he the days of a [L]*Lbn* WHITE
month.

2915-3026 Service 3027-3116

15 And saying is Laban to Jacob, "Seeing that my brother [J]*Ioqb* HEEL
are you, [a]then serve you me gratuitously? Tell[to]me what
is your hire."
16 [a]Now[to]Laban had two daughters. The name of the elder [eld]GREATER
17 is Leah and the name of the younger is Rachel. And the [yng]SMALLER
eyes of Leah are tender, [a]yet Rachel [b]is lovely in shapeli- [L]*Lae* 'No-thing'
18 ness, and lovely in appearance. And loving is Jacob 'Rachel. [R]*Rchl* EWE
And saying is he, "Serve you will I seven years [i]for *17* 396
Rachel, your 'younger daughter." [yng]SMALLER
19 And saying [7]to him[0] is Laban, "Better I give 'her to you
[f]than that I give 'her to another man. Dwell, withal."
20 And serving is Jacob [i]for Rachel seven years. And be- *20* Hol212
coming are they in his [A]eyes as several days, in his love
'for her.
21 And saying is Jacob to Laban, "Grant me 'my wife, for
fulfilled are my days, and I will come to her."
22 And gathering is Laban 'all the mortals of the place and
23 is making a feast. And [b]coming is it in the evening [a]that
[7]Laban[0] is taking 'Leah, his daughter, and is bringing 'her
24 to [7]Jacob,[0] and [7]Jacob[n] is coming to her. And giving is
Laban 'Zilpah, his maid, to Leah, his daughter, [S]for[n] a [Z]*Zlphe* REPLETE-MOUTH
25 maid. And [b]coming is it in the morning, and, behold! She is
Leah. And saying is [7]Jacob[0] to Laban, "What is this you
do to me? Did I not [i]for Rachel serve with you? And why
do you deceive me?"
26 And saying is Laban, "Not so is it being done in our
place, to give the inferior in station before the firstborn.
27 Fulfill the seven of this one, and give will [7]I[n] to you 'this
one, moreover, [i]for the service which you shall serve,
withal, further another seven years."
28 And doing so is Jacob. And fulfilling is he this one's
seven. And giving to him is [7]Laban[0] 'Rachel, his daughter,
29 for his wife. And giving is Laban 'Bilhah, his maid, to [B]*Blee* DISINTEGRATED
30 Rachel, his daughter, for her[to]maid. And coming is he,
moreover, to Rachel, and, moreover, loving is he 'Rachel
more [f]than Leah. And serving is he with him further another seven years.
31 And seeing is Ieue that Leah is hated, and opening is He *31* Dt2115
32 'her womb. [a]Yet Rachel is barren. And pregnant is Leah
and is bearing a son [7]for Jacob.[0] And calling is she 'his name
Reuben for she says, "For see does Ieue[in]my humiliation [R]*Raubn* SEE-son
[7]and gives me a son,[0] for now my husband will love me."
33 And pregnant is [7]Leah[0] again, and is bearing a [7]second[0] son
[7]for Jacob.[0] And saying is she, "For hearing is Ieue that
hated am I, and giving to me is He 'this one, moreover."
34 And calling is she 'his name Simeon. And pregnant is she [S]*Shmoun* HEARER
again and is bearing a son. And saying is she, "Now 'once
more will my husband be obligated to me, for I bear for him *35* 498
35 three sons." Therefore calling is [7]she[n] his name Levi. And [L]*Lui* OBLIGATED

Ieue Will-be-ing-was pregnant is she again, and is bearing a son. And saying is
she, "[7]Now[0] ·once more will I acclaim ‵Ieue." Therefore call-
[J]*Ieude* Acclaimer ing is she his name Judah. And staying is she from bearing.
[stay]STANDING 30 And seeing is Rachel that she does not bear for Jacob.
[R]*Rchl* EWE And jealous is Rachel [i]of her sister. And saying is she to
[J]*Ioqb* HEEL Jacob, "Grant [to]me sons! And, should there be none, I will
die."
2 161-3 2931 2 And [A]hot is the anger of Jacob [i]against Rachel. And saying is he [7]to her,[0] "In Alueim's stead am I, Who withholds
from you the [F]fruit of the belly?"
3 And saying is [7]Rachel to Jacob,[0] "Behold my maidservant
[B]*Blee* DISINTEGRATED Bilhah. Come to her and bear shall she on my knees, and I,
4 moreover, will be built [f]by her." And giving [to]him is she
‵Bilhah, her maid, for a wife. And coming is Jacob to her.
5 And pregnant is [7]Rachel's maid,[0] Bilhah, and is bearing for
6 Jacob a son. And saying is Rachel, "Adjudicated has the
Alueim for me, and, moreover, He hears [in]my [N]voice, and
[D]*Dn* ADJUDICATE is giving to me a son." Therefore she calls his name Dan.
7 And pregnant is she again, and bearing is Bilhah, Rachel's
8 maid, a second son for Jacob. And saying is Rachel, "With
twistings of the Alueim am I twisted with my sister, [S]and[n]
[N]*Nphthli* TWISTED moreover, I prevail." And calling is she his name Naphtali.
[L]*Lae* ?No-thing? 9 And seeing is Leah that she stays from bearing. And
[stay]STAND taking is she ‵Zilpah, her maid, and is giving ‵her to Jacob
[Z]*Zlphe* REPLETE-MOUTH 10 for a wife. [7]And coming is Jacob to her,[0] and Zilpah, Leah's
11 Js1117 127 Is6511 11 maid, is [7]pregnant and[0] bearing for Jacob a son. And saying is Leah, "[7]Coming[0] is a [F]raid!" And calling is she ‵his
[G]*Gd* RAID 12 name Gad. And [7]pregnant is[0] Zilpah, Leah's maid, and is
13 Dt3324 13 bearing a second son for Jacob. And saying is Leah "[i]Happi-
ness is mine, for the daughters call me happy." And calling
[A]*Ashur* PROGRESS is she ‵his name Ashur.
[R]*Raubn* SEE-son 14 And going is Reuben in the days of [=]wheat harvest and
finding mandrakes in the field, and is bringing ‵them to his
mother, Leah. And saying is Rachel to Leah, [7]her sister,[0]
"Give to me, pray, [f]of your son's mandrakes."
15 And saying is [7]Leah[0] to her, "[7]No![0] Is it little of you to
take ‵my husband, [a]then to take, moreover, my son's ‵man-
drakes?" And saying is Rachel, "[7]Not so![n] He shall lie with
you [7]·this[0] night, [u]for your son's mandrakes."
16 And coming is Jacob from the field in the evening, and
forth is faring Leah to meet him. And saying is she, "To
me are you coming [S]tonight,[n] for I hired, yea, hired you
[i]with my son's mandrakes." And lying is he with her in that
·night.
17 And hearkening is the Alueim to Leah, and pregnant is
18 she and is bearing for Jacob a fifth son. And saying is
Leah, "Giving is the Alueim my hire, for [w]I give my maid
[I]*Ishshkr* Forsooth-hire to my husband." And calling is she ‵his name Issachar.
19 And pregnant again is Leah, and is bearing a sixth son for
20 Jacob. And saying is Leah, "Dowering me is the Alueim
with a good dowry ·this time. My husband will prefer me,
for I bear for him six sons." And calling is she ‵his name
[Z]*Zbulun* PREFERRED 21 Zebulon. And afterward she bears a daughter. And calling
[D]*Dine* ADJUDICATRESS is she ‵her name Dinah.
22 And remembering is the Alueim ‵Rachel and hearkening
23 to her is the Alueim and opening ‵her womb. And pregnant

is she and bearing [7]for Jacob[0] a son. And saying is [7]Rachel,[0] [J]Ioqb HEEL
24 "The **Alueim** gathers up ‛my reproach." And calling is she Al u e im
‛his name Joseph saying, "Adding is Ieue to me another SUBJECT-or-to-s (To-subjectors)
son." [J]Iusph Add-er
25 And [b]coming is it, as[w] Rachel bears ‛Joseph, [a]then saying [R]Rchl EWE
is Jacob to Laban, "Send me, and I will go to my place and [L]Lbn WHITE
26 to my land. Give me ‛my wives and ‛my children, [i]for whom
I have served ‛you, and go will I, for you know ‛my service
with which I have served you."

2915-3026 Service 3027-3116

27 And saying to him is Laban, "If, pray, I find grace in
your [A]eyes! I augur [a]that Ieue's blessing me is due to your
28 [7]coming[0]." And saying is he, "Specify your hire [on]to me,
and I will give it."
29 And saying is [7]Jacob[0] to him, "You know ‛[w]how I have
30 served you, and ‛[w]what becomes of your cattle ‛with me. For
little was that which came to be yours before, and breaching is it into much. And blessing ‛you is Ieue, [t]at my foot-
steps. [a]Yet now, when shall I do something, moreover I,
for my own household?"
31 And saying [7]to him is Laban,[0] "What shall I give to you?"
And saying is Jacob, "Naught shall you give [to] me. If you
will do for me ·this ·thing, I will return: Graze will I your thing word
32 flock [7]and[0] [F]keep it, pass will I among all your flock ·today
to [c]take away thence every speckled and flecked flockling,
also every brown flockling among the sheep, and [7]all[0] the
flecked and speckled among the goats, and it becomes my
33 hire. And responding is my [I]righteousness [i]for me, [i]on the
morrow day, for on account of my hire shall [7]it[0] come before
you. Every one in which there is no speck and fleck among
the goats, and brown among the sheep, stolen is it if ‛with
me."
34 And saying [7]to him[0] is Laban, "Behold! O that it shall
[b]come [as]according to your [N]word!"
35 And [c]taking away is he in ·that day the striped and the
flecked ‛·bucks, and ‛all the speckled and the flecked ·she-
goats, [7]and[0] everyone which has white in it, and all the
brown among the sheep, and giving them is he into the
36 [A]hands of his sons. And placing is he a [A]way of three days
between [7]them[0] and [bt] Jacob's. And Jacob is grazing the
‛flock of Laban, ·what is [=]left.
37 And taking is Jacob for himself sticks of smooth white
poplar and of hazel and of the plane tree, and is peeling in
them white peelings, baring the white which is on the
38 sticks. And putting is he ‛the sticks which he peeled in the
troughs, in the drinking ·water, to which the flocks are
coming to drink [to] opposite the flocks. And warm with de-
39 sire are they [7]at the sticks[0] [i]when they come to drink. And
[A]warm with desire are the flocks at the sticks, and are
bearing ·small cattle, striped, speckled, and flecked.
40 And the sheep Jacob parts, and he puts the faces of the puts GIVES
flocks towards the striped and all the brown among
Laban's flock. And he is setting his own droves [to] alone, and
does not set them [on]with Laban's flock.

Ieue Will-be-ing-was sinewy TIE 41 **And it [b]comes, in every [7]season[0] of [A]warming with desire**
of the sinewy of the flock, [a]then Jacob places 'the sticks
[t]before the eyes of the flock, in the troughs, for [7]them[0] to
42 [A]**warm with desire among the sticks. [a]Yet [i]with the droop-**
sinewy TIE **ing ones of the flock he is not placing them. And the droop-**
[L]*Lbn* WHITE **ing became Laban's and the sinewy Jacob's.**

43 **And breaching is the man exceeding exceedingly, and**
[b]coming is he to have many small cattle [7]and herds[0] and
maids and servants and camels and asses.

[J]*Ioqb* HEEL **31** **And hearing is [7]Jacob[0] 'the words of Laban's sons,[to] say-**
ing, "Taking is Jacob 'all which was our father's. And from
2 **that which is our father's he makes 'all 'this '[A]glory." And**
seeing is Jacob 'the [N]face of Laban, and behold! It is not
with him as heretofore.

3 **And saying is Ieue to Jacob, "Return to the land of your**
forefathers and to your kindred, and come will I to be with
you."

[R]*Rchl* EWE 4 **And sending is Jacob and calling[to] Rachel and[to] Leah to**
[L]*Lae* 'No-thing' 5 **the field, to his flock. And saying is he to them, "Seeing am**
I 'the [N]face of your father, that it is not toward me as
heretofore. And the Alueim of my father [b]came to stand by
6 **me. And you know that [i]with all my vigor I served 'your**
7 **father. [a]Yet your father trifles [i]with me, and varied 'my**
allow GIVE **hire at ten countings. [a]Yet the Alueim did not allow him to**
8 **[c]do evil withal. If thus he is saying: 'The speckled shall be[c]**
your hire,' [a]then bear do all the flock speckled. And if thus
he is saying: 'The striped shall be[c] your hire,' [a]then bear do
9 **all the flock striped. And rescuing is the Alueim the 'cattle**
of your father and is giving them to me.

10 2812 13 4816 10 **"And [b]coming is it [i]at the season that the flock is [A]warm**
with desire,[a]that I am lifting my eyes and seeing in a dream
and, behold! [V]The he-goats [7]and the rams[0] 'that go up on the
11 **small cattle are striped, speckled, and dappled. And saying**
to me is a messenger of the Alueim in a dream. 'Jacob!' And
12 Ps5010 12 **saying am I, 'Behold me!' And saying is He, 'Lift your eyes,**
pray, and see that 'all the he-goats [7]and the rams[0] 'going 'up
on the small cattle are striped, speckled, and dappled, for
[B]*Bith-Al* House-of-Al 13 **I see 'all [w]that Laban is doing to you. I am the Al of Beth-El,**
where you anointed the monument [7]and[n] where you vowed
a vow to Me. [S]And[n] now, rise, fare forth from 'this 'land,
and return to the land of your kindred, [7]and I will come to
be with you.[0]'"[V]

14 **And answering are Rachel and Leah, and saying are they**
to him, "Is there further for us a portion and allotment in
15 **the household of our father? Are not we reckoned [7]as[n] for-**
even moreover **eigners [t]by him? For he [F]sold us, and [F]devouring is he, even**
devour EATING 16 **[F]devouring 'our money. For all the riches [7]and the glory[0]**
which the Alueim rescues from our father, ours is it and
our sons'. And now, all [w]that the Alueim says to you, do."

291-14 Return 3117-55 17 **And rising is Jacob, and lifting 'his wives and 'his sons**
18 **on 'camels, and leading away 'all his cattle, and 'all his**
goods which he got, the cattle he acquired, which he got in

Padan, Syria, to come to Isaac, his father, to[d] the land of PPhdn RANSOM
Canaan. See map page 83. ITzchq LAUGH-causer
19 **And Laban goes to shear 'his flock. And stealing is** OKnon SUBMITTER
20 **Rachel 'the household alueim which are her father's. And** 19 3027 352
[F]**stealing is Jacob 'the** [F]heart out of **Laban, the Syrian, on** 21 Nu321 39 361
21 **failing to tell** [to]**him that he is running away. And away is** Dt312-16
he running, he and all which is his. And rising is he and crossPASSING
crossing 'the stream, and is setting 'his [N]**face** toward **mount** setPLACING
·Gilead. GGlod Mound of Witness

22 **And it is being told** [to]**Laban,** ⁷**the Syrian,**° [i]**on the third** LLbn WHITE
23 **·day, that Jacob ran away. And taking is he** ⁷**all**° **his breth-** SArm HEIGHT
ren with him, and is pursuing after him a [A]**way of seven**
days, and hard is he following after 'him in mount ·Gilead. hard folCLINGING
24 **And coming is the Alueim to Laban, the Syrian, in a** See map page 83.
dream in the night. And saying is He to him, [v]**"Beware,** [to] BewareKEEP
you, lest you be speaking with Jacob from good unto evil!"[v] Al u eim
25 **And Laban is overtaking 'Jacob. And Jacob pitches 'his** SUBJECT-or-to-S (To-subjectors)
tent in the mount. And Laban pitches 'with his brethren in
mount ·Gilead.

26 **And saying is Laban to Jacob, "What** have **you done?** JIoqb HEEL
And [F]**stealing are you 'my** [F]**heart, and leading** away **'my**
27 **daughters as captives of the** [A]**sword! Why hide to run away**
and steal from **'me, and not tell** [to]**me,** [a]**that I could send**
you [i]**with rejoicing and** [i]**with songs** ⁷**and**° [i]**with tambourine**
28 **and** [i]**with harp? And you did not let me** [to]**kiss** [to]**my sons and**
29 [to]**my daughters. Now, silly are you to do** so. **Forsooth!** [to] 29 3030
Disposed is my [N]**hand to do** [wi]**to you evil.** [a]**Yet the Alueim**
of your father yesternight spoke to me, [to]**saying, 'Beware,** spokeSAID
30 [to]**you,** [f]**of speaking with Jacob from good unto evil!' And** BewareKEEP
now, go, yea, go, for you long longingly for the household
of your father. Why have you stolen 'my alueim?"

31 **And answering is Jacob and saying to Laban, "For I**
feared, for I said, lest you may be snatching 'your daughters
32 **from** [wi]**me,** ⁷**and all that is mine.**° **With whom you are find-**
ing your alueim, not live shall he. In front of our brethren,
identify what is yours, withal, and take it to you." [a]**Yet not** idenRECOGNIZE
know did Jacob that Rachel, ⁷**his wife,**° **had stolen them.**

33 **And coming is Laban into Jacob's tent, and into Leah's** LLae 'No-thing'
tent, and into the two maidservant's tent, and does not find
them. And forth is he faring from Leah's tent and is com-
34 **ing into Rachel's tent.** [a]**Yet Rachel took 'the household** RRchl EWE
alueim and placed them in the saddle basket of the camel,
and she is sitting on them. And feeling is Laban 'all the
35 [N]**tent,** [a]**yet did not find them. And saying is she to her**
father, "It must not be [A]**hot in the** [A]**eyes of my lord that I**
cannot [to]**rise**[f] **before you, for the** [F]**way of women is** [t]**on me."**
And searching is ⁷**Laban in all the tent,**° [a]**yet he does not**
find 'the household alueim.

36 **And** [A]**hot is** [to]**Jacob, and contending is he** [i]**with Laban.**
And answering is Jacob and saying to Laban, "What is my
transgression ⁷**and**[c] **what is my sin, that you dash after me,**
37 [S]**and**[n] **that you feel 'all the furnishings** ⁷**of my tent?**° [S]**And**[n]
what have you found [f]**of all the furnishings of your house?**
Place it thus in front of my brethren and your brethren,

I e u e 38 **and correct will they the matter between us two. This**
Will-be-ing-was **twenty years am I with you. Your ewes and your she-goats**
were not bereaved, and the rams of your flock I did not
39 **eat. That which was torn to pieces, I did not bring to you.**
I was made a [A]sin offering for it! From my [A]hand you
40 **sought it, be it stolen by day [a]or stolen by night! So became**
devour ATE **I: In the day the drought [F]devoured me, and the ice in the**
41 **night, and flit did my sleep from my [N]eyes. This, for me,**
was twenty years in your household. I served you fourteen
years [i]for your two daughters, and six years [i]for your flock,
42 Ps118 6 7 42 **and vary did you \`my hire at ten countings. Unless the Alue-**
im of my father, the Alueim of Abraham, and the [A]Awe of
[I]*I tzchq* LAUGH-causer **Isaac had come to be[to] with me, then now you would have**
then THAT **sent me away [F]empty-handed. \`The humiliation and \`the**
weariness of my [I]palms the Alueim sees, and correcting you
was He yesternight."

[J]*I oqb* HEEL 43 **And answering is Laban and saying to Jacob, "The daugh-**
ters are my daughters, and the sons my sons, and the flock
my flock, and all [w]that you are seeing, mine is it, and my
daughters'. What shall I do for ·these ·today, or for their
44 1S10 18 44 **sons which they have borne? [a]Yet now, go. Contract will we**
a covenant, I and you, and it will become[to] a witness be-
tween me and[bt] you."

['] And saying is he to him, "Behold! No one is with us. Be-
hold! The Alueim is Witness between me and[bt] you."[?]

raise HIGH 45 **And taking is Jacob a stone and is raising it for a monu-**
46 Ex24 11 46 **ment. And saying is Jacob to his brethren, "Pick up stones."**
And they are [']picking up[o] stones and making a mound. And
eating are they [']and drinking[o] there on the mound. [']And
[L]*Lbn* WHITE **saying to him is Laban, "This mound is witness between**
me and[bt] you today."[?]

[I]*I gr-Shed u tha* 47 **And calling it is Laban[to] Igr-shedutha. And Jacob calls[to]**
Mound-witness **it Galeed.**

[G]*Gl od* Mound-Witness 48 **And saying is Laban [']to Jacob, "Behold![o] ·This ·mound**
raise HIGH **[']and this monument which I raised,[o] is witness between me**
49 **and [bt] you ·today." Therefore he calls its name Galeed and**
[M]*M tzph e* Watcher **the Mizpah which says: "Watching is Ieue between me and[bt]**
you, [t]when we are concealed, each man from his associate."

50 **"Should you humiliate \`my daughters, and should you**
take wives over my daughters, then not a man is with us.
See! The Alueim is Witness between me and [bt] you."

51 **And saying is Laban to Jacob, "Behold ·this ·mound! And**
behold the monument which I aim to be between me and[bt]
52 **you. Witness is ·this ·mound, and witness is the monument,**
that I should not be passing ·this \`·mound to you, and you
should not be passing ·this \`·mound and ·this \`·monument to
[A]*Ab r e m* FATHER- 53 **me, for evil! The Alueim of Abraham and the Alueim of Na-**
HIGH-throng **hor, the Alueim of the forefathers, shall judge between us."**
[N]*Nch u r* SNORTER

And swearing is Jacob [i]by the [A]Awe of his father Isaac.
54 **And sacrificing is Jacob a sacrifice in the mountain. And**
calling is he[to] his brethren to eat [N]bread. And eating are
they [N]bread and lodging in the mountain.

55 **And early is Laban [c]rising in the morning, and kissing is**
he[to] his sons and[to] his daughters and blessing \`them. And
going is Laban, and returning to his place.

32[2] **And Jacob goes** to **his way.**[v][7] **And seeing in a vision, he sees** 2810-22 Mahanaim 321-2
the camp of the Alueim encamped.[r] **And coming upon** in **him** 1 Ps347
2[3] **are messengers of the Alueim.**[v] **And saying is Jacob as** w **he** 2 Dt332 Js514 15 Ps273
sees them, "The camp of the Alueim is this!" And calling is
he the name of ·that ·place Mahanaim. M Mchn im CAMPS

271-40 Deception-Reconciliation 323-3317 323-5 Grace 33-1-17

3[4] **And sending is Jacob messengers before him to Esau, his** J Ioqb HEEL
4[5] **brother, to**[d] **the land of Seir, the field of Edom. And in-** Es Oshu Doer
structing 'them is he, to **saying, "Thus shall you say to my** S Shoir HAIRY
lord, to Esau, 'Thus says your servant Jacob: With Laban E Adum Red
5[6] **I sojourn and it delayed me till now. And mine are becom-** L Lbn WHITE
ing bulls and asses 'and[nc] **a flock, and servants and maids.**
And sending am I to tell to **my lord** 'Esau[o] to' **that your ser-** I e u e Will-be-ing-was
vant[o] **finds grace in your** A**eyes.'"**

6[7] **And returning are the messengers to Jacob,** to **saying, "We** 326 Esau's Approach 331-
came to your brother, to Esau, and, moreover, going is he
to meet you, and four =**hundred men with him."**

7[8] **And fearing is Jacob exceedingly, and it is distressing to** 7-8 Gift 13-23
him. And dividing is he 'the people who are 'with him, and
8[9] 'the flock and 'the herd and the camels, into two camps. And
saying is 'Jacob,[o] **"Should Esau be coming to ·one ·camp and**
smite it, [a]yet the remaining ·camp will come to be delivered."

9[10] **And saying is Jacob, "Alueim of my forefather Abraham** 9-12 Prayer 24-32
and Alueim of my father Isaac, Ieue ·Who saidst to me, A Abrem FATHER-
'Return to your land and to your kindred and I will [c]do HIGH-throng
10[11] good [wi]to you.' Smaller am I [f]than all the kindnesses and I Itzchq LAUGH-causer
[f]than all the A truth which Thou doest to 'Thy servant, for 9 3113
[i]with my stick I crossed ·this '·Jordan, and now I have be- cross PASSED
11[12] come to two M camps. Rescue me, pray, from the A hand of my J Irdn Descender
brother, from the A hand of Esau, for I fear 'him, lest he 10 Ps1465 1P510
12[13] comes and smites me, 'and[o] the mother [on]with the sons. And 12 1316 2813-15
Thou saidst, 'Good, yea, good will I [c]**do** [wi]**to you, and I make** make PLACE
'your A seed as the sand of the sea, which is not being num-
bered [f]for multitude.'"

13[14] **And lodging there is he in ·that night. And taking is he,** 7-8 Gift 13-23
[f]of ·that which is coming [i]to his N hand, a present offering,
14[15] 'and sends[o] **it to Esau, his brother: two** =**hundred she-goats**
and twenty bucks, two =**hundred ewes and twenty rams,**
15[16] **thirty suckler camels and their** S**foals, forty young cows**
16[17] **and ten bulls, twenty she-asses, and ten colts. And giving**
them is he into the A**hand of his servants, drove by drove** to
alone. And saying is he to his servants, "Pass before me,
17[18] **and place an interval between drove and** [bt] **drove." And in-** interval WIND
structing is he 'the first, to **saying, "In case Esau, my brother,**
is encountering you, and he asks you, to **saying, 'Whose are**
you? And whither are you going? And whose are these
18[19] **before you?'** [a]**Then you say, 'To your servant, to Jacob. A**
present offering is it, sent to my lord, to Esau. And, behold!
He, moreover, is behind us.'" behind AFTER
19[20] **And instructing is he** 'the first[o]; **moreover, 'the second;**
[S]and,[n] moreover, 'the third; [S]and,[n] moreover, 'all those who
are going after the droves, to **saying,** "[as]**According to ·this**
20[21] **word shall you speak to Esau,** [i]**when you find 'him. And**

Al u eim SUBJECT-or-to-s (To-subjectors) say, moreover, 'Behold! Your servant Jacob [7]comes[n] after
us.' For," said he, "a propitiatory [A]shelter am I making be-
fore his [N]face [i]with the present offering ·which is going
before me, and afterward will I see his [N]face. Perhaps he
lift favor me(*id.*) will lift up my [N]face."
21[22] And passing is the present offering on before his [N]face.
[a]Yet he lodges in ·that night in the camp.
22[23] And rising is he in ·that night and taking \his two wives
and \his two maids and \his eleven children, and is crossing
cross PASSING 23[24] the \crossing of the Jabbok. And taking them is he and is
JIbq VOIDER passing them over \the watercourse. And passing over is he
See map page 92. [7]all[nc] \which is his.

9-12 Prayer 24-32 24[25] And left is Jacob [to] alone. And wrestling is a Man with
24 Ho12 4 5 25[26] him till the [A]ascending of the dawn. And seeing is he that
he does not prevail [to] against Him. [a]Yet touching is He [in] the
[F]palm of his thighbone. And strained is the [F]palm of Jacob's
thighbone in his wrestling with Him.
26[27] And saying is He [7]to him,[0] "Send Me away, for the dawn
[A]ascends."
let go SENDING And saying is he, "Not letting You go am I save You
bless me."
27[28] And saying is He to him, "What is your name?"
28 25 22 29-34 And saying is he, "Jacob."
JIoqb HEEL 28[29] And saying is He [7]to him[0], "Not Jacob shall your name be
called SAID called longer, but rather Israel [7]is your name.[0] For upright
IIshr-Al Upright-with-SUBJECTOR are you with the Alueim and with mortals, and are pre-
vailing."
29[30] And asking is Jacob and saying, "Tell me, pray, your
name."
And saying is He, "Why is this that you are asking for
My name?" And blessing \him is He there.
PPhni-Al FACING-Al 30[31] And calling is Jacob the name of the place Peniel, "for I
31[32] see the Alueim [C]face to face, and rescued is my [N]soul." And
irradiating [to] him is the sun as [w] he passes \Peniel. [a]Yet he
See map page 92. is limping on his thigh.
sinew TIE 32[33] Therefore not eating are the sons of Israel \the sinew
which was ·benumbed, which is on the [F]palm of the thighbone, till ·this ·day, for He touched the [in F]palm of Jacob's
thighbone [i]at the sinew ·benumbed.

32 6 Esau's Approach 33 1- **33** And lifting is Jacob his eyes and seeing, and behold! Esau,
[7]his brother,[0] is coming, and with him four [=]hundred men.

32 3-5 Grace 33-1-17 And dividing is [7]Jacob[0] \the children [on]to Leah and [on]to
LLae 'No-thing' 2 Rachel and [on]to the two maids. And placing is he \the maids
BRchl EWE and \their children first, and \Leah and her children after
JIusph Add-er them, and \Rachel and \Joseph last.
3 And he passes before them and is prostrating himself to[d]
to FURTHER the earth seven times till he is close [fr]to his brother.
EOshu Doer 4 And running is Esau to meet him. And embracing him
4 45 14 46 29 is he, and falling on his neck and kissing him, and they are
weep LAMENT weeping.
5 And lifting is he \his eyes and seeing \the women and \the
what ANY children. And saying is he, "What are these to you?"

And saying is he, "The children which the **Alueim gra-** *Al u e im*
6 **ciously gives** '**your servant." And close are coming the** SUBJECT-or-to-S (To-subjectors)
maids, they and their children, and they are prostrating
7 **themselves. And, moreover, close are coming Leah and her** [L]*Lae* 'No-thing'
children, and prostrating themselves. **And, afterward, close** [J]*Iusph* Add-er
come **Joseph and Rachel, and they are prostrating** them- [R]*Rchl* EWE
selves.
8 **And saying is he, "What** is **all** ·**this camp to you which I** [what]ANY
encountered?"
And saying is he, "To find grace for '**your servant**' **in the**
[A]**eyes of my lord."**
9 **And saying is Esau, "Forsooth, mine is much, my brother.** [Es]*Oshu* Doer
Be[c] **yours what is yours."**
10 **And saying is Jacob,** "You **must not, pray. Pray, if I find** [J]*Ioqb* HEEL
grace in your [A]**eyes,** [a]**then take my present offering from**
my [A]**hand, for therefore I see your** [N]**face, as if seeing the**
11 [c]**face of** the **Alueim, and accepting me are you. Take, pray,**
'**my** [A]**blessing which** '**I**[n] **bring to you, for gracious to me is**
the **Alueim** [a]**in that it, forsooth, is all mine." And urging it**
[i]**on him is he, and he is taking it.**
12 **And saying is he, "Journey will we and go. and I will go**
in front of you." 
13 **And saying is he to him, "My lord knows that the children**
are tender, and the flock and the herd with unweaned are
dependent **on me, and, if** '**I**[nc] **trot them one day,** [a]**then die**
14 will **all the small cattle. Pray, pass will my lord before his**
servant, and I will conduct them[to]**carefully,** according **to**
the pace of the work which is before me, and to the pace of
the children, till[w]**I come to my lord to**[d] **Seir."** [S]*Shoir* HAIRY
15 **And saying is Esau, "Pray, I will put with you** some [f]**of**
the people who are '**with me."**
And saying is he, "Why this? '**Enough**' is **it that I am**
finding grace in the [A]**eyes of my lord."**
16 **And returning is Esau** [i]**on** ·**that** ·**day** [t]**on his way to**[d] **Seir.**
17 **And Jacob journeys to**[d] **Succoth. And building is he** [t]**for**
himself a house '**there.**' **And for his cattle he makes booths.**
Therefore he calls the name of the place Succoth. [S]*Skuth* Booths

2741 Deception 3318-3431

18 **And coming is Jacob** in **peace** to the **city of Shechem,** [Sh]*Shkm* BACK
which is in the **land of Canaan,** [i]**at his coming from Padan,** [C]*Knon* SUBMITTER
19 **Syria. And camping is he** '**before the city. And acquiring is** [P]*Phdn* RANSOM
he '**a portion of the field where his tent is stretched out,** [S]*Arm* HEIGHT
from the[A]**hand of the sons of Hamor,** the **father** of **Shechem,** [H]*Chmur* Ass
[f]**for a hundred coins, sterling.** *20* 351
20 **And setting** up **is he** there an **altar, and calling** '**on**' **Al-** [setting up]STANDING
Alueim-Ishral. [A]*Al Alei Ishr-Al*

34 **And forth is faring Dinah, the daughter of Leah, whom** SUBJECTOR (of) To-
2 **she bore for Jacob, to see**[in]**the daughters of the** [A]**land. And** SUBJECTORS of Israel
seeing '**her is Shechem, son of Hamor, the Hivite, the prince** [D]*Dine* ADJUDICATRESS
of the [N]**land. And taking** '**her is he and lying** '**with her and** [Hi]*Chui* Living-ite
3 **humiliating her. And clinging is his** [N]**soul** [i]**to Dinah, the** *2* 2933 34 3021
daughter of Jacob, and loving '**the maiden is he, and speak-**
ing [on]**to the** [F]**heart of the maiden.**
4 **And speaking is Shechem to Hamor, his father,**[to]**saying,** [speak]SAYING
"Take for me '·**this** ·**girl for a wife."**

I e u e 5 **And Jacob hears that [7]the son of Hamor[0] had defiled**
Will-be-ing-was **`Dinah, his daughter. [a]Yet his sons came to be `with his**
cattle in the field, and silent is Jacob till their coming.
[S]*Shkm* Back 6 **And forth is faring Hamor, the father of Shechem, to**
[J]*Ioqb* Heel **Jacob to speak `with him.**
7 **And the sons of Jacob come from the field as they hear**
of it. And mortified are the mortals, and [A]hot is their
[I]*Ishr-Al* Upright-with-Subjector **anger exceedingly, that decadence does he in Israel [t]by ly-**
ing `with Jacob's daughter, [a]for so is not being done.
[H]*Chmur* Ass 8 **And speaking is Hamor `with them,[to]saying, "My son**
Shechem's [N]soul is [F]attached [i]to your daughter. Pray, give
9 **`her to him for his wife. And intermarry `with us, and your**
daughters give to us, and `our daughters shall you take for
10 **your [7]sons.[0] And `with us dwell. And the land, [7]behold! Wide**
is it[0] before you. Dwell, and be merchants [7]on it,[0] and have
holdings in it."
11 **And saying is Shechem to her father and to her brothers,**
"Finding am I grace in your [A]eyes, [a]then what you shall say
12 **to me will I give. Increase on me exceedingly a bride-price**
and gift, and I will give as[w]you shall say to me. [a]Yet give
to me `the maiden for a wife."
13 **And answering are the sons of Jacob to `Shechem and**
`Hamor, his father, [i]with deceit. And speaking are they [7]to
[D]*Dine* Adjudicatress 14 **those[0] who had defiled `Dinah, their sister. And saying are**
[7]Simeon and Levi, Dinah's brothers, sons of Leah,[0] to them,
thingword **"We cannot[to]do `this `thing, to give `our sister to a man**
15 **who [t]has a foreskin, for a reproach is that to us. Yea, in**
this consent will we to you [7]and dwell among you,[0] if you
16 **become as[wt]we are [t]by circumcising your every male. And**
give would we `our daughters to you, and `your daughters
will we take for us [7]for wives,[0] and we will dwell `with you
17 **and we will become [7]as[n] one people. And should you not**
hearken to us, to be circumcised, [a]then we will take `our
daughter and go."
18 **And good are their words in the [A]eyes of Hamor and in**
19 **the [A]eyes of Shechem, son of Hamor. And the youth does**
thingword **not delay to do the thing, for he delights in Jacob's daugh-**
ter, and he is the most glorious [f]of all the household of his
father.
20 **And coming are Hamor and Shechem, his son, to the gate-**
way of their city, and speaking to the mortals of their city,
21 **[to]saying, "`These `mortals, peaceable are they `with us, and**
dwell will they in the land, and be merchants in `it. And the
land, behold! Wide is it on all [A]hands before them. `Their
daughters will we take for us for wives, and `our daughters
22 **will we give to them. Yea, in this are the mortals consent-**
ing to us, to dwell `with us, to become one[to]people, [t]by our
23 **circumcising every male, as[w]they circumcise. Their cattle**
and their acquisitions and all their beasts, will they not be
ours? Yea, [7]in this[0] are we consenting to them, and they
will dwell `with us."
24 **And hearkening to Hamor and to Shechem, his son, are**
all faring forth from the gateway of [7]their[0] city. And cir-
cumcised is [7]the flesh of their foreskin[0] of every male, all
who are faring forth from the gateway of his city.

25 And bcoming is it ion the third 'day, iwhen they come to SShmoun HEARER
be in =pain, taking are two sons of Jacob, Simeon, and Levi, LLui OBLIGATED
Dinah's brothers, each man his sword, and coming are they DDine ADJUDICATRESS
26 onto the trusting city, and killing are they every male. And 26 126 Js241-27 Jn45
'Hamor and 'Shechem, his son, they kill tby the edge of the edgeMOUTH
sword. And taking are they 'Dinah from the house of Shech- HChmur Ass
27 em, and faring forth. 7And" the sons of Jacob come upon SShkm BACK
the violated, and plundering are they the city which defiled
28 their sister 7Dinah.c 7And 'all0 their flocks and 7'all0 their
herds, and 7'all0 their asses, and 7all0 wthat is in the city, and
29 7'all0 wthat is in the field, they take. And 'all their estate, I e u e Will-be-ing-was
and 'all their tots and 'their wives, they capture. And plun-
dering are they 7'all wthat is in the city and0 all wthat is in
the 7houses.0
30 And saying is Jacob to Simeon and to Levi, "You trouble JIoqb HEEL
'me to cmake me Fstink iamong 7all0 the dwellers of the
land, iamong the Canaanite and iamong the Perizzite. And OKnon SUBMITTER
I am death-doomed, outnumbered awhen gathered are they PPhrzi VILLAGE-ite
onagainst me and smite me, and exterminated shall I be, I
and my household."
31 aYet saying are they, "As with a prostitute may he deal dealDO
'with our sister?"

2742-285 Departure, Return 351-15

35 And saying is the Alueim to Jacob, "Rise, go up to 7the 1 2743 2819 3228
place0 at Beth-El and dwell there, and make there an altar BBith-Al House-of-Al
to Al 'Who appeared to you iwhen you ran away from the
Nface of Esau, your brother." EsOshu Doer
2 And saying is Jacob to his household and to all who are 2 3428 29
with him, "cTake away 'the foreign 'alueim which are in your
midst, and clean yourselves, and change your garments. changevary
3 And rise will we and go up to Beth-El, and make will I 3 2820 21 313 42
there an altar to the Al 'Who answered 'me in the day of
my distress, and bcame to stand by me 7and saved me0 in the
way which I went."
4 And giving are they to Jacob 'all the foreign alueim which 4 3428
are in their Nhand, and 'the pendants which are in their
ears. And burying 'them is Jacob under the terebinth which
is wiat Shechem.
5 And journeying 7is Israel out of Shechem.0 And bcoming SShkm Back
is the dismay of the Alueim on the cities which surround
them, and they do not pursue after the sons of 7Israel.0
6 And coming is Jacob toward Luz, which is in the land of LLuz DEVIATOR
Canaan (it is Beth-El), he and all the people who are with CKnon SUBMITTER
7 him. And building is he there an altar, and calling is he 7the 6 2819
name0 of the place Beth-El, for there the Alueim was re- BBith-Al House-of-Al
vealed to him iwhen he ran away from the Nface of 7Esau,0 See map page 92.
his brother.
8 And dying is Deborah, Rebecca's wet-nurse, and entombed DDbure Bee
is she below to Beth-El, under the oak. And calling is 7Jacob0 RebRbqe Enthraller
the name of it Alun-Bakuth. AAlun-Bkuth Oak-of-LAMENTATIONS
9 vAnd appearing is the Alueim to Jacob again 7in Luz,0
iwhen he comes from Padan, Syria, and 7the Alueim" is PPhdn RANSOM
10 blessing 'him. And saying to him is the Alueim, "Your name SArm HEIGHT
is Jacob. No longer is your name to be called Jacob, but 10 3228
rather Israel is coming to be your name." And calling is He IIshr-Al Upright-with-SUBJECTOR
his name Israel.

11 171 11 And saying to him is the Alueim, "I am the Al-Who-Suf-
Al u eim fices. Be[r]fruitful and increase. A nation and an assembly of
SUBJECT-or-to-s nations shall [b]come from you, and kings from your loins
(To-subjectors) [A]*Abrem* FATHER- 12 shall fare forth. And \`the land which I gave to Abraham
HIGH-throng and to Isaac, to you am I giving it. [7]Yours it is;[0] and to
[I]*Itzchq* LAUGH-causer your [A]seed after you am I giving \`the land."
13 And ascending is the Alueim from[on] him in the place in
[J]*Ioqb* HEEL which He spoke \`with him.[v]
setting up STATIONING 14 And setting up is Jacob a monument in the place in which
14 Lv2313 18 37 He spoke \`with him, a monument of stone. And libating is
Nu155-10 15 he on it a libation and pouring on it oil. And calling is Jacob
\`the name of the place where the Alueim spoke \`with him,
[B]*Bith-Al* House-of-Al Beth-El.

25 20-22 Rachel 3516-20 16 And journeying [7]is Jacob[0] from Beth-El, and it comes to
[E]*Aphrth* FRUIT-GIV-er be still some distance over ·land to come to[d] Ephrath. And
[R]*Rchl* EWE bearing is Rachel, and hard is she having it in her bearing.
17 And [b]coming is it, [i]as ·she has it hard in her bearing, [a]then
See map page 92. saying to her is the midwife, "You must not fear, for this,
18 moreover, is a son for you!" And [b]coming is it, [i]when forth
[B]*Bn-Auni* Son-of- fares her [N]soul (for she died), [a]that she is calling \`his name
[7]my sighing[0] 19 Ben-oni. [a]Yet his father calls his [7]name[n] Benjamin. And
[B]*Bn-im in* Son-RIGHT dying is Rachel, and is being entombed [i]on the way to[d]
setting up STATIONING 20 Ephrath. (It is now Bethlehem.) And setting up is Jacob a
[B]*Bith lchm* House-bread monument over her tomb. It is the monument, the tomb of
20 1S102 *22* 493 4 Rachel, till ·today.

2523-28 Sons 3521-26 21 And journeying is Israel, and stretching out his tent is he
[I]*Ishr-Al* Upright- 22 [f]beyond[to] the tower Edar. And [b]coming is it, [i]when Israel
with-SUBJECTOR tabernacles in ·that ·land, [a]that going is Reuben and lying
[E]*M gdl-odr* Tower-drove \`with Bilhah, his father's concubine. And hearing of it is
[R]*Ra u bn* SEE-son Israel, [7]and evil appears it in his [A]eyes.[0]
[B]*Blee* DISINTEGRATED 23 And coming are the sons of Jacob to be twelve: The sons
[S]*Shmoun* HEARER of Leah, the firstborn of Jacob, Reuben, and Simeon and
[L]*Lu i* OBLIGATED 24 Levi and Judah and Issachar and Zebulon; [7]and[no] the sons
[J]*Ieud e* Acclaimer 25 of Rachel, Joseph and Benjamin; and the sons of Bilhah,
[I]*Ish shkr* Forsooth-hire 26 Rachel's maid, Dan and Naphtali; and the sons of Zilpah,
[Z]*Zb u l un* PREFERRED Leah's maid, Gad and Ashur. These are the sons of Jacob,
[J]*I u sph* Add-er who are born to him in Padan, Syria.
[D]*Dn* ADJUDICATE [N]*N phthl i* TWISTED [G]*Gd* RAID [A]*Ashur* PROGRESS *29* 2S1223
2519 Birth-Death 27-29 27 And coming is Jacob to Isaac, his father, [7]to[0] Mamre, the
[M]*M mr a* [f]Bitterness[f] town of ·Arba (It is now Hebron), [7]in the land of Canaan,[0]
[H]*Chbr un* JOINED 28 where Abraham and Isaac sojourned. And coming are the
[I]*Itzchq* LAUGH-causer 29 [N]days of Isaac to be a hundred[yr] and eighty years. And ex-
Adm 3674 piring is Isaac, and he died, and is gathered to his people,
[E]*Osh u* Do-er old and satisfied with [N]days. And entombing \`him are Esau
See map page 92. and Jacob, his sons.

69-929 Forefathers 361-8 1 Canaan 6-8 36 And these are the genealogical annals
[E]*Adum* Red of Esau (He is Edom):

2 2634 3624 2-3 Esau's Family 4-5 2 Esau took \`his wives from the daughters
[C]*Kno n* SUBMITTER [A]*Od e* Ornament [E]*Ailun* Oak Canaan: \`Adah, the daughter of Elon,
[H]*Chth i* Dismay-ite the Hittite; and \`Aholibamah, the daugh-
[A]*On e* RESPOND [Z]*Tzboun* STREAKS ter of Anah, the [7]son[no] of Zibeon, the
3 289 [H]*Chui* Living-ite [B]*Bshmth* AROMATICS 3 Hivite; and Bashemath, the daughter of
[I]*Ishmo-Al* HEARING-is-Al [N]*Nb iuth* PRODUCTION-S Ishmael, sister of Nebaioth.

2-3 Esau's Family 4-5 [A]*Od e* Ornament 4 And bearing is Adah for Esau \`Eliphaz,

5 **and Bashemath bears 'Reuel, and Aholi-**
bamah bears 'Jeush, and 'Jaalam, and
'Korah. These are the sons of Esau, who
were born for him in the land of Canaan.

6 **And taking is Esau 'his wives and 'his**
sons and 'his daughters and 'all the [N]souls
of his household, and ʼall° his cattle and
'all his beasts and 'all his acquisitions,
and ʼ'all° [w]that he got in the land of Ca-
naan, and going is he ʼfrom" the land ʼof
Canaan," from the [N]face of Jacob, his
7 **brother, for it [b]comes that they get more**
[f]than may dwell together, and the land
of their sojourning cannot to[F]bear 'them,
in view ʼof the multitude' of their cattle.
8 **And dwelling is Esau in mount Seir.**
(Esau, he is Edom.)

9 **And these are the genealogical annals**
of Esau, father of Edom, in mount Seir:
10 **ʼAnd" these are the names of Esau's**
sons: Eliphaz, son of Adah, wife of Esau;
Reuel, son of Bashemath, wife of Esau.
11 **And coming to be sons of Eliphaz are**
Teman, Omar, Zepho, and Gatam, and
12 **Kenaz. And Timno becomes a concubine**
[t]of Eliphaz, Esau's son, and bearing is
she for Eliphaz 'Amelek. These are the
sons of Adah, wife of Esau.
13 **And these are the sons of Reuel: Na-**
hath and Zerah, Shammah and Mizzah.
These come to be the sons of Bashemath,
wife of Esau.
14 **And these come to be the sons of Aholi-**
bamah, daughter of Anah, ʼson" of Zibeon,
wife of Esau: And bearing is she for Esau
15 **'Jeush and 'Jaalam, and 'Korah. These are**
the sheiks of the sons of Esau: The sons
of Eliphaz, the firstborn of Esau, sheik
16 **Teman, sheik Omar, sheik Zepho, sheik**
Kenaz, sheik Korah, sheik Gatam, sheik
Amalek. These are the sheiks of Eliphaz
in the land of Edom. These are the sons of
Adah.
17 **And these are the sons of Reuel, son of**
Esau: sheik Nahath, sheik Zerah, sheik
Shammah, sheik Mizzah. These are the
sheiks of Reuel, in the land of Edom. These
are the sons of Bashemath, wife of Esau.
18 **And these are the sons of Aholibamah,**
wife of Esau: sheik Jeush, sheik Jaalam,
sheik Korah. These are the sheiks of Aho-
libamah, daughter of Anah, wife of Esau.
19 **These are the sons of Esau, and these are**
their sheiks. ʼThese are the sons° of Edom.

20 **ʼAnd" these are the sons of Seir, the**

[B]*Bshmth* AROMATICS [R]*Roual* Associate-Al
[A]*Aelibme* TENTED-fane-height [J]*Ioush* Do
[Ja]*Iolm* OBSCURER [K]*Qrch* BALD
[C]*Knon* SUBMITTER

1 Canaan 6-8 [E]*Oshu* Doer

Al u eim
SUBJECT-or-to-s
(To-subjectors)

[J]*Ioqb* HEEL

view FACE

[S]*Shoir* HAIRY [E]*Oshu* Doer [Ed]*Adum* Red
See map page 92.

101-119 Sons 369-43 9-19 Sons, Sheiks 20-43

[E]*Aliphz* Al-glitters [A]*Ode* Ornament
[R]*Rou-Al* Associate-Al [B]*Bshmth* AROMATICS
11 Jb211 151
[T]*Thimn* ʼAmazementʼ [O]*Aumr* SAYER [Z]*Tzphu* Watch
[G]*Gothm* Low [T]*Thmno* WITHHOLDER
12 147 Ex178 14 Nu2420 Dt2517-19
[A]*Omlq* PEOPLE-LAPPER

[N]*Nchth* Settled
[Z]*Zrch* RADIANT [S]*Shme* Desolation

[A]*One* RESPOND [Z]*Tzboun* STREAK

[Ko]*Qrch* BALD

See map page 92.

9-19 Sons, Sheiks 20-43 [S]*Shoir* HAIRY

Horite, dwellers of the land: Lotan and
21 Shobal and Zibeon and Anah and Dishon
and Ezer and [7]Rishan.[0] These are the
sheiks of the Horites, sons of Seir, in the
land of Edom.
22 And coming to be sons of Lotan are
Hori and Hemam. And the sister of Lo-
tan is Timno.
23 And these are the sons of Shobal: Al-
van and Manahath and Ebal [s]and[n] Shepho
and Onam.
24 And these are the sons of Zibeon: [a]Aiah
and Anah. He is the Anah who found ‘the
hot springs in the wilderness [i]when graz-
ing ‘the asses [t]of Zibeon, his father.
25 And these are the sons of Anah: Dishon
and Aholibamah, daughter of Anah.
26 And these are the sons of Dishon: Hem-
dan and Eshban and Ithran and Cheran.
27 [s]And[n] these are the sons of Ezer: Bil-
han and Zaavan [7]and Ioukam[0] and Akan.
28 [7]And[n] these are the sons of [7]Rishan[0]: Uz
and Aran.
29 These are the sheiks of the Horites:
sheik Lotan, sheik Shobal, sheik Zibeon,
30 sheik Anah, sheik Dishon, sheik Ezer,
sheik [7]Rishan.[0] These are the sheiks of the
Horites, for their sheiks in the land of
Seir.
31 And these are the kings who reigned in
the land of Edom, before a king reigned
32 for the sons of Israel: And reigning in
Edom is Bela, son of Beor. And the name
33 of his city is Dinhabah. And Bela died.
And reigning [u]in his stead is Jobab, son
34 of Zerah, from Bozrah. And Jobab died.
And reigning [u]in his stead is Husham
35 from the land of the Temanites. And
Husham died.
And reigning [u]in his stead is Hadad,
son of Bedad ·who smote ‘Midian in the
field of Moab. And the name of his city
36 is Avith. And Hadad died.
And reigning [u]in his stead is Samlah
37 from Masrekah. And Samlah died.
And reigning [u]in his stead is Saul from
38 Rehoboth by the stream. And Saul died.
And reigning [u]in his stead is Baalhanan,
39 son of Achbor. And Baalhanan, son of
Achbor, died.
And reigning [u]in his stead is Hadad,
[7]son of Bered.[0] And the name of his city is
Pau. And the name of his wife is Meheta-
bel, daughter of Matred, [7]son of Mezahab.[0]
40 And these are the names of the sheiks
of Esau, their families, for their places

[H]*Chur i* Pale-ites [L]*Lut n* WRAP
[S]*Shubl* TRAILER [Z]*Tzbo un* STREAK [D]*Dish n* SLEEK
[E]*Atzr* TREASURE
[H]*Chur i* Pale-ites [S]*Shoir* HAIRY
[E]*A dum* Red
[L]*Lut n* WRAP
I e u e Will-be-ing-was [He]*Eim m* Discomfit
[T]*Th mno* WITHHOLDER
[S]*Shubl* TRAILER [A]*Olun* ON
[M]*M nch th* STOPPER [S]*Shph u* RIDGE
[O]*Aun m* NEGATION
[Z]*Tzbo un* STREAK [A]*Aie* Falcon
[A]*On e* RESPOND
[D]*Dish un* SLEEK
[A]*Ael i bme* TENTED-fane-height
[H]*Chmd n* COVET
[E]*Ash bn* FIRE-son [I]*I thr n* Looser [C]*Kr n* DIGGER
[E]*Ozr* HELP [B]*Bl en* DISINTEGRATION
[Z]*Zoun* Sweater [A]*Oqn* PRESSURE
[U]*Outz* Counsel
[A]*Arn* PINE
[H]*Chur i* Pale-ites
[S]*Shubl* TRAILER [Z]*Tzbo un* STREAK
[A]*On e* RESPOND [D]*Dish un* SLEEK [E]*Ozr* HELP
See map page 92.
[S]*Shoir* HAIRY
31 176 3511 Dt1714-20
[A]*A dum* Red
[I]*Ishr-Al* Upright-with-SUBJECTOR
[B]*B lo* IN-SWALLOW [Beor]*Bour* Brute
[D]*Dn e b e* ADJUDICATION-in-her
in his stead UNDER [J]*I ub b* Interior
[Z]*Zrch* RADIANT [B]*Btzr e* Vintage
in his stead UNDER [H]*Chush m* HURRIER
[T]*Thim n i* Amazement-ites
in his stead UNDER [H]*Ed d* Splendor
[B]*Bd d* Solitary [M]*M din* Quarreler
[M]*Mu ab* FROM-FATHER
[A]*Ou ith* DEPRAVED
in his stead UNDER [S]*Shm l e* GARMENT
[M]*M shrq* Hisser
[S]*Shaul* Asked-for
[R]*Rchb uth* WIDES
[B]*Bol chn n* Possessor-of-GRACE
[A]*Okbur* Mouse
See map page 53.
[P]*Phou* PUFF-UP [M]*Me i tb-Al* WHAT-GOOD-AL
[M]*M trd* Persistent [Mez]*Mizeb* Who-is-GOLD

ᵀin their lands,ᴼ ⁱby their names: sheik
41 Timno, sheik Alvah, sheik Jetheth, sheik
Aholibamah, sheik Elah, sheik Pinon,
42 sheik Kenaz, sheik Teman, sheik Mibzar,
43 sheik Magdiel, sheik Iram. These are the
sheiks of Edom, for their dwelling places,
in the land of their freehold. He is Esau,
father of Edom.

ᵀThmno WITHHOLD ᴬOlue ᵀONᵀ
ᴬAel i bme TENTed-fane-hight ᴱAl e Terebinth
ᴾPhinn FACE ᵀThimn Amazement ᴹMbtzr Fortress
ᴹMgd i-Al RAIDer-Al ᴵOir m City-FROM
ᴱAdum Red
ᴱOsh u Doer
Al u e im
SUBJECT-or-to-s
(To-subjectors)

51-68 Progenitors 371-5026

37 And dwelling is Jacob in the land of his father's so-
2 journings, in the land of Canaan. These are the genealogical annals of Jacob. See map page 92.

1 3228 *2* 306-8 10-13
ᶜKnon SUBMITTER
ᴵIoqb HEEL

Joseph, seventeen years of ˢage, comes to be grazing ⁱⁿ
the flock ʼwith his brothers, and he, the lad, is ʼwith the sons
of Bilhah and ʼthe sons of Zilpah, wives of his father. And
bringing is Joseph ʼtheir evil mutterings to ᵀIsrael,ᴼ their
3 father. And Israel loves ʼJoseph more ᶠthan any other of
his sons, for a ᴬson of his old age is he, to him. And he
4 makes for him a distinctive tunic. And seeing are his brothers that their father loves ʼhim more ᶠthan any other of
his ᵀsons.ⁿ And hating ʼhim are they and cannot speak
peaceably to him.

372-4528 Joseph 5015-26
372-36 Canaan 391-4157
372-4 Brethren 12-17
ᴮBl e e DISINTEGRATED
anyALL
3 2715 Ex284 39 391
2S1318 19
anyALL
ᴵI shr-Al Upright-with-SUBJECTOR

5 And dreaming is Joseph a dream. And telling it is he to
his brothers. And continuing further are they in their
6 hatred ʼof him. And saying is he to them, "Hear, pray, ·this
7 ·dream which I dreamed.ᵛAnd behold! We were compressing
stooks in the midst of the field. And, behold! Rising is my
stook, and, moreover, takes its station. And, behold! Surrounding it are your stooks, and prostrating to my stook!"ᵛ
8 And saying to him are his brothers, "ʳVerily reign over
us shall you? And should you ʳverily rule among us?" And
continuing further are they to hate ʼhim on account of his
dreams, and on account of his words.
9 And dreaming is he still another dream. And relating is
he ʼit ᵀto his father andᴼ to his brothers, and is saying, "Behold! I dream a further dream. ᵛAnd, behold! The sun and
10 the moon and the eleven stars are prostrating to me."ᵛ And
relating it is he to his father and to his brothers. And re-
buking ⁱⁿ him is his father, and saying to him, "What ·dream
is ·this which you dream? Shall I and your mother and your
brothers come, yea, come to prostrate to you toᵈ the earth?"
11 And jealous are his brothers ⁱof him, ᵃyet his father keeps
ʼthe word.

5-11 Dreams 18-36
ᴶI u sph Add-er
8 Ex214 Lu1914
9 426 4326 4414

12 And going are his brothers to graze ʼtheir father's ʼflock
13 in Shechem. And saying is Israel to Joseph, "Are not your
brothers grazing in Shechem? Go.ᵃSend you will I to
them."
And saying is he to him, "Behold me!"
14 And saying to him is ᵀIsrael,ᴼ "Go, pray, ˢandⁿ see if it is
ʼwell with your brothers, and ʼwell with the flock, and return me word." And sending him is he from the vale of
Hebron.
15 And coming is he toᵈ Shechem. And finding him is a man,
and, behold! Straying is he in the field. And asking him is
16 the man ᵗᵒsaying, "What are you seeking?" And saying is

372-4 Brethren 12-17
ˢShkm BACK
wellwelfare
See map page 92.
ᴴChbr un JOINed

I e u e Will-be-ing-was he, "My brothers am I seeking. Tell [to] me, pray, whereat
they are grazing."
17 And saying is the man, "They journeyed hence, for I
[D]*Dthn* VERDANT[Chal] heard ⌜them⌝ saying, 'Go will we to[d] Dothan.'"
[J]*Iusph* Add-er And going is Joseph after his brothers, and is finding
See map page 92. them in Dothan.
5-11 Dreams 18-36 18 And seeing \him are they from afar, and [in] ere he is com-
18 Mt271 ing near to them. And plotting are they against \him among
19 themselves to [c]put him to death. And saying is each man to
his brother, "Behold! This possessor of ·dreams is coming!
20 And now go, and we will kill him and fling him into one of
devour ATE the cisterns and say, 'An evil animal devoured him,' and see
will we what will become of his dreams."
[R]*Raubn* SEE-son 21 And hearing of it is Reuben, and rescuing him is he [f]out
of their [A]hands. And saying is he, "Not smite will we his
shed POUR OUT 22 [N]soul." And saying to them is Reuben, "You must not shed
blood. Fling \him into ·this ·cistern which is in the wilder-
stretch SENDING ness, [a]yet a [A]hand you, you must not stretch out [i]against
him,"—that he may rescue \him from their [A]hands, to re-
store him to his father.
23 And [b]coming is it, as [w] Joseph comes to his brothers, [a]that
they are stripping \Joseph of \his tunic, \the distinctive tunic
24 which is on him. And taking him are they, and flinging \him
into the cistern.
25 Jd824 25 25 [a]Yet the cistern was empty. No water is in it. And sitting
down are they to eat [N]bread. And [F]lifting are they their
[G]*Glod* Mound-of-Witness eyes and seeing, and behold! A caravan of Ishmaelites are
coming from Gilead [a]with their camels, bearing perfume
[E]*Mtzrim* Narrows and balm and labdanum, going by to [c]go down to[d] Egypt.
[J]*Ieude* Acclaimer 26 And saying is Judah to his brothers, "What gain is it
27 391 27 that we kill \our brother and cover \his blood? Go, and we
[I]*Ishmo-Ali* HEARING-is-SUBJECTOR will sell him to the Ishmaelites, and our [N]hand must not
come to be [i]against him, for our brother ⌜and⌝ our [N]flesh is
See map page 83. he." And hearkening are his brothers.
[M]*Mdnim* Quarrelers 28 And passing are mortals, Midianites, merchants. And
Midianites a sub-tribe of drawing are they and [c]bringing up \Joseph from the cistern,
Ishmael (Jd824) and are selling \Joseph to the Ishmaelites [i]for twenty silverlings. And bringing are they \Joseph to[d] Egypt.
29 And returning is Reuben to the cistern, and behold! No
30 Joseph is in the cistern. And tearing is he \his garments.
And returning is he to his brothers and is saying, "The boy!
There is no one! And I! Whither can I come?"
31 And taking are they Joseph's \tunic, and slaying a hairy
32 one of the goats, and dipping \the tunic in the blood. And
sending are they \the distinctive tunic, and they are bringing
it to their father. And saying are they, "This we found.
iden RECOGNIZE Pray identify the tunic, if it is not your son's."
33 And identifying it is he and saying, "The tunic of my son!
devour EATEN An evil animal has devoured him! Joseph is torn to pieces,
[J]*Ioqb* HEEL 34 yea, to pieces!" And tearing is Jacob his garments, and is placing sackcloth [i]on his =waist, and is mourning over his son
35 3021 35 many days. And rising are all his sons and all his daughters
⌜and they come⌝ to console him, [a]yet refusing is he to be con-
soled and is saying that, "Descend will I to my son, to[d] the
[M]*Mdnim* Quarrelers unseen, mourning." And lamenting over \him is his father.
[P]*Phutiphr* (Egyptian) 36 And the Midianites sell [V]Joseph⌝ to Egypt, to Potiphar,

a eunuch of Pharaoh, chief of the executioners. [Ph]*Phro e* [H]UNCOVERED[b]

38 And [b]coming is it [i]at ˙that season [a]that down is Judah 38[1-30] Judah 42[1]-45[28]
going from ˋhis brothers and is turning aside unto a man, [J]*Ieud e* Acclaimer
2 an Adullamite, and his name is Hirah. And seeing is Judah [H]*Chir e* HEATER
there the daughter of a man of the Canaanites, and his [K]*Kno n i* SUBMITtite
name is Shua. And taking her is he and is coming to her. [S]*Shu o* Implorer
3 And pregnant is she and is bearing a son, and calling is [F]*Oir* Denuded
[S]she[n] ˋhis name Er. *2* 24[3] 26[35] 27[46]
4 And pregnant is she further and is bearing a son, and is Ex34[16] Dt7[3]
calling ˋhis name Onan. [O]*Aunn* NEGATION
5 And continuing further is she and bearing a son, and
calling ˋhis name Shelah. And she comes to be in Chezib [S]*Shl e* EASE
[i]when bearing [V]them.[o] [C]*Chzib* LIAR
6 And taking is Judah a wife for Er, his firstborn, and her
7 name is Thamar. And [b]coming is it that Er, Judah's first- [T]*Thmr* PALM
born, is evil in the [A]eyes of Ieue, and Ieue is [c]putting him to
death.
8 And saying is Judah to Onan, "Come to your brother's *8* Dt25[5-9] Ru4[10] Mt22[24]
wife and wed ˋher, your brother's widow, and raise [A]seed
9 for your brother." And know does Onan that the [A]seed will
not become his. And it [b]comes, when he is coming to his
brother's wife, [a]then he ruins it on[d] the earth, to avoid
10 giving [A]seed to his brother. And evil in the [A]eyes of Ieue is *I e u e*
ˋwhat he does, and, moreover, He is [c]putting ˋhim to death Will-be-ing-was
[7]also.[o]
11 And saying is Judah to Thamar, his daughter-in-law,
"Dwell a widow at your father's house till my son Shelah
shall be grown. For," says he, "lest he, moreover, will die grown GREAT
as his brothers." And going is Thamar and dwelling in her
father's house.
12 And increasing are the days, and the daughter of Shua,
Judah's wife, died. And [7]consoled[o] is Judah, and going up
is he [on]to the shearers of his flock, he and his [7]shepherd,[o]
Hirah, the Adullamite, to[d] Timnah. [T]*Thmn e*[?] COME-TO-END[?]
13 And told is it to Thamar,[to]saying, "Behold! Your husband's father is going up to[d] Timnah to the shearing of his
14 flock." And away is she [c]taking the garments of her widowhood off her, and is covering herself [i]with a veil and she is
bedecking herself. And sitting is she [i]at the opening to the
springs, which are on the way to[d] Timnah, for she sees that
Shelah is grown, and she is not given to him for a wife. grown GREAT
15 And seeing her is Judah, and is accounting her to be a
prostitute, for she covers her face, [7]and he did not recog-
16 nize her.[o] And aside is he turning to her [to]by the way, and
is saying [7]to her,[o] "Prithee, pray, coming am I to you," for
not know does he that she is his daughter-in-law. And
saying is she, "What will you give to me that you shall
come to me?"
17 And saying is he, "I will send [7]to you[o] a kid of the goats
from the flock."
And saying is she, "If you will give a surety till you
send."
18 And saying is he, "What is the surety which I shall give
to you?"
And saying is she, "Your seal and your twist and your
staff which is in your hand."

Al u eim And giving them is he to her, and is coming to her, and
SUBJECT-or-to-s pregnant is she [t]by him.
(To-subjectors) 19 And rising is she and going, and is [c]taking away her veil
off her and is putting on the garments of her widowhood.
20 And sending is Judah ʼthe kid of the goats [i]by the hand of
his ʼshepherd,° the Adullamite, to take the surety from the
21 hand of the woman. [a]Yet he did not find her. And asking
is he ʼthe mortals of ·her place,[to]saying, "Where is the hallowed harlot, she [i]at the springs, on the way?"
And saying are they, "No hallowed harlot came to be in
this place."
[J]*Ieud e* Acclaimer 22 And returning is he to Judah and saying, "I did not find
her. And, moreover, the mortals of the place say, 'No hal-
lowed harlot came to be in this place.' "
23 And saying is Judah, "Take it to her shall she, lest we
[b]come into contempt! Behold! I send ·this ·kid and you did
not find her!"
24 And [b]coming is it, [as]about three months from this, [a]that
it is being told[to]Judah,[to]saying, "Your daughter-in-law
[T]*Thmr* PALM Thamar commits prostitution, and moreover, behold! Pregnant is she [t]by prostitutions."
And saying is Judah, "[c]Bring her forth, and burned shall
she be."
25 Forth is she [c]brought. [a]Yet she sends to her husband's
father,[to]saying, "[t]By the man whose these are am I preg-
iden RECOGNIZE nant." And saying is she, "Identify, pray, whose ·these are:
the seal and the twist and the staff."
26 Mt13 26 And identifying them is Judah, and is saying, "More just
is ʼThamar° [f]than I, therefore, for I did not give her to
[S]*Shl e* EASE Shelah, my son." [a]Yet not continue does he to know her
further.
time SEASON 27 And [b]coming is it, [i]at the time of her bearing, [a]that, be-
28 hold! Twins are in her belly. And [b]coming is it, in her bear-
put GIVING ing [a]that ʼone° is putting out a hand. And taking it is the
midwife and tying on his hand a double-dipped token,[to]say-
29 ing, "This fares forth first." And [b]coming is it, as his hand
is returning, [a]then, behold! Forth fares his brother. And
saying is she, "What! Breached have you. On you be the
[P]*Phrtz* BREACH 30 breach!" And calling is she his name Pharez. And afterward
forth comes his brother, who had on his hand the double-
[Z]*Zrch* RADIANT dipped token. And calling is [S]she[n] his name Zarah.

372-36 Egypt 391-4157
391-2 Potiphar 19-20 39 And Joseph was [c]brought down to[d] Egypt. And bought is
1 3725 36 he by Potiphar, a eunuch of Pharaoh, chief of the execu-
[E]*M tzr im* Narrows tioners, an Egyptian man, from the [A]hand of the Ishmaelites
[Ph]*Phro e* [H]UNCOVERED[b] 2 who had [c]brought him down there. And coming is Ieue to be
[I]*I shmo-Al i* HEARING-is- ʼwith Joseph, and becoming is he a prosperous man. And
SUBJECTOR-ite coming is he to be in the house of his lord, the Egyptian.

3-6 Confidence 21-23 3 And seeing is his lord that Ieue is ʼwith him and that all
4 [w]that he is doing Ieue is prospering in his [A]hand. And find-
[J]*I u sph* Add-er ing is Joseph grace in the [A]eyes ʼof his lord,[n] and ministering
is he ʼto him. And [c]making him is he supervisor over his
household, and all, forsooth, ʼwhich[n] is his he gives into
5 ʼJoseph's° [A]hand. And [b]coming is it, since he [c]makes ʼhim
supervisor in his house and over all, forsooth, [w]that is his,

[a]that Ieue is blessing \the Egyptian's household[in]due to *I e u e*
Joseph, and coming is Ieue's blessing to be [i]over all, for- Will-be-ing-was
6 sooth, which is his, in the house and in the field. And leav- [leav]FORSAKE
ing is he all [w]that is his in the [A]hand of Joseph. And naught *6* 2917
knows he of \his, save the [N]bread which he is eating.

And [b]coming is Joseph to have a lovely shape and a lovely -6-7 Potiphar's
7 appearance. And [b]coming is it after ·these ·things, [a]that Wife 11-12-
[F]lifting is the wife of his lord \her eyes to Joseph and is [thing]word
saying, "Lie with me."

8 And refusing is he, and saying to his lord's wife, "Behold! 8-10 J.'s Refusal -12-20
My lord knows [S]naught[n] of \me in the house, and all, for-
9 sooth, [w]that is his he gives into my [A]hand. No one is
greater in ·this house [f]than I, and he has not kept back
aught from me save \you, in [w]that you are his wife. And
how shall I do·this·great·evil and sin[t]against the Alueim?"
10 And [b]coming is it, as she speaks to Joseph day by day, [J]*Iusph* Add-er
[a]that he does not hearken to her to lie beside her, to be[c]
with her.

11 And [b]coming is a ·day as ·this, and coming is [7]Joseph[nc] to[d] -6-7 Potiphar's
the house to do his work, and no man [f]of the mortals of the Wife 11-12-
12 household is there in the house. And grasping him is she
[i]by his cloak,[to]saying, "Lie with me!"

And leaving is he his cloak in her hand, and fleeing, and 8-10 J.'s Refusal -12-20
faring forth ·outside. [leav]FORSAKE
13 And [b]coming is it, as she sees that he leaves his cloak in
14 her hand and is fleeing [7]and faring forth[n] ·outside, [a]that
calling is she to the mortals of her household and is speak- [speak]SAY
ing to them,[to]saying, "See! He brings to us a man, a Heb- [H]*Obr i* Passer
rew to laugh [i]at us. He [b]comes to me [7]saying,[o] 'Lie with me,'
15 and calling am I [i]with a loud voice. And [b]coming is it, as he [loud]GREAT
hears that I [c]raise high my voice and am calling, [a]that he
is leaving his cloak beside me and is fleeing and faring [leav]FORSAKE
16 forth \outside." And leaving is she his cloak beside her till [leav]FORSAKE
his lord comes to his house.
17 And speaking is she to him [as]according to ·these words,[to]
saying, "There came to me the Hebrew ·servant whom you
brought to us, to laugh [i]at me, [7]and said to me, 'Lie with
18 me.'[o] And [b]coming is it, as I [c]raise high my voice and am
calling, [a]that he is leaving his cloak beside me and is flee- [leav]FORSAKE
ing [7]and is faring forth[o] ·outside."

19 And [b]coming is it, as his lord hears \the words of his 391-2 Prison 19-20
wife, which she speaks to him,[to]saying, "[as]According to
·these words does your servant to me," [a]that [A]hot is his
20 anger. And Joseph's [=]lord is taking \him and is giving him
over to the round-house, the place in which the king's
prisoners are bound. And coming is he to be there in the
round-house.

21 [a]Yet coming is Ieue to be \with Joseph, and He is [F]stretch- 3-6 Confidence 21-23
ing out to him in kindness and is giving him grace in the
22 [A]eyes of the chief of the round-house. And the chief of the
round-house is giving into the [A]hand of Joseph \all the
prisoners who are in the round-house. And \all [w]that is
23 being done there, he comes to be the doer. Naught is the

Al u eim SUBJECT-or-to-s (To-subjectors) chief of the round-house [7]prison[0] seeing \`of all that is in
his [A]hand, in [w]that Ieue is \`with him, and [s]all[nc] [w]that he is
doing Ieue is prospering.

1-8 Dreams 9-23 40 And [b]coming is it, after ·these ·things, that sinned have
thin[g] word the [7]chief[0] cupbearer of the king of Egypt, and the [7]chief[0]
[E]*M tzr im* Narrows 2 baker [t]against their lord, the [to]king of Egypt. And wroth
[Ph]*Phro e* [H]UNCOVERED[b] is Pharaoh over his two eunuchs, over the chief of the cup-
3 bearers and over the chief of the bakers. And giving \`them
is he over in ward in the house of the chief of the execu-
[J]*I u sph* Add-er tioners, to the round-house, the place where Joseph is
4 [A]bound. And the chief of the executioners gives \`Joseph the
supervision over \`them, and he is ministering to \`them.
And coming are they to be some days in ward.
5 And dreaming are both a dream. Each man has his dream
same ONE in the same night, each man [as]according to the interpretation of his dream, the [7]chief[0] cupbearer and the [7]chief[0] baker,
who are the king of Egypt's who are [A]bound in the round-
house.
6 And coming to them is Joseph in the morning, and he is
7 seeing \`them. And, behold! They are turbulent! And asking is
he \`Pharaoh's eunuchs, who are \`with him in the ward of
his lord's house, [to]saying, "For what reason are your faces
[A]evil ·today?"
8 And saying are they to him, "A dream we dream, and
there is no interpreting of \`it." And saying is Joseph to
them, "Do not interpretations belong to the Alueim? Re-
late them, pray, to me."

1-8 Dreams 9-23 9 And relating is the chief cupbearer \`his dream to Joseph
9-11 Eunuch 16-17 and is saying to him, "[v]In my dream, [a]behold! A vine is be-
10 fore me. And in the vine are three intertwining branches.
Ripen COOK And it seems as if budding. [7]Up come blossoms.[0] Ripening
11 are its clusters of grapes. And the cup of Pharaoh is in my
press SLAYING hand. And taking am I \`the grapes and pressing \`them
into Pharaoh's cup. And giving am I \`the cup [on]into Phar-
hand PALM aoh's hand."[v]

12-13 Interpretation 12 And saying to him is Joseph, "This is its interpretation:
18-22 13 The three intertwined branches, three days are they. In
further three days Pharaoh will [F]lift up \`your [N]head, and
restore you [on]to your post, and you shall give Pharaoh's
custom JUDGMENT cup into his hand, [as]according to the former custom, by
which you became his cupbearer.

14-15 Request 23 14 "For, remember me should \`you [as]when it is well [t]with
well GOOD you, [a]then, pray, [do]deal withal in kindness, and mention me
14 Lu2342 15 to Pharaoh, and [c]bring me forth from ·this ·house, for
[H]*Obr i* PASSER [s]verily, stolen was I from the land of the Hebrews, and,
moreover, here have I done naught that they should place
\`me in [7]this[0] cistern."

9-11 Eunuch 16-17 16 And seeing is the chief of the bakers that he interprets
well GOOD well. And saying is he to Joseph, "Indeed, I [7]dreamed[f] in my
dream and, behold! [v]Three trays of [7]cereal[f] food is on my
17 head. And in the uppermost ·tray are some [f]of all food for
Pharaoh, [7]the king,[0] made by baking. And the flyers [7]of
the heavens[0] are eating \`them from the tray, off my head."[v]

18 **And answering is Joseph and saying ʼto him°, "This is** 12-13 Interpretation
19 **its interpretation: The three trays, three days are they. In** 18-22
further three days, [A]lift will Pharaoh `your head off of you, *I e u e*
and hang `you on a tree. And the flyers ʼof the heavens° shall Will-be-ing-was
eat `your flesh off of you."
20 **And [b]coming is it [t]on the third day, the birthday of `Phar-** [Ph]*Phro e* [H]UNCOVERED[b]
aoh, [a]that he is making a feast for all his servants. And
[A]lifting up is he `the [N]head of the chief of the cupbearers,
and `the head of the chief of the bakers in the midst of his
21 **servants. And restoring is he `the chief of the cupbearers** *21* 4113
[on]to his cupbearing, and giving is he `the cup[on]into the hand hand PALM
22 **of Pharaoh. [a]Yet `the chief of the bakers he hangs, accord-**
ing as [w]Joseph had interpreted to them.

23 **[a]Yet the chief of the cupbearers did not remember `Joseph,** 14-15 Request 23
and forgetting him is he. *23* Am66

41 **And [b]coming is it [t]at the end of two years to a day that** 1-36 Exaltation 37-57
Pharaoh dreams and, behold! [V]Standing is he [on]at the water- 1-4 Dream, Cows 17-21
2 **way. And, behold! From the waterway are coming up**
seven young cows, lovely in appearance and plump of flesh.
3 **And grazing are they in the marsh grass. And, behold!**
Seven other young cows are coming up after them from
the waterway, evil in appearance and thin of flesh. And
standing are they beside the young cows on the shore of the shore lip
4 **waterway. And eating are the ʼseven° young cows, evil in**
·appearance and thin of ·flesh, `the seven young cows, lovely
in ·appearance and ·plump.[V] And waking is Pharaoh.

5 **And sleeping is he and dreaming a second time. And, be-** 5-7 Dream, Spikes 22-24
hold! [V]Seven spikes are coming up [t]on one reed, plump and
6 **good. And behold! Seven ʼother° spikes, thin and blasted by**
7 **the burning east wind are sprouting after them. And up**
are swallowing the ʼseven° spikes, ·thin ʼand blasted by the
east wind,° `the seven ·plump and ·full spikes.[V] And waking
is Pharaoh. And, behold! A dream was it.

8 **And [b]coming is it in the morning [a]that agitated is his** 8-16 Interpretation 25-36
spirit, and sending is he and calling `all the sacred scribes
of Egypt and `all its wise men. And relating is Pharaoh to [E]*M tzr im* Narrows
them `his dream. [a]Yet no one is there to interpret ʼ[V]it° for
Pharaoh.
9 **And speaking is the chief of the cupbearers to `Pharaoh,[to]**
10 **saying, "Of my sin am I reminded ·today. Pharaoh was wroth**
[on]with his servants, and gave ʼ[V]us° in ward in the house of
the chief of the executioners, `me and `the chief of the bakers.
11 **And dreaming are we a dream in the same night, I and** same ONE
he. Each man dreamed [as]according to the interpretation of
12 **his dream. And there `with us was a Hebrew lad, a servant** [H]*Obr i* PASSER
[t]of the chief of the executioners. And we related them to
him and he is interpreting for us `our dreams. For each man,
13 **[as]according to his dream, he interpreted. And [b]coming is it**
that, as [w]he interpreted to us, so it comes to be. `Me he
restores [on]to my post, and `him he hanged."
14 **And sending is Pharaoh and calling `Joseph. And running** *J I u sph* Add-er
him are they from the cistern. And shaving is he and chang- change varying
ing his garments, and coming to Pharaoh.

[J] *Iusph* Add-er 15 **And saying is Pharaoh to Joseph, "A dream I dream, and**
Al u eim **there is no one to interpret 'it. And I hear [to] say [on] of you,**
SUBJECT-or-to-s **that you, hearing a dream, [to] interpret 'it."**
(To-subjectors) 16 **And answering 'Pharaoh is Joseph [to] saying, "Apart from**
the Alueim [7] there is no [nc] answer for the welfare of Pharaoh."

1-4 Dream, Cows 17-21 17 **And speaking is Pharaoh to Joseph [7] saying, [o] "In my**
[shore] lip **dream, [V] behold me standing on the shore of the waterway.**
18 **And behold! From the waterway are coming up seven**
young cows, plump of flesh and lovely in shape. And graz-
ing are they in the marsh grass.
19 **"And, behold! Seven other young cows are coming up**
[7] from the waterway [o] after them, poor and exceedingly evil
in shape, and emaciated of flesh. Not seen have I such as
[so] to 20 **they in all the land of Egypt, [t] so evil. And eating are the**
[7] seven [o] emaciated and evil young cows the 'first seven
[7] ·lovely and [o] ·plump ·young cows, and coming are they into
[inwards] NEAR 21 **[7] their [n] inwards, [a] yet not known is it that they come into**
[7] their [n] inwards, and their appearance is evil, as [wi] at the
start. [V] And awaking am I.

5-7 Dream, Spikes 22-24 22 **"And I [7] sleep and [o] am seeing [7] again [o] in my dream, and,**
behold! [V] Seven spikes are coming up [i] on one reed, full and
23 **good. And, behold! Seven [7] other [o] spikes, puny, thin, [7] and [n]**
blasted by the burning east wind, sprouting after them.
24 **And swallowing up are the [7] seven [o] ·thin ·spikes [7] blasted by**
[stat] SAYING **the east wind, [o] the seven ·good [7] ·full [o] ·spikes. [V] And stating**
this am I to the sacred scribes, and there is no one telling [to]
me what it is."

8-16 Interpretation 25-36 25 **And saying is Joseph to Pharaoh, "The dream of Pharaoh,**
[Ph] *Phroe* [H] UNCOVERed [b] **one is it. '[a] What the Alueim will be doing He tells to Pharaoh.**
26 **The seven good young cows, seven years are they; and the**
seven good ·spikes, seven years are they. The dream [7] of
27 **Pharaoh, [o] one is it. And the seven emaciated and ·evil young**
·cows ·coming up after them, seven years are they. And
the seven empty ·spikes, blasted by the burning east wind,
28 **are coming to be seven years of famine. It is the word**
which I speak to Pharaoh: '[w] What the Alueim will do He
29 **shows to 'Pharaoh. Behold! Seven years are coming of**
30 4153 30 **great satisfaction in all the land of Egypt. [a] Yet rise will**
seven years of famine after them. And forgotten will be all
the satisfaction in [7] all [o] the land of Egypt, and finish will
31 **the famine 'the land. And not known shall be the satisfac-**
tion in the land, in view of the famine ·that is afterward,
32 Is40[2] 61[7] Ze9[12] 32 **for [F] heavy will it be exceedingly. And on account of the**
repetition of the dream to Pharaoh twice, it is that the
[matter] word **matter is established [f] with the Alueim. And the Alueim**
will hasten His doing of it.
33 **"And now, see will Pharaoh to a man of understanding**
34 **and wisdom, and set him over the [N] land of Egypt. Doing**
this will Pharaoh, and he will [c] give the supervision to
supervisors over the [N] land and a fifth of [7] all the produce of [c]
the land of Egypt will they take in the seven years of ·sat-
[gt togeth] CONVENE 35 **isfaction. And get together shall they 'all the food of ·these**
[7] seven [n] ·coming ·good ·years, and heap up cereals under the

36 [A]**hand of Pharaoh for food in the cities, and keep it. And**
the food shall **come to be**[to]**supervised** [t]in the **land for the**
seven years of the famine which shall come to **be in** the
land of Egypt, and so **the** [A]**land shall not be cut** off [i]**by** the
famine."

37 **And good is the matter** in the [A]**eyes of Pharaoh and in**
38 the [A]**eyes of all his servants. And saying is Pharaoh to his**
servants, "Find will we one **as this man, who has the spirit**
of the **Alueim in him?"**
39 **And saying is Pharaoh to Joseph, "After** the **Alueim has**
[c]**made known** to 'you 'all this, there is no one as **understand-**
40 **ing and wise as**[wt]**you. You shall be**[c] **over my household,**
and [on]**at your bidding all my people shall bear weapons. But**
on the [N]**throne will I be greater** [f]**than you."**

41 **And saying is Pharaoh to Joseph, "See! Given 'you have**
42 **I** [?]**today**[o] **to be over all the** [N]**land of Egypt." And taking off**
from his hand 'his ring is Pharaoh, and is putting 'it on the
hand of Joseph. And clothing 'him is he in garments of
cambric sheen, **and is placing** a knitted collar of '**gold on his**
43 **neck, and is** [c]**having 'him ride in the second chariot which**
he [t]**has. And calling are they before him, "Kneel!" And he**
[?]**gives**[n] **'him** to be **over all** the [N]**land of Egypt.**
44 **And saying is Pharaoh to Joseph, "I** am **Pharaoh, and**
apart from you shall **no man raise 'his** [N]**hand** [a]**or 'his** [N]**foot**
in all the land **of Egypt."**
45 **And calling is Pharaoh Joseph's name Zaphnath-paaneah.**
And giving[to]**him is he Asenath, daughter of Potiphera,**
priest of On, for a wife. And forth is Joseph faring over
46 the **land of Egypt. And Joseph is thirty years** [s]**old** [i]**when he**
stands before Pharaoh, king of Egypt. And forth is Joseph
faring from[to]the [N]**face of Pharaoh, and passing** [i]**through**
all the land of Egypt.

47 **And** [do]**yielding is the land in the seven years of satisfac-**
48 **tion,** [t]**by fistfuls. And getting together is he 'all the food of**
the seven years [?]**of satisfaction**[n] **which come to be in the**
land of Egypt. And bestowing is he the food in the cities.
The food of the field of the city which surrounds it, he
49 **bestows in its midst. And heaping up is Joseph cereals as**
the sand of the sea, multiplied exceedingly furthermore, so
that he leaves off[to]**numbering, for there is no numbering it.**

50 **And to Joseph are born two sons,**[in]**ere the** [?]**seven**[o] **famine**
years are coming, whom Asenath, daughter of Potiphera,
51 **priest of On, bears for him. And calling is Joseph 'the name**
of the firstborn Manasseh, for "the Alueim makes me ob-
52 **livious of 'all my toil and 'all my father's household." And**
'the name of the second he calls Ephraim, for "the Alueim
makes me [F]**fruitful in the land of my humiliation."**

53 **And concluding are the seven years of satisfaction, which**
54 **come to be in the land of Egypt, and starting to come are**
the seven years of famine, as[w]**Joseph had said. And** [b]**com-**
ing is the famine in all 'lands, [a]**yet in all the land of Egypt**
55 **there comes to be** [N]**bread.** [a]**When famishing is all the** [A]**land of**
Egypt, [a]**then crying are the people to Pharaoh for** [N]**bread.**

Al u e im
SUBJECT-or-to-s (To-subjectors)
[E]*M tzr im* Narrows
matter word
1-36 Exaltation 37-57
37-46 Joseph -56-57
40 458
bid MOUTH
weapons KISS (?eat?)
[Ph]*Phro e* [H]UNCOVERED[b]
[J]*I u sph* Add-er
put GIVING
raise HIGH
[Z]*Tzphn th* [H]SECLUDE[b]
Phonch [H]PUFF-UP-STOP[b]
[A]*Asnth* (Egyptian)
[O]*Aun* [H]NEGATE[b]
47-49 Dreams 53-56
gt togeth CONVENING
50-51 Fruitfulness 52
[P]*Phutiphro* (Egyptian)
[M]*M nsh e* Oblivion
50-51 Fruitfulness 52
[E]*A phr im* FRUIT-s
47-49 Dreams 53-56
54 1210

I e u e Will-be-ing-was And saying is Pharaoh to all [A]Egypt, "Go to Joseph, [7]and[n]
56 what he will say to you, be doing." And the famine comes
to be on the surface of all the earth.

37-46 Joseph -56-57 And opening is Joseph ʽall [7]the cereal[n] stores which are
[J]Iusph Add-er among them, and is [S]retailing[n] to [7]all[o] [A]Egypt. And the
57 [I]famine is holding fast in the land of Egypt. And all [7·A]lands[n]
come to[d] Egypt to Joseph to purchase, for fast is the [I]famine holding in all the earth.

381-30 Joseph 421-4528
421-2 Commission 431-2 **42** And seeing is Jacob that, forsooth, there are victuals in
[J]Ioqb HEEL Egypt. And saying is Jacob to his sons, "Why are you star-
stare[r]SEEING 2 ing at one another?" And saying is he, "Behold! I hear,
forsooth, that there are victuals in Egypt. Go down there
and purchase for us thence [7]a little food[o] [a]that we will live,
and not die."

3 Journey 4315- 3 And down are going ten brothers of Joseph to purchase
cereals from Egypt.

4 Benjamin 433-14 4 [a]Yet ʽBenjamin, Joseph's brother, Jacob does not send
[B]Bn-imin Son-RIGHT ʽwith his brothers, for, says he, "Lest meet will he with a
mishap."

5 Arrival 43-15 5 And coming are the sons of Israel to purchase in the
[I]Ishr-Al Upright-with-SUBJECTOR midst of the comers, for the famine comes to be in the land
of Canaan.

6-24 As Authority 6 And Joseph, he has ·authority over the [N]land. He is the
4316-34 retailer to all the people of the land. And coming are the
6 377 8 brothers of Joseph and prostrating to him, nostrils to[d] the
7 4418-34 7 earth. And seeing is Joseph ʽhis brothers, and is recognizing
them. [a]Yet foreign makes he himself to them, and is speaking ʽwith them obstinately, and is saying to them, "Whence
come you?"

[C]Knon SUBMITTER And saying are they, "From the land of Canaan, to purchase food."

8 And recognizing is Joseph ʽhis brothers, [a]yet they do not
9 375 9 9 recognize him. And remembering is Joseph the dreams
which he dreamed [t]concerning them. And saying is he to
them, "Spies are ʽyou. To see ʽthe [F]nakedness of the land
you come."

10 And saying are they to him, "No, my lord. And your
11 servants come to purchase food. All of us, sons of one man
are we. Established are we. Not spies [b]are your servants."
12 And saying is he to them, "No. For the [F]nakedness of the
land you come to see."
13 And saying are they, "Your servants, twelve brothers
are we, sons of one man in the land of Canaan. And, behold!
The smallest is ʽwith our father ·today, and ·one is not."
14 And saying to them is Joseph, "It is what I speak to you,
15 [to]saying, 'Spies are ʽyou.' [i]By this will you be tested. By
the life of Pharaoh, should you fare forth hence, save your
16 ·smallest brother [in]come hither—! Send one [f]of you, and he
shall take ʽyour brother here, and ʽyou shall be bound, and
your words shall be tested, whether the truth is ʽwith you.
*[Ph]Phroe [H]*UNCOVERED[b] And should it not be, by the life of Pharaoh—! For spies
are ʽyou."

[s]And saying are they, "The youth cannot leave his father. leav FORSAKE
17 [a]When he leaves 'his father, [a]then he will die."[n] And gathering 'them is he into a ward three days.
18 And saying to them is Joseph [i]on the third day, "This do Iusph Add-er
19 and live. 'The Alueim fear I. If 'you are established, one Al u e im
of your brothers shall be bound in the house of your ward. SUBJECT-or-to-s (To-subjectors)
And 'you go [7]and[n] bring the victuals [7]you have purchased[f]
20 for the famine of your households. And 'your 'smallest
brother you shall bring to me. And if faithful be found your
words, [a]then you shall not die." And doing so are they.
21 And saying are they, each man to his brother, "Nevertheless, guilty are we on account of our brother [w]when we saw
the distress of his [N]soul, [i]when he supplicated [to] us and we
did not hearken. Therefore comes [7]on[n] us [S]all[n] 'this 'distress."
22 And answering 'them is Reuben, [to] saying, "Did not I speak speak SAY
to you, [to] saying, 'You must not sin [i]against the boy'? And 22 3721
not hearken did you. And, moreover, behold! His [A]blood is
23 required." [a]Yet they do not know that Joseph is hearing, req INQUIRED
24 for the translator is between them. And around is [7]Joseph[0] tran mock
going, away from [on] them, and is weeping. And returning is weep LAMENT
he to them, and is speaking to them. And taking is he from 24 3425 495
'them 'Simeon and is binding 'him [t]before their [A]eyes. SShmoun HEARER

25 And instruction is Joseph giving, [a]when they are filling 25-26 Money 441-4524
'their vessels with cereals, [a] to return his [=]money to each
man [to]in his sack. and to give [to] them provisions for the [A]way.
And done is it to them so.
26 And up are they lifting their victuals on their asses, and
going are they thence.

27 And opening is 'one 'his sack to give provender to his ass 4227-38 Return 4525-28
in the lodging, and seeing is he 'his money [7]pouch[0], and
28 behold! It is in the mouth of his bag! And saying is he to
his brothers, "Restored is my money, and, moreover, [7]it[n] is
in my bag!" And forth is faring their heart and trembling
are they, each man saying to his brother, "What is this that
the Alueim does to us?"
29 And coming are they to Jacob, their father, to[d] the land IIoqb HEEL
of Canaan, and are telling [to] him 'all 'that had befallen 'them, CKnon SUBMITter
30 [to]saying, "The man, the lord of the [N]land, spoke 'to us
obstinately, and gave 'us over [7]in ward[0] as spies of 'the
31 [N]land. And we said to him, 'Established are we. Not [b]come
32 have we to spy. Twelve are we, brothers, sons of our father. 32 3728
'One is not, and the smallest is 'today 'with our father in
33 the land of Canaan.' And saying to us is the man, the lord
of the [N]land, '[i]By this shall I know that 'you are established.
Your brothers, 'one leave be 'with me. And [7]the victuals
you have purchased[0] for the 'famine of your households, take
34 and go. And bring 'your 'small brother to me, [a]then I will
know that 'you are not spies, for established are 'you. 'Your
brother will I give back to you, and in 'the land shall you
be merchants.'"
35 And [b]coming is it, at their emptying their sacks, [a]behold!
Each man's money pouch is in his sack. And seeing are
they and their father 'the pouches with their money, and
36 are fearful. And saying to them is Jacob, their father, "Me

JIusph Add-er you bereave! Joseph is not, and Simeon is not, and 'Benja-
SShmoun HEARER min you will take! On me bcome all these things."
speakSAYING 37 And speaking is Reuben to his father, to saying, "Two of
my sons cput to death should I not bring him back to you.
Give 'him oninto my Ahand, and I will restore him to you."
ss 3735 38 And saying is he, "Not go down with you shall my son,
for his brother is dead, and he to alone remains. And meets
I e u e him a mishap in the way in which you will go, athen down
Will-be-ing-was will you cbring 'my Ngray hairs iwith affliction tod the unseen."

421-2 Commission 431-2 43 And the famine is Fheavy in the land. 2And bcoming is it,
as wthey finish to eating 'the victuals which they had brought
EMtzrim Narrows from Egypt, athen saying to them is their father, "Return.
Purchase for us a little food."

424 Benjamin 433-14 3 And speaking to him is Judah, to saying, "The man testified,
speakSAYING yea, testified ito us, to saying, 'You shall not see my Nface, if
JIeude Acclaimer 4 your 7'small0 brother fails to be 'with you!' Should you,
forsooth, send 'our brother 'with us, down will we go and
5 purchase food for you. aYet should you not be sending 7our
brother with us,0 we will not go down, for the man said to
us, 'You shall not see my Nface if your 7'small0 brother fails
to be 'with you!'"
IIshr-Al Upright- 6 And saying is Israel, "Why did you cdo evil to me tby tell-
with-SUBJECTOR ing to the man you thave 'still another brother?"
6 4236 7 And saying are they, "In his asking, the man asked tconcerning us and tconcerning our kindred, to saying, 'Still is
your father living? Forsooth, thave you a brother?' And we
bidMOUTH told to him, onat his bidding 'these 'matters 7of which he
matterword asked.0 Did we know, yea, know that he would say 7to us,0
'cBring down 'your brother'?"
8 And saying is Judah to Israel, his father, "Send the youth
'with me, and we will rise and go, and live and not die, both
both and andmoreover 9 we, mrand you mrand our tots. I will be surety for him. From
my Ahand shall you seek him. Should I not bring him to
you and put him before you, athen I sin tagainst you all my
byTHAT 10 days. For, were we not obliged to dally, ttby now we had
returned this twice."
11 And saying to them is Israel, their father, "If so, indeed,
do this: Take from the pruned 7fruit0 trees of the land in
your vessels, and ctake down to the man a present offering,
a little balm and a little honey, perfume and labdanum,
12 pistachio nuts and almonds. And money, duplicated, take
in your hand, and 'the money that 'was restored in the
mouth of your bags, restore iby your hand. Perhaps it was
13 an error. And 'your brother take, and rise Sandn return to
14 the man. And the Al-Who-Suffices give to you compassion
before the man, aso that he lets 'your other brother and
goSEND 'Benjamin go! And I, as w I am bereaved, am I bereaved!"

423 Journey 4315- 15 And taking are the mortals 'this ''present offering and
BBn-imin Son-RIGHT duplicate money take they in their hand, and 'Benjamin.

425 Arrival 43-15 And rising and going down are they tod Egypt. And
426-24 As Brother standing are they before Joseph.
4316-34 16 And seeing 'them is Joseph, 7and" 'Benjamin, 7his brother,

his mother's son,° and saying is he to him who is over his *Al u e im*
household, "Bring 'the mortals to[d] **the house, and slaughter** SUBJECT-or-to-s
a slaughter and [c]**make ready, for 'with me shall the mortals** (To-subjectors)
eat [7N]**bread°** [i]**at** ⁼**noon."**
17 **And doing is the man as**[w]**Joseph says. And bringing is** *JIusph* Add-er
the man 'the mortals to[d] **Joseph's house.**
18 **And fearful are the mortals, for they are brought** [7]**to**[dn]
Joseph's house. And saying are they, "On account of the
matter of the money 'returned in our bags [i]**at the start are** [matter]word
we being brought, to [F]**roll himself upon us, and to fall upon**
us,[a]**to take 'us for servants, and 'our asses."**
19 **And close are they coming to the man who is over Jo-**
seph's household, and speaking are they to him at the
20 **portal of the house. And saying are they, "O! my lord.**
21 **Down, yea, down came we** [i]**at the start to purchase food. And**
it [b]**came that we come to the lodging and opened 'our bags,**
and, behold! The money of each man was in the mouth of
his bag, our money [i]**by its weight,** [a]**yet we will restore 'it**
22 [i]**with our** [7]**hands.° And other money have we** [c]**brought down**
in our hand to purchase food. Not know do we who placed [who]ANY
our money in our bags."
23 **And saying is he, "**[N]**Peace be to you! You must not be**
fearful. Your Alueim and the Alueim of your [7]**forefathers**[n]
gave[to]**you buried treasure in your bags. Your money came**
24 **to me." And forth is he** [c]**bringing 'Simeon to them. And** [S]*Shmoun* HEARER
bringing is the man 'the mortals to[d] **Joseph's house. And**
giving them is he water, and washing are they their feet.
And giving is he provender to their asses.
25 **And preparing are they 'the present offering, till the**
coming of Joseph [i]**at** ⁼**noon, for they hear that they shall**
eat [N]**bread there.**
26 **And coming 'home is Joseph, and bringing are they 'the** *26* 377-10
present offering which is in their hand to[d] **the house to**
him, and prostrating are they to him [7]**with their nostrils°**
to[d] **the earth.**
27 **And asking**[to]**them is he as to their welfare, and saying** [welfare]peace
[7]**to them,° "The welfare of your father, the old man of whom**
you were speaking; still living is he?" [speak]SAYING
28 **And saying are they, "Well fares your servant,**[to]**our fa-** [well fare]peace
ther. Still living is he." [7]**And he said, "Blessed be 'that**
'man [t]**by the Alueim!"**[7] **And bowing are they the head and**
prostrating [7]**to him.°**
29 **And** [F]**lifting is** [7]**Joseph° his eyes and seeing 'Benjamin, his** [B]*Bn-imin* Son-RIGHT
brother, his mother's son. And saying is he, "Is this your *29* 4621
'small brother of whom you said you would [7]**bring° him to**
me?" And saying is he, "The Alueim be gracious to you, my
30 [A]**son!" And hastening is Joseph, for fervid is his** ⁼**compassion** *30* 452
for his brother, and seeking is he to weep. And entering is he [weep]LAMENT
31 **his 'chamber and is weeping there. And washing is he his**
face and faring forth. And checking himself is he, and say-
ing "Place on [N]**bread."**
32 **And placing are they for him**[to]**alone and for them**[to]**alone,**
[a]**for the Egyptians are 'eating 'with him**[to]**alone, for the** [E]*Mtzri* Narrows-ites
Egyptians cannot[to]**eat** [N]**bread 'with the Hebrews, for that** [H]*Obri* PASSER
33 **is an abhorrence to the Egyptians. And sitting are they** *33* 374 8
before him, the firstborn [as]**according to his birthright and**

I e u e Will-be-ing-was **the inferior in station [as]according to his inferior estate.**
And amazed are the mortals, each man [to]at his associate.
34 4522 *34* **And lifting up is he helpings, from ‛before him, [to]for them,**
[B]*Bn-im in* Son-RIGHT **and much** more **is Benjamin's helping [f]than all their help-**
ings by **five handfuls. And drinking are they with him and**
are gratified.

4225-26 Money 441-4524 441-13 Dismissal 4517-24

1-2 The Cup 4-12 **44** **And instructing is [7]Joseph[0] ‛him who is over his household,**
[to] **saying, "Fill ‛the bags of the mortals with food, as** [w] **much**
as they can lift, and place the money of each man in the
2 **mouth of his bag. And ‛my beaker, the silver beaker shall**
you place in the mouth of the bag of the small one **[a]with**
‛his victual money." And doing is he [as]according to the
[J]*I u sph* Add-er **word which Joseph speaks.**

3 Departure 13 *3* When **the morning is light,** [a] **the mortals are sent away,**
they and their asses.

1-2 The Cup 4-12 *4* **They fare forth, not far from ‛the city, and Joseph says to**
him who is over his household, "Rise! Pursue after the
mortals and overtake them and say to them, 'Why do you
forUNDER **repay evil [u]for good? [7]Why** did **you steal my silver beaker?** [c]
5 **Is not this [w]that [i]from which my lord drinks? And he,** when
he augurs, auguring is he in it. Evil [c]do you in what you
do'."
6 **And overtaking them is he, and is speaking to them ·these**
‛·words.
7 **And saying are they to him, "Why is my lord speaking**
words **as ·these? Far be it from** [to] **your servants** [f] **to do [as]ac-**
8 **cording** to **·this word. Behold! [S]The[n] money which we found**
[C]*Kno n* SUBMITTER in **the mouths of our bags we restored to you from the**
howWHEREAS **land of Canaan. And how shall we steal from your lord's**
9 **house silver or gold? Whoever [f]of your servants shall be**
found ‛with **it [a]shall die. And, moreover, we will become** [to]
my lord's [to] **servants."**
EvenMoreover *10* **And saying is he, "Even now, [as]according to your words,**
so be it. [7]The man[0] with whom **[7]the beaker[0] shall be found,**
he becomes my servant, and you shall be[c] innocent."
11 **And hasting are they, and [c]letting each man's ‛bag down**
12 **to[d]** the **earth, and opening are they each man, his bag. And**
searching is he, starting **[i]with the greatest and finishing**
[i]with the smallest. And found is the beaker in the bag of
Benjamin.

3 Return 13 *13* **And tearing are they their garments, and lading is each**
man [7]his bag[0] on his ass, and returning are they to[d] the
city.

4414-34 Explanations *14* **And coming are Judah and his brothers to[d] Joseph's**
451-16 **house, and he is still there. And falling are they before him**
14-15 Joseph 17 **to[d] the earth.**
15 **And saying to them is Joseph, "What ·deed is ·this [w]that**
you do? Not know, do you, **that, by augury a man such as I**
am, is auguring?"

16 Judah 18-34 *16* **And saying is Judah, "What shall we say to my lord?**
What shall we speak? And with what shall we justify our-
selves? The Alueim has **found ‛the depravity of your ser-**

vants. Behold us, servants [t]of my lord, [mr]both we [mr]and he in [both and]moreover
whose hand the beaker was found."

17 **And saying is 'Joseph', "Far be it from [to]me [f]to do this!** 14-15 Joseph 17
The man in whose hand the beaker was found, he shall *JIusph* Add-er
become my servant. And you, go [t]in peace to your father."

18 **And close is Judah coming to him and saying, "O! my lord.** 16 Judah 18-34
Pray, speak will your servant a word in the [A]ears of my *JIeude* Acclaimer
lord, and your anger must not be [A]hot [i]against your ser- *18* 3726 27 438 9
19 **vant, seeing that such a one as you are as Pharaoh. My** [Ph]*Phro e* [H]UNCOVERED[b]
lord asked 'his servants [to]saying, 'Forsooth, [t]have you a
20 **father or a brother?' And said we to my lord, 'Forsooth,** *I e u e* Will-be-ing-was
we [t]have a father, old, and a boy of his old age, the smallest,
and his brother is dead, and left is he [to]alone [t]of his mother,
21 **and his father loves him.' And said you to your servants,**
'[c]Bring him down to me [a]that I may place my [A]eyes upon
22 **him.' And said we to my lord, 'The youth cannot [to]leave 'his** [leave]FORSAKE
23 **father. And, leaves he 'his father, he also will die.' [a]Yet**
you said to your servants, 'Should not your 'smallest
brother come down 'with you, you shall not continue to see
my [N]face.'

24 **"And [b]coming is it that we went up to your servant, 'our'**
25 **father, and we told [to]him 'the words of my lord. And saying**
26 **is our father, 'Return. Purchase for us a little food.' And**
said we, 'We cannot [to]go down. Should, forsooth, our 'small-
est brother 'go down' 'with us, [a]then we will go down, for we
cannot [to]see the man's [N]face [a]if our 'smallest brother is not
'with us.'

27 **"And saying is your servant, 'our' father, to us, 'You**
28 **know that two were borne for me by my wife. And forth** *28* 3731 32 35
is 'one faring from 'me. And saying am I, "Yea, as prey is
29 **he torn to pieces!" And not seen him have I hitherto. And**
take this one, moreover, from [wi]before my [N]face, and a
mishap befalls him 'on the way,' [a] down will you [c]bring 'my
[N]gray hairs [i]by evil to[d] the unseen.'

30 **"And now, as I come to your servant, 'our' father, and**
the youth is not 'with us, [a]when his [N]soul is tied [i]to his
31 **[N]soul, and it [b]comes as he sees that no 'youth is 'with us,'**
[a]he will die, and down will your servants [c]bring the '[N]gray
hairs of your servant, our father, [i]by affliction to[d] the
32 **unseen. For your servant became surety for 'the youth [f]**
with my father, [to]saying, 'Should I not bring him to you
'and set him before you', [a]I sin [t]against my father all my
'days.'

33 **"And now, dwell, pray, will your servant, [u]instead of the** [instead]UNDER
youth, a servant to my lord, and the youth shall go up with
34 **his brothers. For how shall I go up to my father, and the** [how]WHEREAS
youth is not 'with 'us,' lest I shall see [in]the evil which will
find 'my father?"

45 **[a]Yet Joseph cannot [to]check himself [t]before all who are** 44[14-34] Explanations
'stationed [on]about him. And calling is he, "Forth [c]go every 45[1-16]
man from [on]me!" And no man stands 'with him [t]while Joseph 1-2- Joseph 3-15
makes himself known to his brothers.

2 **And giving is he 'his voice [i]to lamentation. And hearing**
are 'all' the Egyptians. And hearing is the household of -2 Pharaoh 16
Pharaoh. [E]*M tzr i* Narrows-ites

1-2- Joseph 3-15 3 And saying is Joseph to his brothers, "I am Joseph. Still
3-4 J. Revealed 9-13 is my father living?"
3 4328 Mt2430 Rv17 And his brothers cannot[to] answer 'him, for flustered are
they [f]by his presence.
4 Ac79 4 And saying is Joseph to his brothers, "Come close, pray,
Al u eim SUBJECT-or-to-s to me." And close are they coming. And saying is he, "I am
(To-subjectors) Joseph, your brother, whom you sold to[d] [A]Egypt.

5 Alueim's Over-ruling 7-8 5 "And now, you must not grieve, and it must not be [A]hot
in your [A]eyes, that you sell 'me hither, for to [c]preserve life
5 Ps10517 Ac317 79 the Alueim sends me before you.

6-2 yrs.-Famine-5 yrs. -6 6 "For this two years the famine is within the land, and
there are still five years in which there is no plowing [a]or
constitutePLACE harvesting.

5 Alueim's Over-ruling 7-8 7 "And sending me is the Alueim before you to constitute
[to]you a remnant in the earth and to [c]preserve your lives for
8 4143 8 a great deliverance. And now, not you send 'me hither, for
constitutePLACE it was the Alueim. And constituting me is He[to] a [M]father to
Ph*Phro e* [H]UNCOVERED[b] Pharaoh, and[to] lord [t]of all his household, and ruler in all
the land of Egypt.

3-4 J. Revealed 9-13 9 "Hasten and go up to my father and say to him, 'Thus
constitutePLACE says your son Joseph, "The Alueim has constituted me[to] lord
J*I usph* Add-er [t]of all [⁷]the [N]land of[°] Egypt. Come down to me. You must
staySTAND 10 not stay there. And dwell in the land of Goshen and [b]come
G*Gsh n* CLOSE-by to be near to me, you and your sons and your sons' sons,
See map page 107. and your flocks and your herds, and all which is yours.
11 And sustain 'you will I there, for there are still five years
of famine, lest destitute you be becoming, and your [⁷]sons[°]
and all who are yours."'
12 "And, behold, your [N]eyes are seeing, and the [N]eyes of my
brother Benjamin, that it is my [N]mouth which is speaking
13 to you. And tell my father of 'all my glory in Egypt, and
of 'all [w]that you see. And hasten and [c]bring down 'my
father hither."
14 And falling is he on the neck of his brother Benjamin
weepLAMENTING and weeping [⁷]on him.[°] And Benjamin weeps on his neck.
15 And kissing is he[to] all his brothers and is weeping on them.
And afterward his brothers speak 'with him.

-2 Pharaoh 16 16 And a 'voice is heard in Pharaoh's house,[to] saying, "Come
have the brothers of Joseph." And good is it in the [A]eyes of
Pharaoh and in the [A]eyes of his servants.

441-13 Dismissal 4517-24 17 And saying is Pharaoh to Joseph, "Say to your brothers,
'This do: Spur 'your brutes and go. Enter into[d] the land of
C*Kno n* SUBMITTER 18 Canaan, and take 'your father and 'your households and
come to me. And give will I to you [⁷]all[°] 'the [N]good of the
19 land of Egypt. And eat shall you 'the [N]fat of the land. And
you are instructed to do this: Take to you from the land of
Egypt cars for your tots and for your wives, and carry
20 'your father and come. And your [A]eye must not commiserate
you over your chattels, for the [N]good of all the land of
I*I shr-Al* Upright- Egypt, yours is it'."
with-SUBJECTOR 21 And doing so are the sons of Israel. And giving to them is
bidMOUTH Joseph cars [on]at the bidding of Pharaoh, [⁷]the king,[°] and he

22 **is giving to them provisions for the ^way. To every to man of** 22 4334
them he gives changes of garments, and to Benjamin he change vary
gives three =hundred silverlings and five changes of gar- BBn-imin Son-RIGHT
23 **ments And to his father he sends as this: ten jack-asses**
bearing f the Ngood Sof the land c of Egypt, and ten she-asses EMtzrim Narrows
bearing cereals and bread and a sort for his father for the
^way. Al u eim
24 **And sending is he 'his brothers and they are going. And** SUBJECT-or-to-s (To-subjectors)
saying is he to them, "You must not be disturbed ion the
way."

25 **And up are they going from Egypt and coming to d the** 4227-38 Return 4525-28
26 **land of Canaan, to Jacob, their father. And telling to him** CKnon SUBMITTER
are they, to saying, "Still is 'your son,' Joseph, living!" And JIusph Add-er
that "he is ruling in all the land of Egypt!" aYet so torpid
27 **is 'Jacob's' Fheart that he does not believe to them. And** IIoqb HEEL
speaking are they to him 'all the words of Joseph which he
spoke to them. aYet seeing is he 'the cars which Joseph
had sent to carry 'him. aThen living is the Nspirit of Jacob,
28 **their father. And Israel is saying, "Much! Still is Joseph,** IIshr-Al Upright-with-SUBJECTOR
my son, living! Go will I and see him in ere I die."

46 And journeying is Israel, 'he', and all wthat he thas. And 1-7 Jacob,Egypt 28-5014
coming is he to d Beer-sheba and is sacrificing sacrifices to 1 Journey 5-7
the Alueim of his father Isaac. See map page 92. IItzchq LAUGH-causer

2 **And speaking is the Alueim to Israel in appearances of** 2 God speaks 3-4
the night, and saying, v"Jacob! Jacob!" And saying is he, 2 2211 3228
"Behold me!"

3 **And saying is He, "I am the Al, the Alueim of your** 2 God speaks 3-4
forefather. You must not fear fto go down to d Egypt, for 3 1513 14 262
4 **to a great nation will I constitute you there. I will go down** con PLACE
with you to d Egypt, and I, moreover, will cbring, yea, bring 4 1514
you up. And Joseph shall set his 'hands' on your eyes."v

5 **And rising is Jacob from Beer-sheba. And carrying are** 1 Journey 5-7
the sons of Israel 'Jacob, their father, and 'their tots and BBar-Shbo WELL-oath
'their wives, in the cars which Pharaoh sends to carry 'him. PhPhroe HUNCOVEREDb
6 **And taking are they 'their cattle and 'all' 'their goods which** 5 4519
they had gotten in the land of Canaan, and coming to d
7 **Egypt, Jacob and all his ^seed 'with him. His sons and sons'** 7 3155 4615 17
sons 'with him, his daughters, and his son's daughters, and
all his ^seed brings he 'with him to d Egypt.

8 **And these are the names of the sons of** 8-25 Sons 26-27 8-15 Leah, Rachel 19-22
Israel 'coming to d Egypt: Jacob and his 8 493-27
sons: The firstborn of Jacob, Reuben. RRaubn SEE-son
9 **And the sons of Reuben: Enoch and** EChnuk DEDICATED
Phallu and Hezron and Carmi. PPhlua MARVELER HChtzrun Court CKrmi VINE-YARDist
10 **And the sons of Simeon: Jemuel and** SShmoun HEARER JImu-Al 'DAY-AL'
Jamin and Ohad and Jachin and Zohar JImin RIGHTER OAed OBTRUDE JIkin 'Establisher'
and Shaul, son of a 'Canaanitess. ZTzchr GREY SShaul ASKED-for CKnoni SUBMITTER-ite
11 **And the sons of Levi: Gershon, Kohath** LLui OBLIGATED GGrshun DRIVER-OUT
and Merari. KQeth 'BLUNTED' MMrri Bitterness 11 Nu2659
12 **And the sons of Judah: Er and Onan** JIeude Acclaimer EOr Denuded OAunn NEGATION
and Shelah and Pharez and Zarah. aYet SShle EASE PPhrtz BREACH ZZrch RADIANT
Er and Onan died in the land of Canaan.
And there come to be sons of Pharez:
Hezron and Hamul. HeChtzrun Court HaChmul SPARER

IIsh shkr Forsooth-hire TThulo MAGGOT 13 PPhue MOUTH JI shub Dweller SShmr un Observer	And the sons of Issachar: Tola and Phuvah and 'Jashub" and Shimron.
ZZbul un PREFERRED SS rd PROBE-DOWN 14 EAl un Oak JI chl-Al Await-SUBJECTOR	And the sons of Zebulon: Sered and Elon and Jahleel.
LLa e 'No-thing' 15 PPhdn RANSOM SA rm HEIGHT DDin e ADJUDICATRESS	These are the sons of Leah, which she bears for Jacob in Padan, Syria, and 'Dinah, his daughter. All the Nsouls of his sons and his daughters are thirty-three.
16-18 Maids' Sons 23-25	
GGd RAID ZTzph i un Watcher HChg i Celebrant 16 SShun i REPEATER EA tzb un STATION ErOri NAKED ArodiArud i Descender AreliAr-Al i Lion-Al-ite	And the sons of Gad: Ziphion and Haggi 'and" Shuni and Ezbon, Eri and Arodi and Areli.
AAshr PROGRESS II mn e RIGHTER 17 II shue EQUAL BB rioe IN-association SShrch Who-scents HChbr JOIN MMlk i Al MY-KING-Al	And the sons of Asher: Imnah and Ishuah and Ishui and Beriah; and Serah, their sister. And the sons of Beriah: Heber and Malchiel.
ZZl pheREPLETE-MOUTH 18 LLbn WHITE LLa e 'No-thing'	These are the sons of Zilpah, whom Laban gives to his daughter Leah, and she bears 'these for Jacob—sixteen Nsouls.
8-15 Leah, Rachel 19-22	
RRchl EWE JI oqb HEEL JoI u sph Add-er 19 BBn imin SON-RIGHT	The sons of Rachel, Jacob's wife: Joseph and Benjamin.
20 EMtzr im NARROWS AAsnth (Egyptian) PPhut i phr (Egyptian) OAun HNEGATE[b] MM nsh e Oblivion EA phr im FRUITS SArmith HIGHESS (fem.) MMchir SELLER GGlod 'ROLL-FURTHER'	And 'sons' are born to Joseph in the land of Egypt, whom Asenath, daughter of Potiphera, priest of On, bears for him, 'Manasseh and 'Ephraim. 'And sons are born to Manasseh, whom a Syrian concubine bears for him, Machir. And Machir begets Galaad. And the sons of Ephraim, Manasseh's brother: Soutalaam and Taam. And the son of Soutalaam: Edem.'
BBn imin SON-RIGHT BelBlo IN-SWALLOW 21 BBkr Firstborn AAsh bl MAN-DISINTEGRATE GGr a STIR NNom n PLEASANTNESS AAch i AH-ME RRash HEAD MMph im HChph im OVERSPREADS AA rd Descender	And the sons of Benjamin: Belah and Becher and Ashbel. 'And sons were born to Belah:' Gera and Naaman, Ehi and Rosh, Muppim and Huppim and 'to Gera is born' Ard.
22	These are the sons of Rachel, who were born to Jacob. All the Nsouls are 'eighteen.'
16-18 Maids' Sons 23-25	
DDn ADJUDICATE HChsh im HURRY- 23	And the son of Dan: Hushim.
NN phthl i TWISTED JI chtz-Al DIVIDER-Al 24 GGun i PROTECTOR JI tzr Former SShlm Welfare	And the sons of Naphtali: Jahzeel and Guni and Jezer and Shillem.
BBl ee DISINTEGRATED 25 I e u e Will-be-ing-was	These are the sons of Bilhah, whom Laban gives to Rachel, his daughter. And she bears 'these for Jacob. All the Nsouls are seven.

8-25 Sons 26-27 26 All the Nsouls ·coming twith Jacob tod Egypt, which fare
26 Summary 27 forth from his thighs, aside from the wives of Jacob's sons
26 Summary 27 27 —all the Nsouls are sixty a six. And the sons of Joseph who
26 1Ch714-20 Ac714 are born to him in Egypt are two Nsouls. All the Nsouls
27 Ex15 Ru411 pertaining to the Ahouse of Jacob ·coming tod Egypt are
See map page 107. 'seventy-five.'

461-7 Jacob, Egypt 4628-5014 4628-4712 Sojourn 4727-5013 4628 Jacob 4711-12

28 3726 4418 28 And 'Judah he sends before him to Joseph, to direct to his
JIeud e Acclaimer Nface tod Goshen. And coming are they tod the land of
GGsh n CLOSE-by Goshen.

29 **And hitching up is Joseph his chariot and is going up to[d] Goshen to meet Israel, his father, and is appearing to him. And falling is he on his neck. And weeping is he longer on his neck.** — 4629-30 Meeting 477-10; [I]shr-Al Upright-with-SUBJECTOR; weep LAMENTING

30 **And saying is Israel to Joseph, "Die will I at once, after my seeing your [N]face, for still living are you!"** — [J]usph Add-er

4631-32 Presentation 471-2

31 **And saying is Joseph to his brothers and to his father's household, "Up will I go and tell to Pharaoh and say to him, 'My brothers and my father's household, who were in the land**
32 **of Canaan, have come to me. And the mortals are graziers of flocks, for they became cattlemen, and their flocks and their herds and all [w]that is theirs have they brought.'** — [Ph]Phroe [H]UNCOVERED[b]; [C]Knon SUBMITTER; -men MORTALS

4633-34 Directions 473-6

33 **"And [b]come shall it that Pharaoh will call to you and say**
34 **'to you,' 'What is your [do]occupation?' [a]Then say shall you, 'Cattlemen [b]are your servants from our youth [a] till now, [mr]both we [mr]and our forefathers,'—in order to dwell in the land of Goshen, for an abhorrence to Egyptians is every grazier of a flock."** — 34 476; -men MORTALS; [G]Gshn CLOSE-by; [E]Mtzrim NARROWS

4631-32 Presentation 471-2

47 **And coming is Joseph and telling to Pharaoh, and is saying [S]to him," "My father and my brothers, and their flocks and their herds, and all [w]that is theirs, come from the land of Canaan. And behold them in the land of Goshen."** — 1 4628; See map page 107.; Ieue Will-be-ing-was

2 **And from the outstanding men of his brothers he takes [S]with him" five mortals, and putting them is he before Pharaoh.**

4633-34 Directions 473-6

3 **And saying is Pharaoh to 'Joseph's" brothers, "What is your [do]occupation?"**
And saying are they to Pharaoh, "Graziers of flocks are
4 **your servants, [mr]both we [mr]and our forefathers." And saying are they to Pharaoh, "To sojourn in the land have we come, for no pasture is there for the flocks which are your servants', for [F]heavy is the famine in the land of Canaan. And now, pray, dwell will your servants in the land of Goshen."**

5 **And speaking is Pharaoh to Joseph, to saying, "Your fa-**
6 **ther and your brothers have come to you. The land of Egypt, before you is it. In the best of the land cause your father and your brothers to dwell. Dwelling are they in the land of Goshen. And should you,[a] forsooth, know able mortals among them, [a]then place them as chiefs over the cattle which are mine."** — speak SAYING

7 **And bringing is Joseph Jacob, his father, and is standing him before Pharaoh. And Jacob is blessing Pharaoh.** — 4629-30 Meeting 477-10; [I]oqb HEEL

8 **And saying is Pharaoh to Jacob, "How have been the [N]days of the years of your life?"**

9 **And saying is Jacob to Pharaoh, "The days of the years of 'my life's' sojourning are a hundred and thirty years. Few and evil come to be the [N]days of the years of my life, and they do not overtake the [N]days of the years of the life of my forefathers in the days of their sojournings."** — Adm 3684

10 Hb77 **10 And blessing is Jacob `Pharaoh and is faring forth from**
[Ph]*Phro e* [H]UNCOVERED[b] **before Pharaoh.**

4628 Jacob 4711-12 **11 And Joseph located `his father and `his brothers, and is**
[loc]dwell **giving to them a freehold** in the land of Egypt in the best
11 Ex111 **of the land, in the land of Rameses, as**[w]**Pharaoh instructs.**
[J]*Iusph* Add-er **12 And sustaining is Joseph `his father and `his brothers and**
[R]*Romss* [f]Son-of-the- **`all his father's household.** And there is [N]**bread for the**
Sun[f] (Egyptian) [N]**mouths of the tots.**
See map page 107.

13-17 Exchange 18-26 **13 And [N]bread there is none in all the land, for [F]heavy is**
the famine exceedingly, and frantic is the land of Egypt
[C]*Kno n* SUBMITTER **14 and the land of Canaan in view of the famine. And gleaning**
is Joseph `all the money ·found in the land of **Egypt and in**
Al u eim the land of **Canaan** [i]for the **victuals which they are pur-**
SUBJECT-or-to-s **chasing for** [7]**their ration.**[0] **And bringing is Joseph** [7]**all**[0] **`the**
(To-subjectors) **money to**[d] **Pharaoh's house.**
15 And spent is [7]**all**[0] **the money** [f]**in the land of Egypt and**
[f]**in the land of Canaan. And coming are all in Egypt to**
Joseph, [to]**saying, "Grant** [to]**us** [N]**bread!** [a] Why should **we die**
in front of you? For the **limit** of **our money has been**
reached."
16 And saying is Joseph, "Grant your cattle, and give it
will I to you, [7N]**bread**[n] [i]**for your cattle, if** [7]**the**[n] **money**
17 reaches its limit." And bringing are they `their cattle to
Joseph, and giving is Joseph to them [N]**bread** [i]**for ·horses,**
and [i]**for cattle of the flocks, and** [i]**for cattle of the herds,**
and [i]**for asses. And** [7]sustaining[0] **them is he** [i]**with·**[N]**bread,** and
fodder [i]**for all their cattle in ·that year.**

13-17 Exchange 18-26 **18 And spent is ·that ·year. And coming are they to him in**
the **second ·year, and saying to him, "Not suppress will we**
from my lord that spent is the money, and the **cattle and**
the beasts belong to my lord, then nothing remains before
19 my lord, barring[if]**our bodies and our ground. Why shall we**
die [t]**before your** [A]**eyes** [7mr]**and our ground be desolate?**[0]
Buy `us and `our ground [i]**with** [N]**bread, and we and our**
ground will become servants [t]**of Pharaoh. And give seed**
[7]**for sowing**[0] **and we shall live and not die, and the ground**
will not be desolate."
20 And buying is Joseph `all the **ground of Egypt for Phar-**
aoh, for the Egyptians sell [7]**to Pharaoh**[0] **each man his field,**
seeing that a fast hold has the [I]**famine over them. And**
21 coming is the land to be Pharaoh's. And `the people [7]**are**[0]
[c]**made to serve `him** [S]**as servants**[n] **from** one end **of Egypt's**
22 boundary [a] unto its other end. **But the ground of the priests**
[7]**alone, this Joseph**[0] does not **buy, for there is a statutory**
dole for the priests from `Pharaoh, and they eat `the
statutory dole which Pharaoh gives to them. Therefore
they did not sell `their ground.
23 And saying is Joseph to [7]**all the Egyptians,**[0] **"Behold!**
Buy do I `you ·today,** [a]**with `your ground, for Pharaoh. Lo! for
24 you there is seed, and sow shall you `the ground. And it
comes, of the incomes, [a]**you give the fifth** [7]**handful**[0] **to Phar-**
aoh, and four handfuls shall become yours, for seed for the
field, and for your food, and for [7]**all**[0] **who are in your house-**
hold, and for food for your tots."

25 And saying are they, "cPreserving are you our lives.
Finding are we grace in the Aeyes of my lord, and we be- JIusph Add-er
come Pharaoh's servants." PhPhroe HUNCOVEREDb
26 And Joseph is constituting 'it for a statute over the conPLACING
ground of Egypt till 'this 'day—to Pharaoh toa fifth. But EMtzrim Narrows
the ground of the priests, theirs alone does not become
Pharaoh's.

4628-4712 Sojourn 4727-5014

27 And dwelling is Israel in the land of Egypt, in the land 4727 in Egypt 4933-502
of Goshen. And holdings have they in it and are Ffruitful, 27 Ex17 1237
and increasing exceedingly. GGshn CLOSE-by See map page 107.

28 And living is Jacob in the land of Egypt seventeen years. 4728 Lives 503-14
And bcoming are the Ndays of the years of Jacob's life to Adm 3701
be a ahundred yr and forty-seven years.

29 And near are drawing the days of Israel's death, and he 4729-31 Burial 4929-32
is calling to his son to Joseph and is saying to him, "Pray, IIshr-Al Upright-
should I find grace in your Aeyes, pray place your hand with-SUBJECTOR
under my thigh and Spray n do deal with me in kindness and 29 4526 28
30 truth. Pray, you must not entomb me in Egypt. a Lay 'me'
with my fathers, and carry me from Egypt and entomb me
in their tomb."
And saying is he, "I will do as according to your word." Al u e im
31 And saying is he, "Swear to me." And swearing is he to SUBJECT-or-to-s (To-subjectors)
him.
And worshiping is Israel on the head of 'his staff.'

48 And bcoming is it after 'these 'things athat someone is 481-20 Blessing 491-28
saying to Joseph, "Behold! Your father is ailing." And tak- 1-2 Sons brought 8-12
ing is he 'his two sons with him, 'Manasseh and 'Ephraim, thingword
and 'comes to Jacob.' MMnshe Oblivion
2 And someone is telling to Jacob and saying, "Behold! Your EAphrim FRUIT-s
son Joseph is coming to you." And encouraging himself is
Israel, and is sitting on the couch.

3 And saying is Jacob to Joseph, v"The Al-Who-Suffices 3-4 Sons blessed 13-16
appeared to me in Luz, in the land of Canaan, and blessing JIoqb HEEL
4 'me is He, and saying to me, 'Behold Me cmaking you Ffruit- 3 2813 19 356
ful. And I increase you, and give you to be an to assembly of LLuz DEVIATOR
peoples. And I give ''this 'land 'to you and' to your Aseed
after you for a freehold eonian.'v See map page 92.

5 "And now your two sons, 'born to you in the land of 5-7 Preference 17-20
Egypt previous to my coming to you tod Egypt, mine are prevFURTHER
they, Ephraim and Manasseh. As Reuben and Sasn Simeon, RRaubn SEE-son
6 shall they become mine. aYet your kindred, whom you SShmoun HEARER
beget after them, are yours. Come shall they to be called See map page 83.
onby the name of their brothers in 'allotting' their allotment.
7 "And I, iat my coming from Padan, 'Syria,' Rachel, 'your PPhdn RANSOM
mother,n died onby me in the land of Canaan in the way, RRchl EWE
iwhile still some distance 'overland to come tod Ephrath. 7 3519
And I entombed her there ion the way tod Ephrath." (It See map page 92.
is now Bethlehem.) BBithlchm House-bread

8 And seeing is Israel 'the sons of Joseph. And saying is 1-2 Sons presented 8-12
he, "anWho are these?"
9 And saying is Joseph to his father, "My sons are they,
who were given me by the Alueim in this place."

[J] *Ioqb* HEEL — And saying is ⌜Jacob,⌝ "Take them, pray, to me and I will
10 bless them." [a]Yet the eyes of Israel are [F]heavy [f]with age
I e u e Will-be-ing-was — ⌜and⌝ he cannot [to]see. And close is he [c]bringing 'them to
11 him. And kissing [to]them is he and embracing [to]them. And
pray MEDIATE — saying to Joseph is Israel, "To see your [N]face I did not pray,
[J] *Iusph* Add-er — and behold! The Alueim, moreover, shows 'me 'your [A]seed."
12 Hb1121 12 And forth is Joseph [c]bringing 'them from [wi]between his
knees, and is prostrating ⌜to him⌝ [t]with his nostrils to[d] the
earth.

3-4 Sons blessed 13-16 13 And taking is Joseph 'the two, 'Ephraim [i]on his right [f]at
Israel's left, and 'Manasseh [i]on his left [f]at Israel's right,
stretch SEND 14 and is [c]bringing them close to him. And stretching out is
Israel 'his right ⌜hand⌝ and is setting it on Ephraim's head,
[a]when he is the inferior in station, and 'his left on Manasseh's head, using 'his hands intelligently, for Manasseh is
15 the firstborn. And blessing ⌜them⌝ is he and saying, "The
Alueim before Whom my forefathers, Abraham and Isaac,
[F]walked, the Alueim, 'my [F]Shepherd from my ⌜youth⌝ till
16 38 151 171 181 Ex2320 16 'this 'day, the Messenger, 'my 'Redeemer from all evil,
21 Js513 Col15 Rv314 — bless ⌜these⌝ 'youths. And called [i]on them shall be my
[A] *Abrem* FATHER-HIGH-throng — name, and the name of my forefathers, Abraham and Isaac.
And prolific shall they be, to make a ⌜vast⌝ increase within
[I] *Itzchq* LAUGH-causer — the land."

5-7 Preference 17-20 17 And seeing is Joseph that his father is setting 'his right
[E] *Aphrim* FRUITS — hand on Ephraim's head, and evil is it in his [A]eyes. And
up is ⌜Joseph⌝ holding his father's hand, to [c]take 'it away,
[M] *Mnshe* Oblivion 18 off of Ephraim's head, on to Manasseh's head. And saying
is Joseph to his father, "Not so, my father, for this is the
firstborn. Place your right on his head."
19 And refusing is his father and saying, "I know, my son!
and moreover — I know! Moreover, he shall become [to]a people, [mr]and he
19 Nu132-35 218 20 — shall become great. [a]Howbeit, his 'smaller brother shall be
Dt3317 Hb1120 21 — greater [f]than he. And his [A]seed shall become a fullness of
20 the nations." And blessing them is he in 'that 'day, [to]saying,
make PLACE — "[i]By you shall Israel bless, [to]saying, 'The Alueim make you
[I] *Ishr-Al* Upright-with-SUBJECTOR — as Ephraim and as Manasseh!'" And placing is he 'Ephraim
before Manasseh.

21 Restore 22 21 And saying is Israel to Joseph, "Behold! I am dying. [a]Yet
the Alueim comes to be with 'you, and restores 'you to the
21 Double 22 22 land of your forefathers! And I, [S]behold![c] I give to you
22 Dt2117 1Ch52 Ez4713 — Shechem, one share over your brothers, of that which I
[A] *Amri* SAYITE — took from the [A]hand of the Amorite [i]with my [A]sword and
See map page 92. — [i]with my [A]bow."
481-20 Blessing 491-28

1-2 Introduction 28 49 And calling is Jacob to his sons and saying, "Gather, and
1 3228 438 4526 28 — I will tell [to]you 'what will meet 'you in the days hereafter.
Nu2414 Dt430 3129 2 Convene and hear, sons of Jacob,
Is22 Jr2320 *2* 468-25 — And hearken to Israel, your father.

3-15 Leah's Sons 22-27 3 Reuben, my firstborn, you are my [M]vigor,
[R] *Raubn* SEE-son — And the beginning of my [M]virility,
With a surplus for bearing and a surplus of strength.
4 Nu161 2 1Ch51 4 Ebullient as 'water, you must not have a surplus!
For up you went to the bed of your father.
Then you violated my berth to which ⌜you⌝ went up.

5 **Simeon and Levi are brothers.** SShmoun HEARER
'They concluded" violence 'out of their covenants.' LLui OBLIGATED
6 **Into their deliberation you must not come, my Nsoul!** 5 3426
'And" in their assembly you must not 'contend,' my Nglory.
For in their anger they killed 'men,°
And in their acceptance they felled a 'chief.' chief bull
7 **Cursed is their anger, for it was strong.** 7 347 Ex3226-29
And their rage, for it was obstinate. Lv2532-34 Dt108 9
Apportion them will I in Jacob, JIoqb HEEL
And scatter them in Israel. IIshr-Al Upright-with-SUBJECTOR

8 **Judah, you your brothers will acclaim.**
Your 'hands" shall be ton the Fscruff of your enemies. JIeude Acclaimer
Prostrate to you shall the sons of your father. scruff NAPE
9 **The Mwhelp of a lion is Judah. From the Fprey, my son,** 8 Ps7211 Ph210
Bow will he, **recline as a lion. [you go up.** 9 Nu23
And, as a parent lion, who will cmake him rise? who ANY
10 **Not withdraw shall the Asceptre from Judah,** 10 Nu2417 Ps456 607
aNor a Astatute-maker's staff from **between his feet,** 1088 Is3322 Ez2127
Till it be that ease shall come 'to him.'
And to it shall the expectation of the peoples be.
11 **Bind to a Avine will he his colt,** I e u e
And to a Ayellow muscat grape the s**foal of his she-ass,** Will-be-ing-was
He rinses in Awine his apparel,
And in the Fblood of Agrapes his coverlet.
12 **Flushed will be his Neyes from Awine,**
And white, his teeth, from Amilk.

13 **Zebulon tat a port of the seas shall tabernacle,** ZZbulun PREFERRED
And at a to port for ships awith its flank 'unto° Sidon. STzidun 'SIDE'
See map page 83.
14 **Issachar 'covets pleasantness,°** IIshshkr Forsooth-hire
Recline will he between the Ahearthstones, and 14 3018
15 **See a resting** place **that is good,**
And a 'land that is pleasant,
a**Yet stretch out will he his Ashoulder**b **for a burden,** sh shoulder blade
And become will he a servant tunder a labor **levy.**

16 **Dan shall adjudicate his people,** 16 Bilhah's sons 21
As one of the tribes of Israel. DDn ADJUDICATE
17 F**Become shall Dan a serpent on a way,** 16 306 Jd1520 Jr816 17
A horned snake on a path, that 'bites the heels of a horse, 17 Lv2410-16 1K1230 2K1029
And fall shall its rider backward.F
18 **For Thy salvation I expect, Ieue!** 18 Is258 9 Mt2413

19 **Gad—a raiding party shall 'raid' him,** 19 Zilpah's Sons 20
a**Yet he shall raid their Nheels,** GGd RAID

20 **Asher—**stout shall be his N**bread,** 19 Zilpah's Sons 20
And he will provide royal luxuries. provide GIVE

21 **Naphtali** is an **'oak'** stretched out, NNphthli TWISTED 16 Bilhah's sons 21
The giver of 'products° that are seemly. stretch SENT

22 A Ffruitful son is Joseph, A F**fruitful son, 'joy' of my Neye,** 21 Jd518
'My son," inferior, 'to me has returned,° JIusph Add-er 3-15 Rachel's 22-27
23 **And bitter were they with him, and 'contended°** 22 Dt3313-17
And begrudging him were the Farchers, 23 Am66
24 a**Yet 'broken° in 'virility° is 'their° Abow,**
And 'slack° are the Aarms of 'their° hands.

Al u eim From the [A]hands of the Sturdy One of Jacob,
SUBJECT-or-to-s Thence is the [F]Shepherd, the [F]Stone of Israel,
(To-subjectors) 25 From the Al of your father, and your Helper,
[J]*Ioqb* HEEL And He 'Who-Suffices, and your Blesser,
[I]*shr-Al* Upright- Blessings of the heavens [S]from[n] above,
with-SUBJECTOR Blessings of the submerged chaos reclining beneath,
Blessings of the [A]breasts and the [A]womb,
26 Blessings of your father 'and your mother.°
Master are they over the blessings of 'my mountains,°
Unto the yearning of the eonian hills,
[J]*Iusph* Add-er [b]Coming are they [t]on the [N]head of Joseph,
[B]*Bnimin* Son-RIGHT And [t]on the [N]crown of the 'governor° of his brothers.
27 Jd315 1S116-11 27 [P]Benjamin is a wolf, tearing to pieces. [apportion the loot."[P]
Ac758 81 3 913 In the morning he'll devour further, And in the evening he'll
devour[EAT]

1-2 Summary 28 28 All these are the twelve tribes of Israel. And this is what
their father speaks to them, [a]when he is blessing 'them.
Each man [was]according to his blessing he blesses 'them.

4729-31 Burial 4929-32 29 And instructing 'them is he, and saying to them, "I am
29 239 10 4730 being [F]gathered to my people. Entomb 'me [to]with my fore-
[E]*Ophrun* SOILER fathers [to]in the cave which is in the field of Ephron, the
[H]*Chthi* Dismay-ite 30 Hittite, in the double cave which is in the field [w]adjoining
[C]*Knon* SUBMITTER Mamre, in the land of Canaan, which Abraham bought 'with
[A]*Abrem* FATHER- the field from 'Ephron, the Hittite, for a freehold for a tomb.
HIGH-throng 31 "[S]And[n] there they entombed 'Abraham and 'Sarah, his
30 2316 31 Hb1113 wife. There they entombed 'Isaac and 'Rebecca, his wife.
[L]*Lae* [F]No-thing[F] 32 "And there I entombed 'Leah. Bought was the field and
See map page 92. the cave which is in it from 'the sons of Heth."

4727 in Egypt 4933-502 33 And finishing is Jacob [to]instructing 'his sons, and gather-
Adm 3701 ing is he his feet into the couch and is expiring, and is
33 258 3529 2S1223 being [F]gathered to his people.
[J]*Iusph* Add-er 50 And falling is Joseph on his father's face, and lamenting
2 3228 436 4526 28 2 over him and kissing [to]him. And instructing is Joseph 'his
Ec127 servants, 'the healers, to embalm 'his father. And embalming are the healers 'Israel.

4728 Mourns 503-14 3 And fulfilling are they for him forty days, for so they
fill the days of the embalmed. And lamenting are the
[E]*Mtzrim* Narrows-ites Egyptians 'with him seventy days.
4 4114 4 And passing are the days of his lamentation, and speak-
[Ph]*Phroe* [H]UNCOVERED[b] ing is Joseph to the household of Pharaoh, [to]saying, "Pray,
should I find grace in your [A]eyes, pray, speak 'for me° in
5 the [A]ears of Pharaoh, [to]saying that my father adjured me
[S]before his death[n] [to]saying, 'Behold! I am dying. In my
tomb which I dug for myself in the land of Canaan, there
shall you entomb me.' And now, pray, up will I go and
entomb 'my father, [S]as I swore,[n] and return."
6 And saying is Pharaoh 'to Joseph°, "Go up and entomb
'your father, as [w]he adjured you."
7 And up is Joseph going to entomb 'his father. And up
'with him are going all the servants of Pharaoh, 'and° the
elders of his household, and all the elders of the [N]land of
See map page 107. 8 Egypt, and all Joseph's household, and his brothers, and
leave[FORSAKE] 'all° his father's household. But the tots and the flocks and
[G]*Gshn* CLOSE-by 9 their herds they leave behind in the land of Goshen. And

up with him go mr **both chariots** mr **and horsemen. And it** both andmoreover
comes to be an exceedingly F**heavy** ·**camp.**
10 **And coming are they unto the threshing site of ·Atad,** See map page 100.
which is in **across the Jordan, and wailing there are they** acrossPASS
with an exceedingly great and F**heavy wailing.** *JIrdn* Descender
11 **And making is he a mourning for his father seven days.**
And seeing are the dwellers in the land, the Canaanites, *CKnoni* SUBMITTER-ite
the mourning *ᵗ***on the threshing site of ·Atad, and saying**
are they, "A F**heavy mourning is this for the Egyptians."** *AAbl-Mtzrim* Mourn-
Therefore its name is called "Abel-Mizraim", which is in Narrows
across the Jordan. acrossPASS
12 **And doing for him are his sons so as** w **he instructs them.**
13 **And carrying \him are his sons to** d **the land of Canaan, and** *13* 2316 Ac716
entombing \him are they in the double cave of the field,
'the cave° **which Abraham bought \with the field, for a free-** *AAbrem* FATHER-
hold, for a tomb, from \Ephron, the Hittite, adjoining Mamre. HIGH-throng
14 **And returning is Joseph to** d **Egypt, he and his brothers** *EOphrun* SOILER
and all those going up \with him to entomb \his father, *HChthi* Dismay-ite
after \his father's entombment. *MMmra* 'Bitterness'
15 **And seeing are Joseph's brothers that their father is** 372-4528 Joseph 5015-26
dead, and saying are they, "What if Joseph is holding a 15-21 Death -26
grudge against us and, is reversing, yea reversing to us
16 **\all the evil with which we requited \him ?" And instructions**
are they giving to Joseph, to **saying, "Your father gave in-**
17 **structions before his death,** to **saying, 'Thus are you saying**
to Joseph: Oh, bear, pray, with the transgression of your
brothers and their sin, that with evil they requited you.'
And now, pray, bear with to **the transgression of the ser-** *Alueim*
vants of the Alueim of your father." SUBJECT-or-to-s
And lamenting is Joseph *ᵗ***as they speak to him.** (To-subjectors)
18 **And going are his brothers, moreover, and falling before** *18* 377-10
him. And saying are they, "Behold us yours for servants."
19 **And saying to them is Joseph, "You must not fear, for** *JIusph* Add-er
20 **under Alueim am I. And =you,= you devised** on **against me evil,** *20* 455 Ps10517
'a**yet**" **the Alueim devises it 'for me**° **for good, that it may**
do**work out as at ·this day, to** c**preserve alive many people.**
21 **And now, you must not fear. I'll sustain \you and \your tots."**
And comforting \them is he, and speaking on **to their** F**hearts.**

22 **And dwelling is Joseph in Egypt, he 'and his brothers,** 22-23 Age 26-
and all° **his father's household. And living is Joseph a hun-** *23* Nu2629 3239 Js171
23 **dred and ten years. And seeing is Joseph** to **Ephraim's sons** *EAphrim* FRUIT-s
to the third generation. Moreover, the sons of Machir, the *MMkr* SELLER
son of Manasseh, were born on Joseph's knees. *ManMnshe* Oblivion

24 **And saying is Joseph to his brothers, "I am dying.** a**Yet** 24 Restoration 25
visit, yea, visit will the Alueim \you, and c**bring \you up from** *24* 263 4 2813 3512 481
·**this ·land to the land which 'the Alueim**° **swore 'to our** Ex224 36 63 4 Lu172 73
forefathers,° **to Abraham, to Isaac, and to Jacob."** Hb1122

25 **And adjuring is Joseph \the sons of Israel** to **saying, "Visit,** 24 Restoration 25
yea, visit \you will the Alueim, and up shall you bring my *25* 4929 30 Ex1319
N**bones 'with you.**°**"**

26 **And dying is Joseph, a hundred and ten years** s**old.** 22-23 Age 26-
And embalming \him are they, and placed is he in a coffer 15-21 Death -26
in Egypt.